Under the
RADAR

When Truth Hides in Plain Sight

D.T. SHANTI

Fulton Books, Inc.
Meadville, PA

Published by Fulton Books 2020

ISBN 978-1-64654-496-7 (paperback)
ISBN 978-1-64654-497-4 (digital)

Printed in the United States of America

For *Bertha* and *Mimi*, two souls whose strength and guidance saved me in many ways. Your light drove away my shadows, allowing who I am to come into clear view.

No more hiding under the radar.

Author's Note

This is my story. It is related with as much love and respect as I have within me for the people who have walked this path by my side. If you are one of the characters found within, understand that you may not remember these experiences the same as you read them here. Perspective is the foundation of memory, and I think it is safe to say that your perspective is and will always be different from mine. Take what you like, and leave the rest.

I acknowledge that my story is written through a thick lens of white and economic privilege. For some, that will have the effect of disqualification, and I can understand that mindset; "first world problems" can be hard to look past when finding compassion for someone's journey. There are many who suffer trauma at higher levels than I have and I honor them for their strength and resilience.

In sharing my journey, my hope is to demonstrate that trauma can cause someone to be oblivious to their own reality; to fly 'under the radar', even to themselves. No matter how deeply buried your truth is, there is value in examining it with the proper support and guidance.

The poems came to me as I was writing the book. They helped me clarify my feelings and allowed for a deeper understanding through imagery as I processed details about my life that I had spent many years working to erase.

Words cannot express my gratitude for those who stood by me while I was living this life and for those who stood by me while I excavated the stories that would allow me to put that life down on paper.

The Miracle of Vulnerability

I look into your eyes
to find my spirit,
to find the light in me
reflected in a hue,
easier for me to grasp.

My pain,
so deeply hidden
in corners I have not passed
since a lifetime ago,
waits for me
to have the courage to find it.

What will happen
if I share this with you?
Will you think me a monster
who deserves no tenderness?
Will you judge me a fool
for the path you cannot imagine exists?

Or will you gently
cup my face in your hands
and draw me close enough
to feel your breath
as you whisper

"It's okay…"

Will you wrap your arms
around me
until our heartbeats touch
and the warmth of your body
melts the ice in mine
as you whisper

"You're okay…"

Part One

September 1990

He started kissing me on the couch. We were both still excited by the fact that we could make love right here, in broad daylight, if we wanted to. One of the perks of being adults. Jimmy was always ready for any action I was willing to give him, but I took a little more time to warm up, especially since I had not been drinking yet today. He was the first man I allowed myself to be intimate with while having no alcohol in my system. I guess putting a ring on my finger made me trust him more than the others.

We were both naked from the waist up. His hands cupped my breasts in the same predictable pattern as he pressed his tongue into my ear, which always succeeded in flipping my switch. The committee in my head was talking me through the experience as if it was a commentator calling the plays during a Braves game when the panic began to rise in my throat. My heart was racing, and my head was filled with a *roar* that sounded like a train was going through my living room. I began pushing with both hands on his chest and yelling, "Stop!" I couldn't breathe, and I had no idea what was happening to me.

Jimmy was frustrated and confused, as I was clearly interested in having sex just a few seconds ago. His frustration sounded like anger as he questioned my sanity, trying to wrap me in an embrace that I struggled to release myself from, like he was a total stranger.

"What is wrong with you?" he asked in exasperation.

I didn't know what to tell him, as I was just as confused as he was. His questions became more and more persistent, and my sense of chaos increased.

I suddenly yelled out, "I think I've been abused!"

I had never said that before (that I knew of), and I had no idea where it came from. I started crying, and he put his arms around me to comfort me. I felt like my whole world was falling apart around me, like glass breaking in large shards and falling to the ground. It was a moment of clarity mixed with the most awful confusion at the same time. What the hell was I talking about?

Chapter 1

I was born in a small town in North Carolina to a seemingly middle-class family. I remember sharing a room with my sister, Mary, who was three years older than me. Our room was down the hall from our parents' room, with a bathroom in between, which the four of us shared. We had twin beds and very little space for any of our things. I remember always being asked to clean up our room, but we never seemed to know how, because it just didn't seem like there was anywhere to put anything! There was one set of shelves for both of our things: books, toys, games, etc. One desk was piled so high with papers and stuff that we couldn't use the tabletop. This was before the days of taking what you don't want anymore to the Goodwill store. Mom never threw anything away, and neither did we.

The room was yellow, with matching comforters and drapes, but it didn't have a "cheery" feeling that you might associate with the color yellow. It was the kind of yellow that was washed out and dingy, and I still have slight reactions to this day when I find myself in a space with a similar color. My only fond memory in that room was listening to my album of *The Jungle Book* soundtrack on my record player. I knew all the words to all the songs, and I would dance around in the space and pretend I was Mowgli with my best friend, Baloo, to protect me. I was big into protection then; I felt the best when I was with people or imagining fantasies where I was being protected or taken care of.

On the outside, we were the classic white American family. A mom, a dad, three children, three dogs, and three cats. We lived in a nice house in "horse country" that my grandmother had built before she built her house. (Hers had a similar layout but was much grander!) We never wanted for anything. There was never any stress about putting food on the table or whether the bills would get paid, but there was an undercurrent that none of us understood; it kept sanctuary and safety just out of reach.

The town we lived in for my first eighteen years of life was very small. The streets were lined with pine trees, and the ground was always covered with pine straw. It was a quaint town nestled between two other towns—one known for being the golf capital of the world and a world-class resort town; the other, a more "working class" location. We always lived on the outskirts among the horse farms, so we were dependent on my mom to drive us anywhere we wanted to go. We didn't live in a neighborhood with kids riding bikes and playing in the backyards, so being with other kids always required effort and planning.

We attended the local Episcopal Church, where my father sang in the choir. The church was also where we went to kindergarten and first grade before moving to a private school that now services K to twelfth grades. I went to that school from second grade through graduation, and there were fourteen people in my graduating class with six of us that had been together the whole time! It was a school where you were never able to reinvent yourself among your peers. The reputations that were developed early on stuck with you no matter how hard you worked to change your stars.

People always knew who our family was. My grandmother, whom we called Tootie, had been a pillar of the community for many years, and she had donated a significant amount of money to the private school we attended to name the gymnasium after my grandfather. Throughout the course of my time there, two more buildings would be named after family members, which always placed us in a particular status among our fellow students. As a result of this notoriety, there was little we could do in town or at school that wouldn't get relayed back to our parents by someone who saw us. I remember walking down Broad Street one day with friends, and a random man whom I didn't know stopped me and said, "You're a Greary girl. Which one are you?" I always felt known no matter where I was, especially within this small community that made up our school.

The town was typical of the south in its level of segregation. There were Black people who lived in our town, but they lived in a certain part of town that we called "the projects." It was a neighborhood with street after street of brick duplexes that all looked the same. We had two people we knew who lived in there: Bertha (our housekeeper) and Sally (our babysitter). The only time we ever went into this neighborhood was to visit them. I remember really liking the times we went to stay with Bertha or Sally because it was the closest I came to being in a neighborhood where kids played in the streets and bounced from house to house.

The segregation of the town never occurred to me when I was a child. I don't remember ever noticing that I saw no other Black people except in this one neighborhood, but as a white child, my life was set up that I didn't have to notice. The only frame of reference I had for "normal" was the way this town was configured, and it wasn't until adulthood that it occurred to me how white and privileged my experience was. There was a total of four Black students during my years at the private school. The demographics have changed a little since then, but the town and the school are still disproportionately white and noticeably segregated. I offer this information not as an excuse but as a framework for my privilege and obliviousness to my role in white supremacy within my town.

My father was born in the Deep South, in Clinton, North Carolina, in 1936. He had a brother, who was seven years his senior, and my grandparents split up when Dad was two years old. My grandfather eventually remarried and had three more children, whom we always had in our lives as Dad's siblings, and his stepmother, we called Grandma Irene. My grandfather died in 1964, so I never knew him except through stories, which were very few. He was an alcoholic, which was why my grandmother kicked him out at a time when women didn't make that kind of decision easily. The stigma of being divorced and the hardship of being a single mother in the late '30s and early '40s suggests their marriage must have been very rough for her to make that choice.

My grandmother moved to Kinston, North Carolina, to live near her mother in order to have support in raising her boys. Then, eventually, she moved to Wilson, North Carolina. She never remarried. Both my dad and his older brother presented as very responsible men who were often fastidious with details, but there was a deep disconnect within both of them. Looking back on them now, I am aware of both men possessing a quiet anger buried deep inside that they worked very hard to keep closed up tight, as if allowing its escape would be devastating to them and anyone in close proximity. I wonder if growing up in a single-parent household during this time in our society had anything to do with those traits being so strong in each of them.

Dad felt like he had to be the "man" of the family when his older brother went off to boarding school and take care of things around the house. They lived a middle-class life, but I know my grandmother (who we always called Baboo) had to go to work right after leaving my grandfather to support her family. She likely worked as a secretary since she wasn't a nurse or a teacher, which were often the only professions available to women at that time. I've been told she was forced to write letters to my grandfather, asking him for money to pay for the boys' education since her meager earnings were not enough to cover private school. I can only imagine how hard it was for her to write those letters. She was a strong woman who likely didn't relish asking him for help.

My mother's childhood story had the outward trappings of a very different life than my father's, but underneath they were much the same. Mom was born in 1940 in New York, New York, and grew up in Fairfield and Weston, Connecticut. She is the youngest of three girls, who are five and eight years older than she is, and they were raised in a *very* upper-class family. My maternal grandmother was the granddaughter of William Rockefeller, brother to the infamous John D. Rockefeller. Being from William's line, instead of John D.'s, had all the perks and none of the familial responsibility. We didn't have Rockefeller in our names (that ended with my grandmother), so we didn't have to walk in that limelight all the time, but we benefited from the monetary security that being from one of the most famous American dynasties can provide. We were able to fly under the radar, which is how my mother liked it—living in a modest home in a small town in North Carolina with no outward indications of the lineage from which she came.

Mom grew up in a world of nannies, tea parties with real china cups that had hand-painted flowers on the porcelain in her nursery, horses to ride on the grounds of their home, black and white marble floors in the foyer with a grand curving staircase to the second floor, in-ground pools with manicured gardens all around, a full staff of household servants that lived on site in the servants' quarters, and family photos by world-renowned photographers with matching outfits and well-groomed poodles; and she rebelled against it *all!*

In the home of her childhood, children were to be seen and not heard. Nannies were the primary caregivers of the children and my grandparents traveled and partied quite a bit. Mom remembers very little nurturing contact between Tootie and her as she was growing up, which explains why when it came time for her to nurture us, she struggled to find the skills within her to make that happen.

Of course, this life was very different from my dad's, who grew up in a single-parent household and had a mother working to make ends meet in the Deep South, but there was one similarity that balanced it all: alcoholism. My maternal grandfather was also an alcoholic who died when my mother was fifteen years old of phlebitis in his sleep at the age of fifty-two. Both Tootie and Baboo never remarried. They were best of friends when I was growing up even though they could not have been more different in their life journeys.

As I picture them now in my mind's eye, I remember them being similar in size and stature but wrapped in different packaging. They were both white women, just above five feet tall and had rounded bellies, skinny legs, and ample bosom. The biggest outward difference was their clothing. Tootie always wore fully put-together outfits made of cotton, silk, and wool with an owl somewhere in the ensemble. I remember Baboo's clothing choices to be simpler and more flowy, made of synthetic fabrics. She didn't have an extensive wardrobe, and I don't remember ever seeing her in pants. I never saw Tootie in her sleep clothes, as she was too formal to receive visitors without being fully coiffed. Baboo was looser with her appearance, and because we had sleepovers with her more often than we did with Tootie, she allowed us to see her in a more relaxed state.

Tootie had angular features and a small smile that allowed her face to look soft sometimes, but rarely did we see her in a full-throated laugh. Her jewelry was always small and tasteful, while Baboo's jewelry was bigger and chunky, mostly what we would call costume jewelry today. Baboo's features were rounder and fuller, and she wore glasses all the time. I barely remember Tootie wearing glasses as I think they were just for reading and I am not sure she allowed herself to wear them too often with others around. When Baboo laughed her whole body shook. Her face seemed to be made of her smile, and it wasn't often that Baboo's laugh didn't get everyone else in the room laughing. It was just that infectious. They both knew how to ballroom dance, as it was common for girls who grew up in their generation to be taught at least the basics of waltz, fox trot, lindy, and cha-cha. But Baboo *really* knew how to tear up a dance floor, and she truly *loved* dancing.

In my early childhood years, Dad was a banker and was in charge of handling all financial decisions within the family. I don't know when I learned that it was all Mom's money and that he had virtually nothing of his own wealth. He went to work each day, while she stayed home with us, and it seemed like every other family you might see. I now know that his paycheck was probably paying for barely any of our expenses, but I appreciate the fact that he still went to work. He could have stayed home, but I think that would have driven them crazy, being on top of each other.

As a family, we took trips every year to places like Hawaii, Alaska, and the Grand Canyon, and every summer, my parents went fishing in Saskatchewan, Canada, with friends. They each got new vehicles about every two years. For a long time, I never owned a vehicle longer than three years. It just didn't seem natural. To the outside world, we looked like we had it made, but there was a different side to our family that only very close friends and immediate family got to see.

Mom has a mood disorder called bipolar disorder. She didn't get diagnosed until after my little sister was born, which was six years after me. So for the first years of my life, she was explosive and down-right abusive at times. They called it manic depression back then, and the science of how to manage it was very new and rudimentary. She also smoked like a chimney, inhaling three packs a day by the time she quit when her lung collapsed after my younger sister's birth. I remember her lighting her next cigarette with the previous one before she put it out.

Mom was almost always the disciplinarian in the house, and she would spank us with what we called the switch. It was made of natural fiber, without a handle so to speak. In the early years, it lived propped up in the corner of their bedroom for easy access. In later years, she kept it in the closet at the bottom of the stairs to the attic or what became my older sister's room when they converted it. I remember the fights and the screaming leading up to the whipping, but memories of the whipping itself eludes me today. I know my older sister took more of the punishment, as she was older and more combative with Mom then I was.

If Dad ever decided he needed to do the whipping, it was with his leather belt. I remember him folding it over, holding it with both hands at either end, bringing his hands together to bow the belt out into a circle, then pulling his hands apart, and *snapping* it as he approached for the spanking. It didn't happen often, but he was good at it when he did it. We would discuss how many strokes we were going to get, and I remember focusing on the shoe-shining buffer in the corner next to his closet while I prayed for it to be over quickly.

My role in the family was the peacemaker. When others clashed on things, it was my job to come in, sort it out, and set it straight. Looking back on it, I was given a lot of power in that position, and I know it made me feel important. In other areas in the family, I was pretty unimportant. I was a white, gawky kid, long-legged and skinny as a rail, for most of my growing up years. I had limp, life-less hair that was consistently cut in various versions of a bowl cut and crooked and jagged teeth that made me look like I had fangs. Because Mary and I did not have a loving sisterly relationship. She was not interested in counseling me on improving these things, so my "frugly" years lasted longer than most.

Mary was the pretty one. She had blond hair, blue eyes, and very white beautiful teeth. She seemed to have a better fashion sense than I did and, like Tootie, always looked put together. She knew how to curl her hair to get just the right flip, as was the style then, and even though I knew how hard she worked to achieve her look (she took upward of three hours to get ready to go anywhere), to me, it was like she just woke up looking fabulous. I never understood why she seemed to have such anxiety around her appearance.

Picture days in our family and for school were horrible! When she came downstairs to present herself after her daily regime, it was always a toss-up how to answer the inevitable question: "How do I look?" If we said she looked great, she told us we didn't know what we were talking about and then would run upstairs to change. If we said she should change, she would stomp upstairs and take another half hour to come up with a new outfit. Our choice of response depended largely on how soon we had to leave, but we never knew what the outcome might be or how long this daily process would take before we could get in the car.

Mary and Mom are a lot alike in temperament, which made for some pretty intense clashes over the years. Explosive anger was the expression of choice for both of them, so when one would throw down the gauntlet on an issue, the other would counter with the same force, if not more. I tried, on occasion, to react like Mary did to Mom's temper tantrums, but it never lasted long, and I would crumble pretty fast. Mom scared the hell out of me, and I didn't have the intense anger inside me to sustain the fight. I had been taught that my expression of choice was to lie down and show my belly, like a submissive dog does to its pack leader. That seemed to be the way I reacted to authority. I was the first to back down and change my view.

When it came to clashes between Mary and myself, it was a different story. She stirred up so much anger in me that I felt I might spontaneously combust at times. I remember a time when we were standing in the kitchen together, and she was needling me into fighting with her. She did this often, as she had to know she would win, and so I think it became her path anytime she needed an ego boost.

18

I don't remember exactly what started it, but I became so angry at her that I began to pummel her with my fists. She put her right hand on the top of my head and held me at arm's length so I couldn't get to her. I was swinging my arms madly, trying with each swing to just make contact, but it was no use. She may as well have been a mile away. It looked like something out of a cartoon. I remember feeling such intense rage inside me that I thought at one point: *If she lets me get to her, I* am *going to kill her!*

I truly believed I was capable of murder in that moment. That event stuck with me, because I had envisioned hurting her before, but I really *believed* I would kill her if given the chance. She was always the object of my most intense anger, and I allowed myself to hate her with every hate cell I had. I couldn't do that with anyone else. I was afraid of being rejected from my parents or friends if I even had a mean thought about them, but I felt I had never had her acceptance or love, so it didn't matter what I did. I believed she was going to hate me no matter what.

Childhood was all about protecting myself. This protection needed to be supplemented with some sort of self-esteem boost because I wasn't getting that support from anyone in my family. With Mary, the boost lived in the fact that I was the "good child" to her "bad child." Mary and Mom were crashing their heads together all the time, so I looked like an angel compared to her. Looking back, I imagine this only heightened her dislike for me, because she would be compared to me and she would always fail. This was, at the time, the only validation I got for anything.

Unfortunately, Mary was her own worst enemy when it came to me, because she always seemed compelled to do things to me that I would be only too kind to report to Mom so that she would get into trouble. It was a vicious cycle of Mary abusing me, me crying to Mom, and Mom scolding Mary. One of the few times this was reversed was when I broke my glasses in fifth grade and lied about it to get a new pair.

If Mary always failed in comparison to me with regard to behavior. I always failed in comparison to her with regard to school. I struggled with every subject and was found to have "learning disabilities" along the way. It was suggested that one of the reasons I had trouble in school was because I couldn't see to read well, so in fourth grade, I started wearing glasses. I was still the awkward kid who was being bullied daily for not fitting in, so wearing glasses with really dark frames that were *way* too big for my face was just the icing on the cake. I begged Mom not to make me wear them, but she was unrelenting. She would ask my teachers if they had seen me wear them in class, and if they said no, there was hell to pay. It was either wear them and incur the wrath of my classmates, or not wear them and incur the wrath of Mom. It was often not clear which was worse.

There were three girls in my class that were the ringleaders of the grade. Becky and Patty were constantly bullying me, which made it difficult to concentrate on little else. They didn't like anything about me, and they never hesitated to make it known. The third girl, Tina, was an on-again, off-again friend. Some days, she would be my pal, and on others she was squarely aligned with the other two. In many ways, she was the hardest one to navigate because I never knew which I was going to get. I was skilled with dealing with unpredictable people, but I just couldn't catch a break with Tina most times. I really liked her, which made it even harder. She lived down the street from me on a horse farm, and her family life was seemingly just as crazy as mine, so we had that in common.

One day, I was having a particularly "accepted" day with the Three Musketeers (as I called them), and we started talking in the locker room after gym about my glasses.

"I wish these glasses would just disappear so Mom would have to get me a new pair. Maybe I could get a pretty set of frames that don't make me look like a bug!" I said.

"Well...what if they got broken by accident? Then she would have to get you a new pair!" Becky said.

There was a small voice in my head that questioned why Becky was trying to help me, but I decided to ride the wave. After all, it felt like the first hit of heroine to be accepted by her.

"We could break them, then put them under your jacket in your seat, and you could say you sat on them by accident!" Patty offered.

"I guess so…" I said. I got so caught up in the fact that they wanted to help me that I didn't think about how many ways it could go wrong.

"I'LL DO IT!" yells Tina, grabbing the glasses and wringing them at the nose like a wet towel.

Snap!

It was done. They were broken, and there was no going back. The story sounded foolproof: These girls were always playing tricks on me. Mom would *have* to believe that they had put them under my jacket and I had sat on them. Of course, my fifth grade mind didn't consider that they didn't look sat on. They looked like they'd been through a tornado! But that was of no concern to me. This was going to work, and I was going to get a new set of glasses and finally be cool.

That night, the story was told, and Mom seemed to buy it! Mom was always a sucker for a story where there was an underdog to be supported. We talked about when we could go back to the glasses store to get a new pair, and all was well with the world. This was my first dabble in high crimes and misdemeanors, and it felt good to get away with it! I was on top of the world, and there was no knocking me off.

The next day, as we rode the bus home from school, I looked behind me to see Becky, Patty, Tina—and Mary—huddled together in the back corner of the bus. They would whisper and laugh. Then Mary would turn to me with a knowing in her eyes. *They had told her!* I was dead! I was finished! Mom was gonna kill me, and Mary had her finger on the trigger. I had rarely seen her so happy. We lived at the end of a dirt road that stretched about a half a mile from the point where the bus let us off to our driveway. When we came off the bus and began the long trek home, the taunting began.

"Mom's gonna kill you… You're gonna get it!"

She said it all the way home. I was hysterical by the time we got in the driveway and was deeply relieved to see no cars in front of the house. Whew! She wasn't home. I had just a little more time before my trial and subsequently swift execution. Maybe I could catch my breath and be able to speak in my defense by the time she returned.

I stood in the front hall, staring out the window, waiting for Mom's return. Mary was giddy with excitement. She had never really known me to do *anything* like this and was beside herself to see how much trouble I would get in.

"You are in so much trouble! You are going to be *grounded* forever, and you're gonna have to do *all* the chores for *months*!" The predictions went on and on.

Finally, Mom drove in the driveway. Time stood still, and movements became slow motion as she came through the front door. Mary began spilling the details, and all I could hear was "Waaah waah waah waah waah!" like Charlie Brown's teacher. I leaned against the doorway to the den and watched Mom's face as she listened to the details of her middle daughter's descent into hell.

As expected, when Mary was finished, it became Mom's turn to yell.

"What have you got to say for yourself?"

"It was Becky's idea…"

"Do you know how expensive those glasses are?"

"But Tina was the one who broke them…"

"What were you thinking?"

"I DON'T KNOW! I just hate them so much, and everybody makes fun of me all the time!"

"GO TO YOUR ROOM!"

This was always the final demand. I stomped as loud as I could down the hallway and slammed my door with a force I had never known before. I was *livid*! Not only had I gotten in trouble worse than I had ever in my life, but I had given Mary the ultimate ammunition against me *and* I had been betrayed by the three musketeers. Again.

I paced inside my room, thinking about how upset I was, and I just wanted to break something. I picked up my alarm clock and threw it against the wall as hard as I could, and it smashed and fell to the floor. I'd never done anything like that before, and I think it surprised everyone in the household. I was grounded for a month, which Mary never let me forget, and it culminated in the deeply embarrassing parental conference between my parents and Tina's mother, where it was said out loud that I was a bad influence on Tina and that we couldn't see each other for a while. The final blow was Mom taking me back to the glasses shop and ordering me the exact same pair of frames, which was to be worn every day under penalty of death. Needless to say, that was the end of my crime spree. Mary was much better at being "bad." She could have that family job!

Mom and Dad fought about everything. They never seemed to love each other in my eyes, and the amount of picking that Mom would do to him seemed unbearable to us as we watched the dance between them. They met in our hometown in 1961 when they were both visiting family over the holidays and ended up at the same New Year's party. Dad was in the Navy at the time, and Mom was a sucker for a man in uniform. Mom remembers him being strong and capable, and she was smitten from the start.

They dated for two years before marrying in 1963 in Fairfield, Connecticut. Mom had witnessed his drinking habits and had serious reservations about marrying him just before the wedding, but the invitations had been sent and the dresses had been bought. It seemed impossible to call off the inevitable. She quickly learned that his drinking was way beyond what she had thought, and they hadn't gotten past the honeymoon before she shut down into survival mode. It was a marriage that was doomed from the start but would last another thirty years.

I was compelled from an early age to try to fix their relationship and smooth over all the ruffled feathers so the house would be peaceful. Dad was completely passive when it came to Mom. He would take her shit and take it until *I* thought I was going to explode just watching it! Then when he had had enough, he would explode and storm off into the night, leaving us to wonder if he was coming back, and hating her for her behavior toward him.

Her needling was her way of trying to get him to engage. She recalls manifesting illnesses, some that led to hospitalization, because he would connect with her and take care of her when she was sick and she was desperate for his attention. Despite his height of over six feet, he moved through the house quietly, keeping to his routine and letting her make all the household decisions. When he was home, he was working at his desk or sleeping in his chair with golf on the TV. I remember him in my story as if he was the wallpaper—always there but you forget the pattern if someone asked you to recall what it looked like later. It worked for him to be inconsequential. He was comfortable in the shadows.

Dad was always a drinker. On family trips, he had this leather case that he always carried with him. We would get to our destination, and the first thing he would do is pull out this case and open it up. In it would be a bottle or two of some kind of liquor (usually scotch), a shot glass, a low-ball glass, miscellaneous stir sticks, and things to go with it. I remember that his drink was "scotch on the rocks with a splash and a twist." Mom hated his drinking and never let him forget it. Her father's alcoholism had created a deep hatred in her for drinking from a very early age. I know that Dad went through periods of time when she thought he was abstaining, but it never lasted long. My guess is, he wasn't really abstaining; he had only perfected how to *look* like he wasn't drinking.

He went to work every day without fail and was as consistently emotionally absent as many fathers can be when the household is dominated by females. Dad was always skinny, and one of his shoulders was lower than the other from a childhood bout with polio. He played golf and had an assortment of those goofy golf pants with pictures of horses, sailboats, or lobsters on them that he would wear on the course or to someone's house for dinner if the mood struck him. His head was inordinately large, and I always remember him with the obligatory "comb over," which is the trademark of men who lose their hair at an early age. I have memories of pulling one hair only to have the whole flap lift off his scalp as a unit. The one good thing I got from him was the dance gene, and he taught me well. I love ballroom dancing, especially the lindy, also known as the swing.

Holidays were always observed with us wearing matching outfits and having big smiles even if we weren't feeling it at the time. Mom would make our dresses for Easter and Christmas, and we always looked like the picture-perfect family. Each year we took a Christmas picture to send out to three hundred of their closest friends, and Mom always wrote a letter telling of our escapades for the year to mail with the picture. Both grandmothers and my Aunt Gay and Uncle Haskell (Mom's middle sister and brother-in-law) lived in our tiny little town, so any relatives who lived outside of this sphere traveled to us for the Thanksgiving and Christmas holidays. It never occurred to me that people traveled for these special occasions because they always came to us! Tootie was the matriarch of the family, and she held court in grand style.

Dinner at Tootie's was always formal. We got dressed up and went to her house about an hour and a half earlier than dinner for cocktails and hors d'oeuvres. She had a cook named Bernice, who was such a wonderful and loving lady. She always had on the traditional white outfit, which actually looked like an old nurse's uniform, and I never saw her in "street clothes." Her eyes and smile were warm and inviting, and I would sneak into the kitchen to see what she was cooking and to hear her laugh. She was my safe space at Tootie's, just like Bertha was my safe space in our house.

The hors d'oeuvres were always the same: mini sweet pickles, cheese crackers that were more like a cookie then a cracker, nuts of some kind, and my favorite, peanut butter logs. They were some kind of wafer with a peanut butter mixture all around them, which made them look like logs. They were sweet and crunchy, and I would fill up on them easily if I weren't watched. Tootie would expect the children to pass the hors d'oeuvres around to the adults as they sipped their cocktails and chatted.

Mary was in charge of this for the first few years of my life, and then I got to try when I got about five or six years old. We were always expected to act properly when we were at Tootie's. She was the "grumpy" grandma, the one who never wanted us to act like children, but mind our manners and not be heard from unless spoken to first. She loved us—I know that—but she didn't seem to know how to relate to us. She was not the grandma we wanted to spend the night with. We only spent the night at her house a handful of times in my childhood, and those were only when no one else was available.

When Bernice came into the living room to let us know that dinner was ready, we would rise and go into the dining room. Sometimes there would be place cards to tell us where to sit if we had guests who were outside the family, but family members usually knew where we expected to sit. The youngest grandchild *always* sat to Tootie's left. Mary only had a couple of years of this until I came along, and then I was in the hot seat for at least seven or eight years until my younger sister, Christy, was old enough. Boy, this was a tough place to sit!

"Eat your vegetables," "Drink your milk," "No, you can't have any bread"—these were all I would hear during dinner. The only fun thing I can remember about sitting in the "hot seat" is that Tootie had a small brass turtle that if you pressed his head down, a bell would ring. This is how she would let Bernice know that we needed something or that everyone was done with dinner and the table needed to be cleared. Every once in a while, if I was good during dinner and she hadn't had to fuss at me too much, she would let me ring the turtle. It was a small thing, but I sure looked forward to it!

I remember those formal dinners with warmth, even though they were tough sometimes. There was something about the sparkle of the crystal and the clinking of silver on fine china that made it so special. Everyone behaved themselves, and we didn't have outbursts at Tootie's house; she wouldn't allow it. In that way, dinners at her house were safe. You knew what to expect, and for the most part, everyone had a good time. After dinner, we would return to the living room and sit around the fire while the adults had coffee. Bernice would bring out the silver coffee service and china cups on a silver tray. It was then the children's job to walk the cups and saucers to the adults who wanted coffee without spilling anything. Thank goodness for saucers!

The kids would try to keep their behavior in check, tired though we were, until Mom and Dad were ready to go home. I would sit on the bench in front of the fire and marvel at how hot my back would get from the fire, but the front of me would still be cool. I would sit as long as I could take the heat, then fall off the bench, and turn to let my back cool down. It was something that kept me occupied while we waited to go home.

At Baboo's house, it was the complete opposite! We didn't have many large family gatherings there because her house was smaller, and it would have been difficult to accommodate all of us. Baboo didn't have a cook, and she loved to make "throw everything" soup, which is where you throw everything in your freezer into the soup. I also remember her making cabbage a lot, which assaulted your senses when you walked in the door. Man, cabbage stinks when it's cooking!

My main memories of Baboo's house were when just us girls spent the night with her. Baboo was the "fun" grandmother. We usually stayed with her when a sleepover was required instead of just having a babysitter, and it was something I really looked forward to! She would let us watch all the TV we wanted (of course, those were the days of four channels, so that wasn't saying much), and she would cook us anything we wanted to eat, even if it was two different meals! These little gestures felt like such deep love at the time. Mom would never cook us different meals, nor did we ever have open access to the TV.

I felt special when I was at Baboo's house, even if I had to share her with Mary and then Christy later on. She would paint our nails and let us wear her nightgowns with the straps bound together with rubber bands in the back to keep them on. Baboo was barely five feet tall, so her knee-length nightgowns were full gowns on us as little girls. They were light and flowy and felt like princess dresses to us as we twirled around the house.

The furniture in Baboo's house was mostly dark-wood antiques from the antebellum South. These were pieces that had been passed down to her from her mother and grandmother who had deep roots in the South, especially in North Carolina, stretching back before the Civil War. Her home reminded me of a museum because of this furniture. Thinking back on it, it wasn't her style at all to have her home furnished like this. She was fun and light and loved to dance, which was not the impression you got when you walked through the door. My guess is, she had collected this furniture from her family over the years and considered it a way of honoring them by using it in her home, regardless of the mismatch in style to her own.

Her bed was made of solid mahogany with a large headboard and footboard stained black. This bed played a significant role in my history because if it hadn't broken at just the right moment, my father would have not survived his birth. Dad's head is huge, and Baboo was a tiny woman who was struggling to bring him into the world. Rumor has it that the bed broke during the delivery and that the force of the bed collapsing to the floor was what rendered the final push to get his head to pass through into the light. I guess I owe that bed a debt of gratitude.

The bed I got to sleep in when I was at her house was a tall, four poster rice bed, also made of mahogany. The bed was so tall she had a step stool to use to get into it, which I thought was the coolest thing ever! I remember her getting me into bed and lining both sides of my body with pillows to prevent me from falling out. When I think of it now, I can't imagine putting a small child to sleep in such a tall bed without safety rails. If I had ever fallen out during the night, there was a good possibility of broken bones. My fondest memories of time with a grandmother was with Baboo. She always made me feel loved and safe in her warm arms, nestled against her ample bosom. Her smile was infectious, and she never had a bad word to say about anything or anyone.

The house we grew up in was a smaller version of Tootie's house. It had a gravel driveway that wound around a center grassy area full of trees and bushes; we called it the circle. We would have our Easter egg hunts in the circle because we didn't really have a backyard. While there was plenty of space behind the house leading down to the lake that was between Tootie's house and ours, it was fenced in where the dogs could run and was not a space for us to play. Our house was made of brick, white-washed and slightly sanded so that some of the brick was exposed. There was a brick porch that spanned the front with four white columns evenly spaced. On the porch was the same filigree white iron furniture that Tootie had at her house, as well as a marble-topped table with plants on it, just like Tootie's.

Inside the house, the decor stayed the same my entire eighteen years living there. There was wood paneling made from a wood called pecky cypress that had lots of holes in it in every room. The trim color and carpeting throughout the house was army green. I remember the house being very dark, probably due to the green color that permeated every room, which gave the house a dingy and depressing feeling. Only the kitchen and the bedrooms had white trim, brightening them up a bit. The countertops in the kitchen were muted yellow laminate that stained if you spilled Kool-Aid on them and didn't clean it up right away. The big black rotary phone was hanging on the wall with a cord so long it could stretch to adjoining rooms. That phone receiver was so heavy it could have been a murder weapon if needed.

Dinners at our house were much more casual but still stressful because Mom did all the cooking, which was not her forte. We only really did the "formal" dinners when it was a holiday, but we would sit in the dining room if there were enough of us that we couldn't fit anywhere else. Kids had to help with setting the table, clear afterward, and do the dishes. Hors d'oeuvres were more basic, like cheese and crackers, and there were plenty of cocktails. Mom liked to do things like spaghetti dinners. They were fairly easy, and she could time them right. One thing Mom was good at was baking cakes. When we had birthdays or if the gathering was around a birthday, she always baked a cake, and it was delicious!

We had more toys to choose from at our house, so we spent a lot of the time leading up to the meal in what we called the big room. The big room was where all our toys could be found, as well as a baby grand piano and a pool table. It was a large room above the garage that I think my parents added on to the house after they moved in. I always knew it to be there, so it was just part of my experience. It was always a mess, and the constant demand of "clean up the big room" was so commonplace that it got tuned out most of the time. Sometimes the adults would go to the big room to play pool before dinner, and it was fun to watch the grown-ups compete. We didn't like sharing space with them, though, as we were always being reminded to quiet down, which was aggravating because we thought of this as our room and them as the visitors.

I remember one of Mom and Dad's biggest fights taking place around that pool table. Mom's best friend was Maria, and her husband, Mark, was Dad's best friend; we called them Aunt Maria and Uncle Mark. Their kids, Christian and Amy, were Mary's and my best friends, although that worked better for me because Amy was a girl. Mary tolerated Christian, but she would have preferred he be a girlfriend. Our ages were what they called stepladder, configured with Mary as the oldest, then Christian, then me, then Amy, then Christy at the end.

The whole family was over for dinner one night, and Dad and Uncle Mark were playing pool before dinner. Mom and Aunt Maria were in the kitchen, doing dinner stuff, and the kids were in the big room, trying to stay out of the men's way. Mary had built a tower with the heavy wooden block set we had in the big room, right next to the pool table. As the men moved around the table throughout the game, the location of the tower began to be an issue.

It was Dad's turn. He leaned over to take his shot, and as he drew the pool cue back, the tip of the cue hit the top of the tower squarely. *Bam!* It all came tumbling down with a loud crash!

"Look what you've *done*!" Mary screamed at Dad as her masterpiece lay in shambles on the floor.

"Well, if you didn't build that thing so close to the table, it would still be there!" he retorted.

"I'm telling Mom!" Mary went running into the kitchen to get reinforcements, as the rest of us realized we weren't breathing.

There was gonna be a showdown, and it wasn't clear who was going to come out the victor. Mom came stomping down the hall while being peppered with details of the great fall of the tower of Mary and how Dad (a.k.a. Godzilla) had destroyed the city.

I don't remember Mom taking this type of vested interest in our plight often, but she must have been spoiling for a fight with Dad, and this particular event seemed to suit her just fine. She accused Dad of being a hurtful monster to not be able to avoid the kid's creations so that he could "play his precious pool game" and for yelling at Mary when *he* was the one who had committed the infraction.

Mom didn't hesitate to yell at Dad in front of Uncle Mark, Aunt Maria, and us kids, which was embarrassing and emasculating, ending in him leaving the house in a huff, slamming the screen door behind him, and breaking it off the hinges. Dad rarely did anything explosive, so when he got to the point where he was screaming and slamming doors on his way out, you knew it was bad.

All of us kids were scared. We weren't sure how it was going to end. Would we still eat dinner? I remember thinking that I couldn't believe Mom would act like that in front of people, even if it was Aunt Maria and Uncle Mark. I was always the "fixer" of the family, so my main concern was how were we going to resolve this and make sure everyone is still friends. Since Dad had stormed out and we didn't know where he was, Aunt Maria, Uncle Mark, and their kids went home without eating.

The next morning, when we came into the kitchen for breakfast, Dad was sitting at the table, and there was an unexplained peace that made us all question whether the storm we had witnessed last night had even happened. Mom recalls this fight, or one similar in intensity, was the impetus to her receiving her diagnosis. Dad invited the doctor over to the house to discuss the severity of her behavior in the privacy of our kitchen and thus began the journey with these new words in our house: manic depression.

The one predictable person in our household was our housekeeper, Bertha. Bertha came to work with our family part-time at first, when Mom was experiencing postpartum depression after Mary's birth. Then Bertha went full time when I was on the way. She was the dearest, most loving adult in my life as I was growing up. She was an African American woman with a warm smile and a great laugh, which I can still hear today if I close my eyes. Bertha was always there, and I was her shadow most of the time as she moved about the house, keeping it together for us. She did this physically and psychologically for all of us kids as she was the one who was sane, predictable, and stable.

I called her Bubba because I couldn't pronounce Bertha. She wore what looked like a white nurse's uniform with matching white shoes, and she always had a piece of gum in her mouth, popping her gum, making loud "snaps" with it each time she chewed. She would also hum while she worked. I would walk down the hall toward the big room, passing Mom's sewing room, which was a small alcove with accordion doors that closed to hide the disarray, and as I got closer to the laundry room, I could hear Bertha humming over the sound of the clothes tumbling in the dryer.

Bertha drove a banana-yellow car with a black top, and I used to love it when I could ride with her somewhere because it was different than anything my family had ever owned. There was something about Bertha's presence that grounded me. I knew I was safe and secure when she was around. One of my favorite stories with Bubba was the day I found out people could be afraid of frogs.

I loved frogs. They were my favorite animal, and each time someone gave me a gift, it often had a frog theme. Living in the country, toads were everywhere, and I played with them often. One day, Mom had gone to the store. As I remember it, Bertha and I were the only one's home when I found a bullfrog outside. I picked it up and had it cupped in my hands, talking to it and telling it all my deepest secrets. I took it into the house and walked back to the laundry room to introduce Bertha to my friend. As I approached the room, she saw me speaking softly into my hands.

"Who are you talking to?" she asked.

"My friend," I said as I gently held my cupped hands together.

"Who is your friend?"

"HIM!" I exclaimed, opening my hands and thrusting the bullfrog toward Bertha.

Well, I have never heard such a bloodcurdling scream as the one that came out of Bertha in that moment! She burst past me, ran to the bathroom down the hall, and locked herself inside. I was shocked! I had no idea what had caused my dear friend to act like that. I went and stood outside the door, asking if she was okay and asking her to come out.

"NOT UNTIL THAT THING IS GONE!" she exclaimed.

I didn't get it! I was three or four years old, and I couldn't conceive of someone being afraid of frogs. I stood outside the door, imploring her to come out, but to no avail. When Mom returned home, she assessed the situation and knew of Bertha's fear. She screamed at me to take that thing outside because Bertha was afraid of frogs! I started crying and took my friend outside to let him go so I could go back in and try to make this right. I was mortified that I had hurt her, and I needed to apologize to her, even though I couldn't figure out how in the *world* she could be afraid of something so innocent.

Bertha was my light in the darkness. She was often the only person in the house that smiled when I came in the room. She spent much of her time in the small laundry room that was just down the hall from the big room, and I remember her picking me up to sit on the dryer while she ironed and folded clothes. We would talk for hours about goodness knows what, and she never seemed to tire of my company. I would follow her around when she changed the sheets on the beds and get in her way as often as I could.

As an adult now, I have a different understanding of the dynamics of our relationship from the perspective of a Black woman who was working for a white family, charged with caring for the white children in that family. I know she loved me, but I wish I could talk with her, knowing what I now know, about her experience in our household. I was not aware of my privilege at the time; I was clueless to the imbalance of power within the situation and how that might have affected her on a daily basis.

Watching her make a bed was magical for my young self. She would hold the flat sheet by the corners and flip it out and up as it expanded from its folded state. The sheet would be high above the bed, hovering in what seemed suspended animation, and I would jump onto the bed just in time for the sheet to lightly float down on top of me, brushing my skin every so lightly in a soft touch. Bertha would exclaim, "Where did Dee go?" And I would giggle under the sheet and thought she truly had lost me for a moment.

I am sure it took her twice as long to get this simple task done, but she never scolded me for being in the way. Of course, I know now she wouldn't have likely scolded me about anything as she probably didn't feel like she had the power to do so, but at the time, her grace felt like expressions of love that I did not experience with anyone else in my life. To this day, I think of her each time I make a bed, flipping the sheet high in the air and making crisp hospital corners, or when I hear someone popping their gum or humming a soft tune under their breath. I love her so much.

The Small-Town Promise of Time

I am built on familiar frequencies.

Potholes in the streets
send familiar vibrations to my seat
as my car tires pass through them
for the thousandth time.

I can close my eyes
knowing what road I am traveling
simply by the sway of the vehicle.

A world of familiar senses
passes by my open window:
the smell of fresh doughnuts
from the bakery,
the taste of ice cream
from the corner parlor,
the *tap, tap, tap* sound
of beginner shoes
from the dance studio.

I don't need to know the street names
because I know the stories
of the families who have lived
generation after generation
on this tree-lined grid.
Folks smile in greeting
while their hearts
cry hidden tears.

Descriptions are framed
in family lineage,
because you are not just you

but the compilation of all
who came before you.

I am built on familiar rhythms.

I wonder if there is room
for the truth of my pain.
Would you welcome me
through the doors of the church
if you knew how unholy my story is?

Many revere the unchanging
energy of this space.
The lines and sounds bring comfort
in their predictability,
but for me...they bring horror.

They remind me
that my stars won't change
as long as I am seeing them
from within the boundaries
of this echo chamber of lies.

I can break free,
but first,
I must shatter the chains
around my ankles
and begin to *run*.

I know these familiar streets
will always be there.
This small town whispers to me
as I begin to move my feet...

"Don't worry.
Your secrets are safe with me."

Chapter 2

Daily life in my house as I was growing up had one constant: only the unpredictable was predictable. At the head of this monster was Mom, who seemingly made all decisions of movement governed by her state of mind in the moment. She was a small woman in stature—five feet, three inches with a slim build. She had freckles all over her body that never seemed to join each other no matter how much time she spent in the sun. She was born with bright red hair, and her freckled skin had remained even after her hair had darkened with age. She wore her hair in a fixed hairdo typical of the time and very little makeup that I can recall. She was a casual dresser but would dress up for the occasion if it was required. I believe her preference for jeans was a direct result of her rebellion against her high-level upbringing. She wanted the simple life that came with middle-class living and was not eager to attend events that required formal attire.

One of the things we could count on was Mom's naptime every day. This usually happened around 3:00 or 4:00 p.m., right after we had arrived home from school, and we were expected to be quiet to ensure her nap would be undisturbed. Thinking about this timing now, I am more aware of why this was so hard for us to maintain. We had been expected to behave quietly all day at school, only to come home to more expected quiet time. This was more problematic in the early years when our bedroom was down the hall from Mom and Dad's room, as anytime we went down there to get something out of our room, we inevitably made too much noise and woke the sleeping giant. Thank goodness for the big room and its location on the other end of the house; we had a place to get our sillies out and make some level of noise without disturbing her.

Even with this safe space, I remember that we held our breaths that time when the castle we had made with wooden blocks fell to the floor and sounded like bowling pins crashing during a strike. As our bodies froze, we listened for the tell-tale stomping through the kitchen as she came to let us know she didn't appreciate being woken up. Depending on the severity of our infraction and her temperament that day, punishment could range from grounding to a spanking with what we called the switch.

Much time was spent thinking and predicting what Mom's reaction would be to any given stimulus. I had the added pleasure of trying to predict Mary's movements and moods, which proved to be just as difficult to read. Life was a minefield, and I often just tried to keep my head down and keep it moving.

Dad was predictable in his daily movements and in his lack of connection to us at home. He went to work every day, giving us all sloppy kisses as he left us at the kitchen table, eating breakfast, and then he returned later that day after Mom's nap time but before dinner. He walked in the door, went straight to his room to change out of his work clothes, then stopped at the bar for a drink before landing in his recliner in the den to watch the news and wait for dinner. I don't remember he and Mom talking about their day together, debriefing as married couples often do after spending the day apart.

If Mom's day had been difficult, she would often needle him with snide comments until he engaged. She didn't seem to have any idea how to release tension in herself and relied on the emotional release only a fight could provide her. If Dad wasn't feeling like engaging in this dance, she would turn to one of us for the release. A loving gesture from my mom at this time in my life was to not "go after" someone, culminating in an emotional explosion. We didn't get hugs or an unsolicited "I love you," but the gift of a quiet night was just as precious.

In many ways, we had a sixth member of our family—*the Crazy*. The Crazy of my childhood was a genderless being whose form was flexible and could morph into spaces and people's eyes at will. The Crazy could be the scapegoat, the rawhide whip, the belt, the silence

37

during Mom's naps, the dark room after bedtime, the nightmares, the fear of knives, the hatred of a big sister, or the three hours spent at the dinner table until I ate my cold food. It showed up often without warning, wrapping its arms around me and suffocating me before I even knew it was there.

I didn't have any defense against the Crazy. It was prominent in my life before I was even in consciousness, becoming as familiar as the air I breathed, and I had no specific awareness of its form. It was the hidden force with which I was in constant battle. If I could only find the perfect phrase or the timely look to put the person in front of me in a better space, I could best the Crazy and stay safe. But the Crazy jumped from person to person like a glance, so fast I couldn't follow it. I was powerless to it because I didn't know what I was fighting. It was an energetic whisper that manifested into storms within the eyes of my loved ones that would last until it grew tired of playing with my safety.

Mary was a consistent host to the Crazy. One night when I was around six or seven years old, Mom and Dad went out to dinner and left Mary in charge. As they walked out the front door, I was completely unprepared for what came next. Mary turned around with the Crazy in her eyes, and we were off to the races!

She retrieved the switch and chased me into the big room, cornering me while determinedly stating, "I'm going to *kill* you! I'm going to *kill* you! I'm going to *kill* you!"

Each exclamation came with a *snap* of the switch. This continued until Mom and Dad returned, and by that time, I was completely hysterical. I remember Mom questioning Mary about my state of mind, of which she had no explanation. I was put to bed, trying to catch my breath with the staccato gasps that come when you've been crying for such a long time. It wasn't until well into adulthood that Mom learned the truth of what happened that night. Mary was only acting out her version of the Crazy, but it solidified in my mind that she was not to be trusted—a belief that I am still working on five decades later. It also confirmed that Mom and Dad could be easily manipulated to believe anyone other than me when I tried to tell my truth.

From my early memories, I was labeled the liar of the household. No story I told was immediately believed, and it was a mystery to me which came first—my lying or their lack of belief in me. I was the quiet one, the invisible one, which worked for me most days as I navigated the unpredictable world in which I lived. But there were times when being invisible was agony. I had tried to be like Mary and be confrontational to get attention, but I was never as good at it as she was.

Being "the good one" had its perks from time to time, but only when compared to Mary's combative nature, which was reliant upon Mary's mood and Mom caring enough to engage. I began embellishing stories just enough that they still sounded believable but were more intriguing than what I believed my life to be at the time. I would come down the stairwell from Mary's room and miss a step, free-falling until my foot found solid surface further down than I anticipated. When I rounded the corner to the kitchen, I had "fallen down the stairs from Mary's room," and inquiries into whether or not I had broken anything enveloped me for at least three minutes.

My life felt so boring on any given day that punching up the details seemed like a good way to keep things interesting. Part of having the Crazy as a permanent resident in the family is the phenomenon of experiences happening, like family fights or threats of harm, and then everyone behaving the next morning as if nothing had happened. Reality was like a bar of soap: the harder I tried to hold on to it, the more it slipped out of my hand. If everyone else was going to play so fast and loose with the truth, why couldn't I make my little life experiences seem a little more interesting?

A classic example of the Crazy manifesting to limit my safety was the tale of the Buster Brown shoes. Since shopping was limited in our small town, we always went elsewhere to buy clothes and shoes for school. One day, we went to a nearby town to buy Buster Brown shoes! The ones I chose were brown leather lace-up shoes with a green and blue panel on the sides, and I thought they were the best shoes *ever*! As always, I asked to wear my new shoes out of the store, and the saleslady put my old shoes in the box to be carried home. I walked out of that shoe store with such pride and loved looking down at my shoes and seeing them move on the sidewalk. As we were making our way to the car, I lost my balance and fell into the street, busting my forehead wide open! I started screaming immediately, and Mom scooped me up and set me on the hood of someone's white car that was parked at the curb.

The blood was immense—as happens with head wounds—and I remember seeing Mom's white blazer and the hood of someone's white car starting to look like a horror film set! Mom whisked me off to the emergency room, and we sat in the waiting room for what seemed like forever because of a multicar pileup that had come in just before us. A little cut on a forehead was not a priority, and we had to wait.

The cut was right above my right eyebrow, and when we finally got back to see the doctor, he quickly assessed the need for stitches. As the nurse laid me down on the gurney, with her soothing voice assuring me it would be okay, the doctor approached from above my head with a very large curved needle that had what looked like thread protruding off the end of it. He told me to lay still, and he quickly began to sew up my forehead with no anesthesia! The sharp rush of pain as the needle pierced my skin, coupled with the fact that this was all happening in front of my face, facilitated blood-curdling screams from me. I was inconsolable! The doctor started yelling above my screams, telling me to shut up and warning my mom that if she didn't keep me quiet, he was going to make her leave. Bedside manner was not in his toolbox of skills, and the Crazy was in his eyes.

Several weeks later, the stitches were removed, and I was so glad that was over. Within a week, Mary and I were fighting over something in the den, and she pushed me so hard that I fell against the coffee table, hitting the edge right on the site of my previous wound. When I started screaming and bleeding again, she quickly assessed the situation and knew she had to act fast. She found a shoebox lying nearby and placed it on the floor, telling Mom I tripped over it to explain how I had hit the table. To this day, I have a scar on my forehead, and it was decades later that Mom heard the story retold and realized her error in believing in my clumsiness more than Mary's capability of dastardly deeds. The default seemed to be to believe Mary's explanation and dismiss mine. It wasn't until many years later that I had a better understanding of why that was, but for the moment, I was not to be believed, supported, or trusted.

In the early years, before Mom was diagnosed, we didn't have a word for her mood swings. The key in our world was watching her facial expressions to gauge how far away we needed to stand. During the day, our goal was to do as we were told and stay out of her way. At night, irritated by Dad's drinking and the stressors of cooking dinner and getting everyone to bed so she could finally turn her brain off, she was much faster to trigger. I tried to find solace in my big sister, who at times would remember she loved me and act as my protector. We would find ways to play together to pass the time, and I relished those moments when I felt like we were on the same team in this daily survival walk.

One thing we had in common was our love for all things ABBA. "Dancing Queen" was a favorite from the album *ABBA*, which came out in 1976, and we wore that record out, listening to the songs that are now known by more recent generations from the *Mamma Mia* movies. Our back porch, open to the humid North Carolina air during our early childhood and later closed in for year-round enjoyment, was the second place we were allowed to play. We would set up the Victrola (record player for you kids today) on the porch and play it over and over and over again, twirling with crochet scarves on our heads to mimic the long hair adorned by Agnetha Faitskog and Anni-Frid Lyngstad, the two women members of the band.

Another fond memory of good sister time together was Mary teaching me the hustle to the song "Car Wash." I can't hear those songs today without cell memory kicking in, feeling the dizziness you feel when you've been twirling through a song or how my feet still know the steps to the hustle that we watched on *American Bandstand*. Living out in horse country with no neighborhood kids to play with created a vacuum that forced us to play together in the early years. Television was limited to Saturday mornings or after-school specials, so coming up with ways to get lost in a make-believe world together was to both our benefits.

Happy sister time while playing together was the exception rather than the rule. In the early years, games were decided on by Mary, and I was just happy to be able to participate—until she grew tired of my company. I don't mean to make it sound like it was always horrible. There were times when we felt like the dynamic duo warding off the Crazy when it appeared in Mom's eyes. During one particularly hot argument between Mom and Dad when the Phillips were over for dinner again, Mary gathered all of us kids and ushered us into the stairwell going down to the garage to wait until the storm passed. We *never* went into this stairwell because it was dark and full of spiderwebs, but it was next to the big room and was easy access to hide from the Crazy that had shown up for dinner. We could make a good team when we were in survival mode—until Mary needed to remember she wasn't powerless over everyone. Then I was often in the crosshairs again.

Christy—or CC, as she is known in adulthood—is often an absent member of our family in my childhood remembrances. I don't remember her at all as an infant in the household and, in fact, would say she joined our family as a toddler if I was left to my own memories. You might find it odd that she is rarely mentioned in these stories, but there is a dynamic in play that still exists within our family. I call it the Bermuda Triangle. This triangle consists of Mom, Mary, and me and is fueled by the patterns and history that the three of us share. CC was never inducted into this triangle, which is a gift to me and her. The toxic patterns that the members of the triangle are still working to unravel do not include CC.

In reflecting on who in my life has offered the safest space, Bertha and CC are the two that stand out. Mary, Mom, and I have made a lot of progress on dismantling the patterns that make up the Bermuda Triangle, but I suspect this will be a lifelong process. With CC, I can be myself with no fear of repercussion, which is a gift of such magnitude that I don't think I can ever express to her how much it means to me. I still find myself talking with her and can feel my body physically bracing for a reaction that never comes, and I am always relieved. If Bertha was my security within the family structure in my childhood, CC is that for me as an adult. This provides a life-line for me that I am still discovering the value of to this day.

I was jumpy as a child and didn't like to be sneaked up on or scared. Of course, this was Mary's action of choice because she could get me so easily. Our regular chores were that one of us set the table and one of us cleaned the dishes on alternate weeks. The way our kitchen was set up, the galley was a U-shaped configuration with the side-by-side double oven at the curve. The sink was in the part of the counter that looked out into the room, and when you stood at it, the doorway to the living room was to your left.

When I was on dish duty, Mary would love to crawl on her hands and knees from the living room door, along the counter to where the sink was. Because I was on the other side, I couldn't see her below the counter. I would be cleaning the dishes, trying to get done, and she would pop up from below the counter and yell, "Boo!" I can't tell you how many times this happened, and it terrified me *every time*! Suds and sometimes dishes would fly into the air, and a couple of times, I got in trouble for breaking things in my hysteria. It would take me hours to recover from these frights, and she seemed to love that. But I did get back at her!

Mary's room was the upstairs space that had been converted to a bedroom from attic space when Christy was born. When you went up the stairs, there was a door to your left that led to attic storage space. Built-in shelves were at the top of the stairs and then you turned right to go into the greater space. Directly across the room from the top of the stairs was a closet with slats in the door to increase air circulation. It was a small clothes closet, and then in the back, there was another door that led to more attic space. I don't think Mary liked that closet very much because of the access to the attic. It kind of gave us all the creeps. She had another double-door closet that she kept most of her clothes in, so she rarely went into the small closet.

One day, when Tina and I were going through a friendly phase enough for her to be over for a playdate, we decided we were going to scare Mary and get back at her for all the times she scared the hell out of me. We knew she was on her way home, so we went up to her room and hid ourselves in the small closet. The light was off inside, and we could see out the slats in the door so we knew when she came in. The excitement was overwhelming for me. I rarely got a chance to get her back for anything, and I had much more courage because of Tina's willingness to be with me.

She got home and came up the stairs as we expected. She had no idea we were there, and at first, it was all we could do to squelch our laughter at having gotten away with the perfect plan. After about a minute or so, we realized there was a part to the plan we had not fully considered: How long would we wait in the darkness before jumping out of the closet? As more time passed, we got uncomfortable, knowing that she was going about her business clueless that we were there. She was changing clothes and had her music on and was dancing around the room as teenagers do when they think they are alone. We had a change of heart and wanted to try to sneak out without going through with the scare. Somehow it had turned a corner, and we didn't think it was a good idea to go through with it. So after lots of whispering, we decided to open the door very quietly and sneak out of the room when she had gone into her bathroom. She would never know we were there—no harm, no foul. I turned the doorknob ever so slowly, feeling like every click of the mechanism would give us away. We poked our heads out and peeked around the corner to see if she was in her bathroom as we thought. Thinking the coast was clear, we started our trek to the top of the stairs.

She was not in her bathroom but was inside the double door closet, and she saw us out of the corner of her eye. She began to scream this primal, guttural scream that sounded like she was being slaughtered! Because she was not where we expected her to be, she scared us equally. We began to scream just as loud, and we were all hopping in our spots with mouths wide open! I think it lasted for about thirty seconds before we realized that if we were going to survive this encounter, we better get the hell out of dodge before she came to her senses.

Tina and I made a beeline for the top of the stairs and couldn't get down fast enough, heading straight for the front door and out of the house! I think I have blocked out the retribution for that event, which I'm sure was severe. There were not many more scares after that. I think she may have learned a little of what I had been dealing with all these years in that one moment.

There was never a time when the Crazy spent more time in each member of our family than during the Christmas holidays. We moved as a unit through the ritual of the holidays, but each of us had our own version of our outer facade and our inner anguish. We each had roles to play to make sure this holiday highlighted just how blessed and wonderful our family was, and we were each expected to fulfill those roles to the best of our ability. This was another version of flying under the radar of reality, and we were all quite skilled at the facade.

Dad's role started Thanksgiving weekend with the advent of putting up the Christmas decorations. The boxes of Christmas lights (big bulbs with multicolored lights) and ornaments for the tree came out of the attic and into the living room in an organized fashion, covering every chair and sofa until there was no longer anywhere to sit. The tree would arrive on the truck of the man who worked for Tootie named Eddie. These Christmas trees were always at least ten to twelve feet and real (fake trees were not a thing yet) and would completely fill a corner of the living room and ascend all the way to the vaulted ceiling. Dad was over six feet tall himself but would have to use a twelve feet ladder to get all the way to the top for the lights and the star. The decorating ritual would begin by stringing the lights on the trees, starting at the top and winding his way down to the bottom of the tree. This would take at least three or four strings of lights, and they each had to be perfectly spaced for the best effect. Next, he would unwrap all the ornaments and spread them out on the furniture. This was done for inspection and to remind himself to make sure that all the most important ornaments made it on the tree. They were old and fragile, collected over the years as gifts for each of us with our names and the year given. It seems to me that it took an entire day to decorate that tree, and while we were allowed to place one or two ornaments, the bulk was done by Dad to ensure proper spacing and balance. The final touch was the silver tinsel strands that had to be placed, one by one, on each tree limb. No clumping was allowed!

But when it was done, it was a twinkling masterpiece! Once the tree and lights outside were done, Dad's role in the holidays was complete until Christmas morning for the annual video recording of the reveal and the obligation of putting away all the decorations before New Year's Day or we were sure to fall prey to the bad luck that would ensue in the coming year. His purpose shifted to party host, drink maker, and buffer when the pressure got too much for Mom.

There were times over the years when his role as "Mom buffer" took a starring role in our holiday experience. There were threats over the years of "canceling Christmas" and giving all our gifts away to children "who would really appreciate them," insinuating those children were different than those standing in front of her. He was often the voice of reason when this possibility reared its ugly head, and we relied on him to get us through the weeks between Thanksgiving and Christmas with our holiday promises intact. To the world, he looked like the poor man who had to deal with his wife's mood swings, always willing to fall on the sword for his family.

For us, the holidays were a minefield that stretched as far as the eye could see with a beautiful Oz-like twinkly city on the other side that beckoned us to make the journey with promises of bliss. When the tree was up and the stockings hung and the lights were put up on the outside of the house, we eagerly awaited the arrival of Tootie's gifts. This was a holiday in and of itself, and we waited with bated breath for the moment when Eddie arrived in his blue and white truck with a bed full of gifts. Tootie bought paper towels and toilet paper by the case (which seems overkill for someone living alone) and the *huge* five-foot-by-five-foot cardboard boxes that these shipments came in became the vessels for her abundant splendor! She would have at least five or six gifts for each of us, and the delivery boxes were always filled to the brim! Because all extended family who were not local traveled to our town for the holiday, these gifts included gifts for them as well, which was why there were so many of them. None of these gifts were high in value; for Tootie, it was always quantity over quality. She would leave any of the big presents to Mom and Dad under the guise of Santa, but we always knew we would have lots to open when Christmas morning rolled around.

The overflowing delivery boxes would be hauled into the living room, and it would be our pleasure to take each gift out of the boxes to place them under the tree. We had to be strategic in placement because there was so much that we had to make full use of the space underneath while allowing for a clear path to add water to the base so the tree didn't die before it was time. Each present had a tag on it with our name, and all you would hear were giggles and speculation about what each gift was as it was announced who it was intended for before it went under the tree. When all were unloaded, the presents spread at least four to five feet from the base of the tree outward. Getting to the actual tree was no longer an option.

We were *overjoyed* with the anticipation of Christmas morning and the mysteries of what was in each package wrapped in color-ful paper with curling ribbon bows. These gifts were always under the tree at least a week or two before the big day, so what began as excitement became the carrot that was dangled and threatened with eradication during those two weeks. If someone came into our house, they would see such abundance it might make their eyes water. To us, that abundance was wrapped in thinly veiled threats that became more prominent the closer we got to Christmas Eve and the more exhausted Mom got by her preparations and anticipation of entertaining.

Mary and I had a tradition of spending the night together on Christmas Eve. With CC being so much younger, I don't have any memories of her participating in this tradition. We would stay up late after lights out, dreaming about what the gifts from Santa would be. We were always required to make a Christmas list because Mom never trusted her knowledge of our wants enough to make those decisions on her own. It was common knowledge that if you didn't make a list, you weren't gonna get much for Christmas. I understand the value of knowing exactly what your loved ones want so that you don't disappoint, but for the receiver, it is powerful when someone knows you so well that they can surprise you with a gift that they just *know* you would like. I didn't get the pleasure of this moment of connection until many years later—ironically from Mary—when a Christmas gift she gave me made me cry because I hadn't asked for it but she knew I would love it and got it anyway. The fact that this came from her made it all the sweeter.

One Christmas Eve, Mary and I were upstairs trying to go to sleep and giggling about our expected bounty the next morning.

She sat up in bed and suggested a ninja assignment. "We should sneak downstairs and see what we got!" she whispered as we fantasized about the bounty that awaited.

"Do you think they'll know? How do we know they've gone to bed? We can't see if they are still up, with the doors closed." I was agonizing over all the ways this plan could go wrong. Would they give our gifts away if we got caught? I wasn't sure the knowledge was worth the risk.

"The doors to the living room will be closed. If they are still there, the light will be on, and we can see that under the door. If they are in there, we'll just sneak back upstairs. Come on, scaredy-cat!" This was Mary's favorite name for me when I was putting a damper on her plans.

We made the descent downstairs and headed for the living room. There were two entrances to this grand room, one from the kitchen and one from the front hall. Each entrance had double doors that when closed were about the width of a traditional single door. The tradition on Christmas Eve was after dinner we were allowed to open one gift, which was always matching Christmas pajamas. We would run to our rooms and get changed into our new PJs then come running back in to say good night. After we went to bed, Mom and Dad would close the doors to each entrance to the living room and they would not be opened again until Christmas morning.

As we tiptoed up to the closed doors, we could see that the lights in the living room were out, and all was quiet. On the other side of the living room were Mom and Dad's room and bathroom, so sneaking in was always a risk because they may still be up and wandering the halls just on the other side of the space. If we were spotted, we were sure that Christmas would be canceled. The next obstacle to jump was opening the doors quietly. Neither one of us breathed as Mary pulled ever so gently to make sure the "pop" sound that happened when the catch released itself would be as quiet as we could muster. When the inevitable sound rang through the hallway like a church gong, we held our breath to see if they heard and were coming to investigate. The coast looked clear… We were *in*!

Each person would have a designated space in the living room where their Santa gifts would be displayed. These did not get wrapped, so the response would be immediate without ripping of paper and bows. I think Mom just ran out of steam to wrap anything, but I think her explanation was that Santa didn't have time to wrap all the gifts he delivered all over the world, which made sense to me. He was a busy man! We quickly found our spot and marveled at the gifts we would have to pretend surprise for in the morning. Then we got out of there and back upstairs before we were discovered, giggling and talking a mile a minute about what we were getting and how exciting it was that we didn't get caught! Of course, it didn't occur to me the timing of it all. If we were so worried about Mom and Dad not being up, why did we not question the fact that Santa had come already? It's funny how kids don't seem to have an accurate concept of timing.

The next morning, we would be up with the sun, eager to begin the rampage of unwrapping that would ensue. We would come down to the kitchen to have breakfast and go through the yearly ritual of asking when Baboo was going to arrive. The process was that my grandmother would come to the house around eight thirty, and we would be expected to wait for her to eat breakfast, taking her time eating every morsel that Mom made for her, while we watched in anticipation for her to be a member of the "clean plate club" so we could go in to the living room for the reveal.

Dad had one of those massive video cameras that required a tripod to hold it up because it was so heavy. We could hear him setting up the camera as we pressed our ears to the doors, and our excitement continued to build, even though we had seen the big stuff the night before. All of us had to eat breakfast (which none of us children could stomach), then line up shortest to tallest in front of the doors, and wait for Dad to give the okay. Once he did, we went *bursting* into the living room to find our Santa gifts in our designated spots, all caught on film by our videographer. This footage has no sound, so you can see us bounding around in our excitement and our matching

Christmas PJs with big smiles on our faces. The process was that we would open our stockings first, then move to the gifts under the tree. There were few moments in our world that were more filled with excitement and glee than Christmas morning, but that glee came with obligations.

We had to write thank-you notes each time we got a gift. From the time that we could write our names, thank-you notes were expected, and the resistance to writing them a highly punishable offense. Each Christmas morning, we had to have a pad of paper and a pencil next to us where we would write down each gift giver's name and an itemized list of the gifts received. If we were too young to make this list ourselves, it would be Mom's job to record the bounty. This came with a lot of demands and anxiety since we would open presents so fast that she wouldn't keep track of who gave what and our notes would be incomplete. Opening our stocking was always a relief because we knew we didn't have to write notes for any of those items. All other gift unwrapping came with stress, making sure that Mom was paying attention and that all gifts were recorded. In the early years, we had to unwrap gifts in rotation so that Mom could keep up with what was Mary's and what was mine, which was very hard to achieve for two little girls who just wanted to open their Christmas presents.

Thank-you notes were expected to be done within the first week after Christmas, and each note was to follow a similar template: "Dear so and so, thank you for the … [each item had to be stated no matter how many]. I really like it, and it makes me happy. I hope you have a merry Christmas. Love, Dee."

As we got older, we were expected to elaborate, including how we might use the gift or asking about their holiday plans. I spent many years between Christmas and New Year's grounded because I wouldn't do my thank-you notes. I *hated* this ritual and resisted it with every fiber of my being. It felt so contrived and seemed another example of showing "happy, happy, happy" to the outside world when I wasn't feeling it in my heart. I appreciate being taught the importance of thanking people for their generosity and tried to instill the same in my daughter. My one change was, we did nonitemized thank-you notes, which Mom did not like, when my daughter was little!

For Mom, the holidays seemed to be a time of expectation, obligation, and exhaustion. It began in the weeks leading up to Thanksgiving and didn't end until approaching New Year's, when the decorations came down and the house was returned to normal. Each year, she would be responsible for one big turkey dinner (she, Aunt Gay, and Tootie would rotate between Thanksgiving, Christmas Eve, and Christmas Day dinners) for at least fifteen people, which manifested as high anxiety for her. The years when she got the Thanksgiving meal were the best because she wouldn't have the added burden of managing the meal on top of the Christmas expectations she put on herself every year.

To the outside world, she looked like she had it all together. The house was beautifully decorated with all the traditional Christmas trinkets that only came out of hiding this time of year, the tree was full of gifts, and her daughters would be dressed in similar or matching dresses for our attendance at Christmas Eve services at church. To anyone looking through the window illuminated by candlelight, we looked like a family who had it all.

The reality began weeks before Thanksgiving with the lists. Mom made lists for everything! There were lists for food shopping and gift shopping that she relied on heavily to keep track of what was coming next and what she had gotten done. These lists lived in her purse, and if she ever couldn't find them, all life *stopped* until they were recovered. At the top of the list was the obligatory Christmas card. Sometime around Thanksgiving, Christmas card day was declared and we were expected to present in our finest to have the picture taken (if there wasn't an option from pictures taken earlier in the year of us girls). This was challenging in the early years because we were little and didn't want to sit still long enough. In later years, the challenge was getting us to sit at all because hair and makeup was never good enough, mostly for Mary. Along with this photo, a letter was mailed informing all about our year and what progress we had made as children. Mom took this all on herself and got them all mailed out to probably two hundred to three hundred people around the country.

Next was gift shopping, which all had to be done the old-fashioned way—going to individual stores and purchasing each item, since online shopping wasn't a thing yet. She had each of our Christmas lists to guide her through this process, plus all the stocking stuffer items, gifts for Dad and all other family members, especially those who would be visiting for the holidays. It would have been so much easier if the adults in the family had said they would only get gifts for the kids, but that was not the expectation, and she didn't have lists from these adults. She had to guess what they would want, which I remember being highly stressful for her.

She stayed up until one or two o'clock in the morning every night for at least ten days before Christmas Eve to wrap all items, including each stocking stuffer no matter how small. Exhaustion was probably the biggest component to her mood swings during this time, but she never knew she could do it any other way. I remember seeing her sitting in the living room on Christmas morning surrounded by all the gifts that had her name on the tag. She would sit there for *hours* before she would unwrap the first one, paying endless attention to what each of us were unwrapping to make sure we were ok with her choices.

It was almost painful for her to see what others gave her, like she didn't believe she deserved the love encased in brightly colored paper and bows. When she did finally unwrap a gift, it was excruciatingly slow. She had to make sure removing the tape didn't tear the paper; then she would fold each piece of paper, no matter the size, to reuse. This was indicative of the mentality that we all grew up with. You have *everything*, but you must save what you can to be frugal. I remember being so aggravated with how slow she moved through her gifts. It seemed to us like an exercise in control or that she had worked so hard for so long to get to this day that she wanted to savor each moment. But I wonder if there was a deeper reason she seemed repulsed by the gifts scattered on the floor around her feet. How could anyone love her enough to give her a gift?

The Past Is a Silent Mirror

I hung you
on the wall today.
You came from my childhood,
and I have always loved
the golden leaf frame
that surrounds your
reflective gaze.

I pass by you often,
never taking the time
to really look into your glass
for fear of what
I might see.

Even in the dark,
you reflect the inner workings
of my heart,
memories that don't need light
to exist.

The truth of my first steps
through life
hang suspended
until I choose to look.

No one is forcing me
to ask you questions,
but I know if I don't,
I will never truly see

myself in your surface.
I can choose to avoid,
to ignore,
to run…
Ignorance is bliss, right?

This bliss comes
with a cost.
It costs me time.
It costs me love.
It costs me life!

This bliss is death,
and I choose to look
into the pain and live!

Chapter 3

I took my first drink at the age of ten. It was the launch of a journey of "checking out" rather than "checking in." As an adult, I work every day to make the conscious choice to "check in" with God or my guidance, going within to the place of quiet where spirit resides. But as a young person, checking out was much more accessible. Alcohol was easy to acquire, ingest, and provided me a false sense of control. I didn't understand those who took pills or snorted cocaine. Once you put those substances in your body, you are at their mercy until it goes away. I was enough of a control freak to like knowing exactly how many beers it took to get to a certain level of numb. In fact, I prided myself on that knowing and looked at those who did other drugs to be lowlifes. Funny how the ego will find a rationalization for its own choices: taking care to place someone's behavior below yours to prop itself up.

The Crazy of my teenage years and twenties was 110 proof. Instead of finding the perfect posture to control the Crazy, I decided that anesthetizing was the best way to avoid it or to beat it at its own game. This began the semiconscious efforts to "check out." If I was numb, the Crazy didn't hurt so bad. If I could just check out enough, I wouldn't feel the Crazy when it slapped me across the cheek or grabbed my arms leaving fingerprint bruises or penetrated my being in my quest for love.

I was thirteen when I found myself at my first "real" party. A classmate of mine named Teri lived down the road from us in deep horse country. Her family owned the wooded field across the street from their house that had a small lake (which usually wasn't much bigger than a large mud puddle) nestled deep among the pine trees.

That night, twenty to twenty-five cars made their way down the dirt road to the lake's edge and parked willy-nilly to cram as many in as we could. The ground was red clay and uneven with ruts caused by hard rains in days before. Nothing mattered except the music playing from the multiple radios and access to coolers in each car with the drinks of choice of the owner, usually a case or two of beer.

It was dark, so navigating the space and trying to look "cool" was difficult enough for my thirteen-year-old self without the added complication of getting fairly drunk by my second beer. Most of Mary's friends were there, so I had to do my best to stay away from her for two main reasons: to give her space so that she wouldn't kill me (she had given me a ride, but that was the extent of her need to be near me) and to avoid the inevitable embarrassment she would foist on me if she knew I was drunk. Teri might have been an ally to me in this situation, as she was my age, but she had become the new "Becky" in the current version of the "Three Musketeers"—Teri, Nikki, and Patty. She was cool and knew how to handle herself in these situations, something I aspired to be and do. She also did something that many of us at our private school didn't do: she invited kids from the public high school to her parties. Pinecrest was a big school, and the kids typically wouldn't be caught dead partying with the wimpy private school crowd. But sometimes there were people who created bridges for the two schools to meet, and Teri was one of these bridges.

As I tried to find the best place to stand, I was happy for the darkness. If I was in a well-lit room, it would be painfully obvious that no one was speaking to me. Under the cover of night, however, I could stand among a crowd of people, and no one noticed that I wasn't saying a word. The beer was cold and comforting as I took mouthful after mouthful until the first was gone; then the second was gone; then the third. Maintaining my balance became a struggle, and I found myself laughing at others' conversations from my place of invisibility, like a ghost who doesn't know she's dead and wonders why no one will respond to her questions. I was participating by proxy in my life, a part of every conversation and of none. I marveled at how easy it was for the girls to flirt and tease the boys and tried to pick up pointers as I watched through the thick lens of my buzz. Whoever's radio was the loudest was responsible for the music, usually consisting of classic southern rock that could be sung at the top of one's lungs with the obligatory "air guitar" accompaniment. Led Zeppelin, ZZ Top, Lynyrd Skynyrd, and AC/DC were just a few of the favorites that bounced around in the treetops on that dark night.

Three years of dabbling in drinking had culminated to this moment. My first drink was with Tina. She had sneaked some from the unlocked liquor cabinet: vodka with a Kool-Aid chaser to mark the occasion. It was her first drink too. As we drank from paper dixie cups, we huddled in her room sitting on the lower bunk bed while her little sister Heather banged on the door frantically wanting to get in to see what we were doing. I had taken a sip from Dad's beer before—and never more than a sip—but I had never drunk hard liquor before. It was strong and burned as it went down. As soon as I started feeling the warmth that spread around my cells when the numbness arrives, I was hooked. My anxiety was lessened and life seemed much funnier than before. I was also doing something "bad," which had always been something I had tried to do, but had never found the best way to be bad without putting my immediate health at risk. Maybe this was my way to rebel with the added bonus of numbing the pain of my existence and lowering my anxiety in one fell swoop.

This same concoction of numbness, and rebellion was the goal each time I drank. As the evening progressed by the lake, I had settled into a lovely state of duality: being there in body, but flying somewhere else in spirit. When curfew was approaching, Mary found me to say we were going home. I didn't want her to know how drunk I was. I wasn't even *sure* how drunk I was! We found the car (which is an accomplishment when you are stumbling around in the dark) and somehow made it out of the chaos of parked cars without hitting anyone. We were only just a mile or so down the road from home, so the drive was short. Mary explained how our return would go down. We both were expected to make an appearance in Mom and Dad's room to "pass inspection." This consisted of a series of questions about our night posed by Mom, which seemed easy enough, but they were cleverly crafted to engage both of us in conversation to assess just how drunk we were. I stumbled into the house and followed Mary to Mom and Dad's bedroom after hearing her threats about what she was gonna do to me if she got in trouble for my drunkenness.

"You better keep your shit straight or this is the *last* time you will *ever* go with me to a party! If I get in trouble for your bullshit, that's *it*!" she repeated to me over and over during our short ride home.

As we approached the bedroom, we passed through the dark living room without turning on the light because we knew where every piece of furniture was placed. I really thought I was fine! This was gonna be a piece of cake.

"Hello... how was your night?" Mom began, luring us into a false sense of safety with questions that suggested care and camaraderie for her wandering daughters. I let Mary answer first to see how it was done. She gave short answers containing the bare minimum of details so as to satisfy that she wasn't hiding anything, but nowhere near the depth of the experience we had enjoyed together. Then Mom turned her gaze to me.

"How was your first party? How did it go? Did you have fun?"

Oh shit! My impaired brain was swirling with all the sights and smells of the evening. I had a lot riding on this exchange. I could get grounded by Mom, and I could get killed by Mary for getting her into trouble for allowing me to get drunk at thirteen. Mom was lying in bed with Dad snoring lightly next to her. She stared directly into my eyes daring me to answer with anything other than the truth.

I hesitated, but then finally spoke.

"Oh, it was *great*!" I said too loudly. "There were *soooooo* many people there!" I said with too much emphasis. "It was *soooooo great*!" I repeated.

This went on and on and on. I didn't know how to stop the steady stream of words coming out of my mouth, most of which were the same sentences jumbled in different orders each time I uttered them. Mom listened with great interest, a slight smirk on her face, with the knowing of a mom who was experiencing her drunk daughter for the first time.

Mary was tugging on my jacket, trying to get me to wrap it up and head for the door. She knew that this was a "get in and get out" operation, and any lingering was sure to lead to dire consequences. I didn't get the cue because I was too busy digging a hole to China with the metaphorical shovel in my hands and because I was so drunk. Cues didn't have any relevance.

"Well, good night!" Mary said as she turned me around and pushed me toward the door to exit.

"Good night! Sleep well" Mom said as we left the room and headed to the other side of the house. Mary was berating me in whispered voices that I talked too much and repeated myself and that I better get better at the "inspection" phase of partying if I wanted to keep going out with her.

The next morning, the hangover was *severe*! I had never felt that bad before in my life! My head was throbbing, my mouth felt like the Sahara, and any light at all felt like the sun was in the room with me. I stumbled out of bed and wandered into the kitchen, greeted by a very loud "Good morning" from Mom. She must have known that my head was splitting and was gonna milk this for all it was worth. I think she decided that the natural consequence of the hangover was the best punishment for her little girl after her first drunk. Mary didn't get in trouble for her part in the evening's shenanigans either, which meant I was spared execution by proxy.

I often wonder if the punishment had been more severe at this junction, would I have gone down the road I went in the coming years? Punishments were often severe for such infractions as waking Mom up during her nap, but coming home blasted at the age of thirteen went relatively unnoticed. These types of paradoxes were not uncommon in my world. When the Crazy wasn't showing up specifically in someone's eyes, it was the air we breathed. Up was down, down was up, and any time spent trying to reconcile my "normal" with what other families considered "normal" would bring nothing but frustration and disappointment.

Lack of guidance was a recurring theme in our household. Punishment and retribution were often swift and painful, but the guidance before the boundary was crossed did not seem to exist. You would think that having an older sister who got into a fair amount of mischief would have sparked many family conversations about rules and consequences. Those talks never seemed to happen for me. In a typical family, the parents are the mature adults, who have seen it all and done it all. They help their children navigate the pitfalls of life by imparting wisdom to them—often *before* the situations occur so that they can learn from their parents' mistakes. In this house, we were somehow expected to know better than we did. When the line got crossed, it was as if my parents didn't feel qualified to "parent" us with clear, recognizable boundaries. Mom took on a voyeuristic stance during our high school years, like she was living vicariously through us. Instead of instilling a strong sense of self and an instinct for self-protection, we gave detailed accounts of the shenanigans of our friends at parties, and she reveled in the knowing, as if she was one of the group. Dad never took part in these conversations, nor did he participate in the daily routine of life in our house. Even when the parties happened at our place, Mom was in the middle of the action, while Dad was absent. I often wondered if the fact that Dad worked at the school where most of the partygoers attended had anything to do with his habit of turning a blind eye to underage debauchery happening under his roof.

A huge part of our identity growing up was our attendance at the local private school. The school was a set of five double-wide trailers with a grade in each side separated by an accordion wall for grades second through sixth when I started. Eventually they built the first brick and mortar building we called the "upper school" before my sixth grade year. I transitioned to the upper school in junior high and had two years of being in proximity to high school students but always on the outside of the "cool factor" as a junior high student. Mary was already in high school and never gave me the time of day, even when we found ourselves in the same space. The building was square, attached to the gym and pool that had already existed when this building was erected. The gym was named the H. C. Tate Gymnasium, which always gave me a flutter of pride in my stomach, as it was named for my maternal grandfather whom I never knew. This was not because he was someone of consequence to the school but because my grandmother gave the money to build it and had naming rights. Before my graduation in 1986, there would be two more buildings named for Tootie and Aunt Gay, which morphed from pride to embarrassment, as it was just another illustration of the money our family had. I didn't get teased about the money because I was among many other kids who came from privilege, both racial and monetary. Conversations about whose family had more money were so common the comparison lost its ability to embarrass or shock. We were a bunch of entitled white kids with no awareness of our bubble existence.

The upper school was a series of classrooms along the front elevation of the building, all with their own exit doors to the outside, as well as an inner door that led to the hallway lined with lockers. This hallway was crazy busy in between classes as students shuffled to their lockers to swap out books before the next class. I can still hear the slam of the metal doors as we rushed to get down the hall, spending all our precious minutes socializing, flirting, and laughing with each other. There were the few students who were *always* late to class, even though the lockers were steps away from the classrooms. At the end of the hallway were the double doors that led to the library. If you followed the hallway around to the left, you got to the office, the student lounge across the hall from the office, and another set of double glass doors that led to the lobby outside the gym, pool, and locker rooms. The lobby was lined with trophy cases full of trophies for basketball, volleyball, softball, and soccer. Basketball was the top sport of the school and was the only sport that had cheerleaders. The school was not big enough for football, so homecoming, and all special celebrations were wrapped around the basketball season.

This building was like a second home to me. My father worked in the office as the director of development, which means his job was to raise money for the school. How ironic. The secretary in the office was Ms. Jan. She had been my father's secretary when he worked for First Union Bank, and she had known all of us our whole lives. I called her mom (come to think of it, I called a lot of women mom), and if I ever needed any nurturing, she was there for me. When I found myself with time to kill, I would always go hang out with her.

When you don't have friends, it's great to have a place to go where someone will always greet you with a smile and never ask why you are hanging around. Jan was my safe zone, she always had my back, and would shower me with compliments and reinforcement without any prompting. I loved her so very deeply for her consistent love and nurturing of me over those years.

Outside of the student lounge, behind the gym and locker rooms, was the smoking section. Yes, it was actually called that by all, students and teachers alike. We all smoked in high school, and this courtyard was where we could go to have a cig in between classes or during lunch. It was just a square space where no grass grew. The dirt had big ruts in it that were caused by heavy rain that came off the building and had nowhere to go. There were picnic tables out there sometimes; it was always nice to have somewhere to sit while you inhale lung cancer at the tender age of fifteen with no one telling you not to. This was another example of the lack of guidance from the adults in the space. This school was small and we often called the teachers by their first names or nicknames that the students had come up with, fully accepted by the teachers themselves. There was a familial sense between the student body and the faculty that would have made for a perfect opportunity to guide these young minds to make good, sound choices for their lives and futures. The smoking section is just a perfect example of where that opportunity failed.

When I was in ninth grade, Mary was a senior, and her class ruled the roost. There were twelve of them, and they were a tight group. I was still struggling with popularity but had made some strides in this area because I had started drinking more regularly and was the life of the party! I had cultivated my own group of friends to hang out with, but Mary and I often found ourselves at the same parties. I tried to stay clear of her because she did not like having a tag-along little sister. During freshman year, I got asked out on a date by one of Mary's classmates and also her good friend—a boy named Allen. Originally from Germany, Allen was tall, skinny, and awkward, but he drove and was exotic to me because I had really never left this small town, and his German accent and European ways were intriguing to me. Besides, *he asked me out*, and he was a senior, which definitely upped my cool factor! Win-win for me!

Mary didn't agree. She and Allen were actually pretty close before he and I started dating, but boy, that cooled quick when he asked me out. She was *not* happy about having her little sis encroaching on her territory, especially with one of her friends. Our song was "Telegraph Road" by Dire Straits, and I remember parking in his car on an undeveloped road in his exclusive gated community to listen to that fifteen-minute song and make out. I didn't know what the hell I was doing, but he wanted to spend time with me, and that was an entirely new feeling for me.

The next boyfriend was not new to me. In fact, I was going back in time with this one. He was my first love, Freddie Fredrick. Freddie and I were born two days apart. His mom and mine were in the hospital together, and Ma Fredrick loved to tell the story of how my mom needed to pee so she brought me into Ma Fredrick's room and handed me to her while she ran into the bathroom. When the nurse came in looking for the Greary baby in a panic, Ma Fredrick said in her abrasive and condescending tone that she was right here! (She held two babies in her arms.) The nurse ran up to the bed and said, "Which one is she?" to which Ma Fredrick yelled, "THE ONE IN THE PINK BLANKET, YA TWIT!" Ma Fredrick was another woman I called Mom all my life.

Freddie was at all my birthday parties and is in all the silent videos of the same. When we were in kindergarten together, he gave me a ring out of a Cracker Jack box, and Mary married us during recess on the playground. Freddie had been in my life ever since, and now he was attending the same private school. We would rotate between three houses for our parties each weekend: Jake Billingsley's, Freddie's, and my house. Parents were always there, often making room in their refrigerators for all the beer we brought in to drink. It never seemed to occur to the parents that allowing this underage drinking was problematic, especially for my parents. My father worked at the school where most of us attended. He would be *under* the jail nowadays if this was the norm in this day and age.

I remember one party at Freddie's where we were down in the basement, which was the hangout room with couches, tables, a TV, and a bar. The washer and dryer were also down there in an "unfinished" part of the space next to the small bathroom, which always had a line that was too long when you had beer needing to get out. Ma Fredrick was downstairs, hanging out with us, and I had to go to the bathroom. As I was standing in line, I remember feeling like I was going to throw up and must have said so out loud. Next thing I knew, Ma Fredrick was leading me to the washing machine, opening the top, and thrusting my head into the machine as I lost my cookies, all the while holding my hair.

I remember lifting my head at one point and, with a confused and slurred voice, saying, "I'm puking in your washing machine!"

Ma Fredrick said, "It's okay, honey. It'll wash out." And she thrust my head back into the bowl.

My mother's favorite saying was "You're gonna do it anyway. Might as well do it under my roof so I know you are safe." I know that is gonna sound "cool" to most of you, but with no guidance, it was actually pretty fucked up. I don't ever remember Mom talking to me about the dangers of drinking or about what could go wrong when I was under the influence. She even patched up the ass cheek of one of my friends who fell into a glass-topped table and cut himself as the glass broke into shards big enough to cause serious harm (this was before tempered glass). He sliced the shit out of his ass, and she patched him up without missing a beat. Parties would end with people passed out on the floor all over the house or in any available bed. How none of this got reported by anyone is beyond me.

The next big milestone in any teenage girl's journey is sex. Allen had respected that I was not ready to have sex with him, even when some of those sessions in his car got pretty intense. When Freddie and I began dating, I was determined to control this situation as long as I could. There were lots of almosts, and we got pretty creative when managing our adolescent urges. Our sex life, or lack thereof, was a topic of conversation within our high school circles, enough to give me the nickname of Fort Knox with the fellas.

Freddie and I would be walking down the hall between classes, holding hands, and someone would walk past him and ask if he had "gotten the key yet." We would giggle, knowing what they meant. It never occurred to me to be upset that the entire high school seemed to know that I was holding out on this momentous step in maturity. Nor did I consider that when I finally did cave, I'm sure a play-by-play account was shared with all.

The night I finally gave in, I had been drinking with friends and decided I was hungry, so I stopped through the drive-thru at McDonald's. I was thinking about Freddie and how much I loved him, and I decided I might as well cross that imaginary bridge. Tonight was the night. I was drunk enough to feel ready. I called Freddie before I left the party and told him to meet me at my house. By the time I got home, he was waiting in his car in the driveway. We entered the house together and went upstairs after a few words of hello to my parents. We spent plenty of time in my room alone before, so Mom and Dad wouldn't care about this time either.

I actually have little memory of the event itself, except to know that I had done it with the man I loved and had survived. While he was getting dressed and ready to leave, I remember looking for the blood I thought would be on the sheets and was confused when I didn't see any. Wasn't there supposed to be blood when you lose your virginity? The next week at school, there were no more jokes made about Fort Knox. Freddie had found the key, and I had been in control of the timing, story, and aftermath.

The "If you're gonna do it anyway, might as well be under our roof" philosophy also pertained to having sex. Freddie was my boyfriend, and at the age of sixteen and seventeen, he was allowed to stay the night in my room. We would watch TV together in the den with the rest of the family, and around 11:00 p.m., Mom and Dad would say goodnight and go off to bed, knowing Freddie and I would go upstairs together. The next morning, we all got up and had breakfast together—parents, teenage daughter, and boyfriend. It was a bizarre time. Freddie would sit at the table, shirtless, while Mom made breakfast for the two of us. This was another experience of feeling out of body, like reality didn't meet up with what *should* be happening. I wasn't gonna risk losing the privilege, but there was something in me that wondered where the limits were?

Mary had had a similar level of freedom with her boyfriend, Len, whom Mom adored! This was another clear example of Mom living vicariously through us with our boyfriends because she never experienced the dating scene like we were. When CC got into her teenage years, she had guys stay over all the time, but they were not necessarily sleeping in her room. We had a pool house that was the size of some people's homes, which was where CC had all her parties. It had a sleeper sofa in it, and one morning, Dad went up to the pool house to find CC sleeping on the pulled-out sofa between two young Black men. He *flipped out*, not because she was sleeping between two boys, but because they were both Black! The inconsistency, irrationality, and racist bent of his anger was a common theme in our household.

I was skilled at managing the landmines of my life—predicting the unpredictable and acting accordingly. Through these life moments, I learned how to read the minds and body language of my parents to try to know what their next moves might be. This was a survival tactic that felt well-honed at the time. I realize now that it was a complete false sense of control. It sold me a bill of goods that I was powerful enough to know how they were going to react to protect myself appropriately. I often fell short in my abilities to navigate their cycles of unpredictable behavior. Alcohol gave me a well-needed respite from this exhausting world.

My "checking out" times increased as high school went on. I don't think other teenage girls had the same level of freedom with their boyfriends, but because I had very few girlfriends at this time in my life, I don't remember having those girl conversations with others about what their parents allowed and didn't allow. I got lucky, because Freddie was such a good guy. He cared about everyone around him. He was always the one who would stay the soberest so he could drive those of us who had no business driving. Of course, this was codependent behavior, but I owe him a debt of gratitude for probably saving my life more than once. To this day, he is a fireman, saving people every day.

I was a cheerleader on the junior varsity cheerleading squad in seventh and eighth grade, then got to move to the varsity squad in ninth grade, where Mary and I got to serve together. Mom made a cheerleading outfit for CC, who was nine at the time, and the three of us in our uniforms was our Christmas picture that year. Being on the same squad as Mary was hard because she still did not like me and rarely missed an opportunity to put me in my place. But as a dancer, I was good at cheerleading, and so she didn't have much room for argument on my skill set.

Those were prime times. The basketball team (the Falcons) were super good. Games were highly attended affairs, and I got to prance around in a short skirt and be a part of the "in" crowd. It also didn't hurt that I was dating a basketball player whose friends were also on this winning team. It was the quintessential high school fantasy during the basketball season. When we rode the bus back home from away games, the late-night drives in the dark had a certain romanticism that was not lost on any of us.

When we attempted stunts on the squad, I was often one of the "flyers" because I was skinny as a rail and small. Andrea (my best friend throughout high school) and myself were the smallest of the squad, and so we were the ones that were the tops of the pyramids. After Mary graduated, being on the cheerleading squad on my own was *glorious*! I didn't realize how much in her shadow I had been until she was gone, and now I could step into the sunlight! I was even the captain of the squad for a year or two, which was a highlight. I was not athletic, but I had success as a cheerleader, always remembering the routines and cheers and often being the teacher for those who couldn't seem to get it. I even had the honor of being on the homecoming court one year, but I did not remember this until I looked at yearbooks from 1986 some thirty years later.

Memories are a funny thing when you are swirling in trauma. They can often not stick to the sides and slip away forever. I literally did not remember being on the court until I was looking at the pictures and saw myself being escorted by Freddie in his basketball uniform. It is a surreal moment to see a picture of yourself doing something that to most would seem a pivotal moment, but to me, it's like watching someone else perform in the play that is my life.

Junior and senior years are a blur. I was drinking a lot and never in minimal amounts. Moderation was not in my repertoire. Freddie and I were broken up more than we were together. To deal with that, I had sex with almost every guy in our circle at one time or another. I heard them judge girls who slept with them indiscriminately all the time, but no matter how many I slept with, they never seemed to turn their judgment on me—or I was just too drunk to notice.

One of the more horrific experiences were at a party at Allen's house (he was home from college). He lived in an exclusive gated country club community that had a high-end golf course running through it. One of Freddie's closest friends was Tony. I had been hard crushing on him all during high school, but we had both just ignored our attraction to each other all the time because I was dating Freddie and he was Freddie's best friend.

On this particular night, during a time when Freddie and I were "taking a break," I found myself on the golf course in the moonlight with Tony, consecrating our mutual lust for each other amongst the pine trees on the well-manicured fairway. I vaguely remember being in a fog of giddiness as this moment was finally coming true for me—until I heard a familiar voice. "Oh my god!" Freddie had wandered down to the fairways edge to find his best friend and his love in an unclothed embrace. I have never felt so humiliated and disgusted with myself in all my life. I hurt him so badly in that moment, and I am sure he never forgave me. Of course, I blamed it on the alcohol, but this was just another example of this demon liquid erasing my inhibitions and severely clouding my judgment. Couple that with the desperate need to be loved and the only understanding of love to be that of a sexual nature, and you have a recipe for disaster.

*****

I knew from my preteen years that I wanted to be a special education teacher. Mom was on the board of directors of a preschool that serviced kids with disabilities, and I would come with her when she had meetings and play with the kids while she worked. When I got to junior high, I volunteered in the classroom helping the teachers and then spent summers during high school as a teacher's assistant. I adored these kids and had dreams of having a child of my own with Down's Syndrome. They were so loving and always had hugs for me, and I really thought that having a child with a disability would be so much better than having a typical child. These kids never rejected me, which in my book was the ultimate gift.

I also found acceptance through other helpers at the school. The preschool had an arrangement with a local corrections facility where inmates who were nonviolent and had either shown their progress through good behavior or were close to the end of their sentences, could come to the preschool to help with the kids in the classroom as a work release program. Many of these men had children of their own at home that they hadn't seen in a while and the time they spent with these kiddos often gave them parenting skill sets that they didn't have before. Many of these guys had typical children, so experiencing what it was like for kids with disabilities made them appreciate their kids even more. I don't know if this type of program could exist today with everyone's fears of abuse, but this was in the early to mid '80s, and no one was really talking about the slippery slope of abuse back then, especially given that these were all men coming to the school, no women. It's interesting to ponder the efficacy of this program in today's world.

It was problematic for me as a teenage girl who equated sex with love because these guys *loved me*. I still have letters written to me from some of the guys professing their love for me. I don't remember any of them actually touching me, but the attraction was there, and I had no idea how messed up that was. I even remember going to visit one of them at the facility where he was housed when I could drive myself. I have a memory of us sitting at a picnic table, holding hands. He was a grown-ass man! I shake my head now when I think about how much this could have gone wrong on so many levels. I was desperately searching for acceptance and love and would take it anywhere it manifested.

Mom and Dad were oblivious to this relationship, but even if they had known, I don't know that any restrictions would have been placed. Mom always had a soft spot for "strays," as we would refer to them—people, usually young men, who had had a hard life and whom she could actively try to rehabilitate. My relationship with this inmate was a perfect example of this compulsion to help those who had struggled in life. Throughout the years, we knew we could get what we wanted from Mom as long as the ask came wrapped in a sob story. She was a sucker for these tales, and we got very good at weaving them over the years to get any outcome we desired.[1]

I look into the eyes of my teenage self, and I don't recognize her. The absence of light in her eyes is stunning to me, and my heart aches for her. She seems like a shell, walking through life with someone else providing the forward momentum. I was in complete survival mode during that time in my life. Breath was unconscious, needs were undiscovered, and passions were frivolous. I was just trying to take my next step in a world where each look around the corner revealed another battle to navigate. These battles were the energy that moved me through space. The bitching and moaning about my life were the propulsion that moved my feet. I did not know it at the time, but negative energy was the fuel in my engine. It wasn't until many years later that I would identify this negativity and make the conscious choice to shift my paradigm to a positive flow.

Days before I headed off to college, I received the most peculiar invitation in the mail. It was on beautiful heavyweight paper with gold lettering and embossed emblems inviting me to be a debutante at the International New Year's Ball at the Plaza Hotel in New York City! We were all stunned by the invitation, especially me! Mary hadn't been invited to attend this ball when she was eighteen, so this was an experience that was unique to me, which was equal parts thrilling and terrifying. I wasn't even sure what a debutante was, except that Mom had been one. And this would put us in New York for New Year's Eve, which was so exciting! The ball wasn't the

---

[1] I am appalled by the reference to humans being "strays," and I apologize to those who we used this term to describe them as if they were less than human.

big draw for me, but being able to ring in the new year in NYC was beyond thrilling! We discussed it as a family, thinking about logistics and wondering if it was good timing with everything that was going on with the family. In the end, it was decided. Why not!

I got to go dress shopping as a sort of practice run for my future wedding. I chose a lovely white satin dress with beads on the bodice, sweetheart neckline, and puffy sleeves (it was 1986 after all)! I had to wear long satin white gloves, which made me feel like a princess. Mary and Mom got their dresses, which determined the color theme of the family to be blue. Mom was in periwinkle, Mary in navy, and CC got a dress that was electric shiny blue! As we got closer to the time to leave for New York, Mom became increasingly stressed. CC's dress needed to be hemmed, and there wasn't enough time to find someone to do it, so Mom took on the task.

She had CC stand on the ottoman in the library of what used to be Tootie's house but was now ours (we moved in after she passed away) so that she could pin the hem of her skirt. Unfortunately, CC had some sort of stomach bug that day and was desperately trying not to throw up on her dress. She was eleven years old and was pleading with Mom to let her go because she thought she was going to hurl, and all Mom could focus on was the need to get this dress hemmed before we had to leave for NY.

"Mom, can I *please* go to my room? I'm gonna hurl!"

"*Stand still!* If I don't get this hem right, you will stand here until I do!"

Back and forth they went, with voice levels getting higher and higher. Mary finally came downstairs to see what all the commotion was about and found Mom threatening to slap CC into silence if she didn't shut up and that she *better* not throw up on the dress!

"*Mom!* Will you leave her alone? She's *sick* and needs to go lie down. What the hell is *wrong* with you!" Mary demanded.

CC was looking green, and Mom turned her fury toward Mary. As their screaming match escalated CC, jumped off the ottoman and took off to her room to get out of the dress just in time to throw up in the bathroom. The dress did get done on time, but we were all on notice that the next ten days before we left for NY was going to be beyond anything we had seen in a long time from the Crazy in Mom's eyes. I remember sitting in the corner, thinking there was no way they were even gonna let us in New York, much less at the Plaza Hotel!

When we arrived in New York, the Plaza was undergoing renovations. They had two rooms reserved for us; one was on a floor that had been renovated, and one was not. The room on the renovated floor was *huge*. The ceilings were ten feet tall, the carpet was a pastel color green that was soft under my feet, and the bathroom was about the size of my room at home. It was something right out of a storybook, and to my great astonishment, it was suggested that I get to stay in the bigger room because it was my special trip. CC and Mary stayed with me, while Mom and Dad stayed in the smaller room on the unrenovated floor. I truly felt like a *princess*!

The purpose of the debutante ball is to introduce young women who have come of age into society. Your father presents you to the "court," and you have an escort, who is usually some strapping young man full of potential to change the world through finance or law. My boyfriend at the time and I broke up just before the trip, so my escort ended up being my father's best friend. He had white hair and a white beard and mustache and was a fifty-year-old alcoholic! He was at least thirty years older than all the other escorts, drunk, and making horribly inappropriate jokes when we all sat for the group photo. The girls and their escorts in all their finery got together for a group photo, and he stood out like a sore thumb. The white hair was a dead giveaway of his age, and the red face was a dead giveaway that he had not been drinking water all day. It was a disaster!

The day of the rehearsal, we sat at round tables in the ballroom, watching as each young woman had her time to practice the moment when she was presented to the court, which included a curtsy to society. The grand ballroom of the Plaza Hotel has twenty-foot ceilings gilded in gold leaf and swirling sconces with painted scenes in between that felt like a queen or king should be in attendance. The wooden floors were highly polished, but you knew from their appearance they had been there a long time and had supported many a dignitary over the years.

In a twist of irony, the orchestra that was playing for the ball was the Lester Lanin Orchestra, which played at my mom and dad's wedding reception many moons ago. One of the young women from the Ivory Coast of Africa sat at my table, and she was completely alone. She barely spoke English, and her parents had not traveled to the States with her for this event. I felt so sorry for her and really didn't have a way to communicate with her to offer her comfort. I identified with her loneliness even though I had my whole family with me.

After arriving in New York, I realized the source of much of Mom's anxiety. She didn't remember her own debut! She knew she had experienced similar things we were seeing and feeling, but she couldn't share the stories with me. The only advice she could offer was not to lock my knees while standing in the receiving line to avoid passing out. I could tell there was a sadness in her about this disconnect with her memories that she didn't know how to process. I could identify later with this absence in memory when I realized I had been on the homecoming court but didn't remember it happening.

It's unnerving to know that experiences happened to you but you have no recollection of them. She was also in close proximity to the lifestyle she had willingly given up by marrying my father and living in small-town North Carolina. This was the life she had lived growing up in NYC and Connecticut, with all the finest families experiencing the high life. She had rebelled against all of it; now she found herself smack dab in the middle of all she had left behind, and it terrified her.

*****

The only other time I remember seeing this type of disconnection by my mom in a high-society setting was the year we attended the Rockefeller family reunion at John D.'s estate, called Kykuit in Sleepy Hollow, New York. The family was going to award the estate to the state of New York to be classified as a historic site of the National Trust for Historic Preservation and decided to have one last family reunion to mark the occasion. Mary was sixteen, I was thirteen, and CC was seven when we readied ourselves for this adventure. We went shopping at Thalhimers in Fayetteville to choose dresses that, in retrospect, made us look like we just stepped off the prairie, and we were off to rub elbows with the members of our family who always felt like they belonged anywhere but our family tree.

I remember driving down the long winding driveway as we arrived at the estate in the acclaimed Hudson River Valley, marveling at the fact that the gravel on the driveway reminded me of the pristine gravel of the driveways leading to Tootie's homes in North Carolina and Maine. The first home that appeared over the treetops was a massive building built in the Tudor style with high peaks in its roofline and a beautiful circle of perfectly cultivated greenery surrounding a working marble fountain.

As my eyes widened at the sight, we approached the entrance to the drive leading to this structure with a sign that read "Playhouse" with an arrow indicating that this grand home that took my breath away was not the home of my great-great-uncle but the place they went to *play* when the mood struck. When we took a tour of the building later, we found it housed an indoor pool with roman numerals of granite indicating the water depth, an outdoor pool surrounded by Greek goddess statues, a bowling alley with floors so polished they looked like mirrors, a game room with every possible gaming table you could imagine, including two billiards tables and an indoor basketball court. In my wildest dreams, I never imagined anyone being so rich that they could have a house that was bigger than my grandmother's house that served as the equivalent of our plastic playhouse, molded to look like a log cabin in the backyard next to our swing set.

The main house was five stories high, constructed of brick of varying shades, shaped like a box. We began the day with tours of the Japanese sculpture garden, the "carriage house" (where John D.'s collection of classic cars was housed), and the infamous Playhouse, where the wonder of this day for me had begun. Everywhere we went, we stood with mouths agape at the opulence of the estate and marveled at how different this life was from the one we were living in small-town North Carolina.

The evening was spent in the garden just off the back of the main house with cocktails, and a large sign that must have been twenty yards long with the family tree carefully printed out for all to find themselves. John D.'s descendants wore name tags with a red border around the edge, while William's descendants wore name tags with blue around the edges. The elders of the family, Happy Rockefeller (who was the widow of the late Vice President Nelson Rockefeller), and his son Lawrence Rockefeller were the hosts of this affair, and we did not see them until we adjourned to the big white tent erected next to the main house, where dinner would be served.

Happy was dripping in diamonds around her graceful neck and on her ears as she welcomed us all to what would be a five-course meal the likes of which I had never experienced. I thought I knew what it was like to enjoy a formal dinner with china and silver, but this put anything I had seen at Tootie's to shame. The waiters were wearing white gloves as plates full of the most beautifully prepared food kept arriving. As we drove away that night, I closed my eyes, feeling the rhythm of the car's movement lull me into slumber with a smile on my face. I had always heard of this storied family we belonged to, but I had no idea of the magnitude until we ran among the topiary trees in the perfectly crafted garden, giggling, while Mom and Dad sipped cocktails and tried desperately to look like they belonged among the company they kept.

*****

As we sat at the tables in the grand ballroom of the Plaza Hotel during rehearsal, watching all the young women and their escorts and fathers practice for the big day, Mom was chewing her gum like a cow! All I could hear next to me was *smack, smack, smack,* and I was completely mortified. She was so uncomfortable in this setting, and I suppose her anxiety was being released through the very loud chewing. All my life, Mom had dressed in attire that would suggest she came from a modest upbringing, mainly to escape from the reality of her family's wealth. Being in this setting brought all that back for her, and she seemed to be rebelling against its resurfacing. This part of the day could not end soon enough.

That night was New Year's Eve. We had tickets to go to the Limelight nightclub to see Cab Calloway perform. The Limelight is in an old church, which I remember saying must be why I couldn't get a buzz on that night. The drinks were ridiculously expensive but had barely any alcohol in them. CC didn't go with us, because she was eleven years old at the time, but she had a better time than we had. Back then, the windows opened in the rooms at the Plaza, so she sat in the windowsill with the window open, listening to the crowd in Times Square and watching the ball drop on TV. I'm not sure why Mom and Dad thought it was okay to leave an eleven-year-old in a room alone in NYC, and I cringe when I think of her sitting in an open window and what could have happened if she had fallen, but that was what we did.

The next night was the debutante ball. I was presented to society to the tune "Nothing could be finer than to be in Carolina," which I thought was hoky at the time, and I couldn't breathe most of the time because my strapless bra was too tight. At one point, Mary took me into the bathroom and suggested I take off the bra. I couldn't *believe* the difference! We threw it in the trash and went back to the table. That was one of the most liberating moments of my young adulthood, but I was so *aware* of the fact that I was going braless in the grand ballroom of the Plaza Hotel. It seems silly to me now, but at the time, I felt like a *rebel*.

After the ball, Mary decided to go out and party with the daughter of my escort who had attended with the rest of his family. I didn't have anything to wear except my debutante dress, so I didn't go. Thinking back on it, I could have gone in what looked like a wedding dress and woven stories of how I left my intended at the altar. But I was afraid and didn't trust Mary and her cohort to have my back, so I stayed in the hotel room. As I lay in my bed, I fell into a deep despair, wishing I had the courage to go with them. What had come easily for me as a small child—spinning hyperbole—seemed impossible in the city that never sleeps.

Debutante balls are about legacy. Rarely does a daughter get invited unless the mother was before her and the grandmother before her. Mom and I were face-to-face with that legacy from the moment the invitation arrived in the mail. Legacy of money, prestige, hopes, and expectations was prominent in the days and weeks leading up to the trip to New York. We crumbled under the weight of it all. I imagine our experiences were very similar, a collective "out of body" phenomena that few can describe or relate.

But here's the thing: just when you think your experience is unique to you, legacy reminds you that we've all been here before. What happens to me is just a continuation of what happened to her, which is just a continuation of what happened to her mother and so on and so on. Generation after generation, we try desperately to change our stars, but legacy just keeps pulling us back to the energetic patterns of the ages. Legacy patterns are also mired in layers that take years to unearth and strength to endure.

Happiness Is a Desperate Blessing

I reach for you
in every corner,
desperately trying to hold on
as you slip
through my fingers.

You hold the wisdom
of the ages.
The colors I connect to you
are bright,
existing in the form
of a smile.

When I find you,
I feel calm,
the angry flare
of pain is soothed,
and I can relax.

Why are you so fleeting?
Why can I not hold on to you
long enough to make
this calm the rule
rather than
the exception?

In my mind,
I run frantically,
searching for
the next fix,

the next touch,
the next kindness
that will continue
the feeling of bliss
that feeds the addiction.

Happiness is
a desperate blessing.

I am transfixed
by the sound
of my cry
as it passes.

Chapter 4

In February of my senior year in high school, just before my eighteenth birthday, Tootie died. She had been treated for lung cancer in the years prior, and we were told that was all behind her. One day, I remember her calling the house to talk to Mom.

"Hi, Dee. Can I speak to your Mom, please?" Her voice was always formal—not light and familiar as a grandma to her granddaughter might sound.

"She's not here," I replied. Tootie rarely called the house. Something was wrong.

"Well, I'm going to the hospital right now, and I need your Mom to bring me some things when she gets home. It's just pneumonia, no big deal. Can you tell her and have her call me at the hospital?"

Cell phones didn't exist yet, so I had to wait for Mom to get home to tell her what I knew. Tootie was a powerhouse, so this was nothing more than a blip on her radar. It didn't even occur to me that she might really be in trouble. If Mom was worried, she didn't let on and our daily lives went on as usual. Tootie was in the hospital for a week or so, and they decided to send her home, but each time they began preparations for discharge, her heart would behave in a funny way, which would prompt them to keep her a little longer. This happened twice, and on the third time, she was noticeably going downhill. Mom and Aunt Gay made the calls, and everyone came in to see her and say their goodbyes. This was really happening.

She had kicked everyone out of her room, even the nurses, after spending time visiting with each family member. We all found ourselves sitting in the waiting room outside the elevators, wondering what to do next. When the elevator descended and ascended to our floor three times, opening to an empty car, we determined it was time to go home. The next morning, I rolled over in my bed and looked at the clock to see the time 6:10 a.m. That was *way* too early to be out of bed on a weekend, so I rolled over and went back to sleep. A couple of hours later, Dad came up to my room and woke me to tell me Tootie was gone. In my half-asleep stupor, I rolled over and began to cry.

When I finally came down to the kitchen, the room was full of silent family members. Everyone's eyes were buried in their coffee or breakfast, and the air was heavy. I asked Dad what time she died.

"Six ten a.m.," he replied.

We all used to say Tootie had powers. She always knew what others were thinking, and you couldn't pull the wool over her eyes for anything. I truly believed she had come by that morning to say good-bye, and I envisioned her spirit flying around the room above my sleeping body. We would have more conversations with Tootie from beyond the veil in the future, especially with my daughter, but for now, the thought that she came by to say goodbye to me was one of the most intimate interactions I had ever had with my grandmother. We learned through the autopsy that the lung cancer was not gone and that she would likely have died within a year from the disease in slow-suffocation. She would have truly hated being sick and frail and a burden to anyone, so her exit in this timely manner made all the sense in the world to all of us. She was a woman who took control of her world with both hands. Why would her final moments on this earth be any different?

We were prepared to lose Baboo first. The year before Tootie passed, Baboo had a stroke that rendered her paralyzed on her left side. Just two weeks before the stroke, she was on a cruise with one of her closest friends, Aunt Liz, dancing her heart out every night. She was a lively ballroom dancer and would laugh nonstop while her feet glided her around the floor. The doctors said she could get most of her movement back if she worked hard in the rehab center and really focused. Baboo was always full of life, and we all knew that a little thing like a stroke was not going to hold this ball of fire down. She needed to get dancing again!

She was moved to a rehab center from the hospital and her rigorous schedule was established. The first time I came to visit her, I was mortified to find her flatly refusing to do any of the exercises the therapists were asking her to do. I found her lying in her bed, complaining about how hard the exercises were and how much it hurt to move. This refusal to cooperate in her recovery was nothing like the grandmother I knew.

"Baboo, what is going on? You have to do the exercises if you want to get better."

"I can't! It hurts too much! I'm tired. I can't do it! I wouldn't wish this on my worst enemy," she would exclaim over and over.

"Baboo, I want my grandmother back! If you can't do it for yourself, can you do it for me? I love you so much, and I want to see you dancing again." I tried everything I could to get her to do the work to no avail. She would cry and come up with every reason why she couldn't do the exercises they were asking her to do.

Within three weeks, the administrators of the rehab center were telling Dad that if she didn't start cooperating, they would have to ask her to leave to make room for someone who would benefit from therapy. She couldn't be persuaded to engage, and they kicked her out.

Dad moved her to a nursing home in a neighboring town, which smelled like urine and death. I would go visit briefly but couldn't stand to be there for too long, especially to eat. Baboo was always asking us to have a meal with her, but I couldn't ingest any food in that atmosphere. After Tootie died, we moved into her house across the lake. With this move came access to the farm, including the "gatehouse" at the top of the driveway, where Eddie used to live while he managed Tootie's barn and grounds. It seemed the perfect fit to renovate the house to make it wheelchair accessible and move Baboo out of the nursing home and into this fresh space.

Dad would hang her paintings on the walls and fill it with her furniture so she could be surrounded by her own things. Maybe being in this better space would help her find the will to live again? Mom and Dad could afford to do the renovations and pay for around the clock care for her, which was such a loving gift to give her for whatever time she had left with us. We did not know she would live another nine years at this level of incapacity, which was pure torture for her. When Tootie died, Baboo was probably the most crushed out of all of us.

She just kept murmuring over and over, "It should have been me. It was supposed to be me first."

Just a few months after burying Tootie, Mom's middle sister Gay was diagnosed with an aggressive form of brain cancer. They did surgery to remove as much of the tumor as they could, but we knew they would not be able to get it all without stripping her of her ability to communicate. So it was decided, since the cancer was going to kill her anyway, that they would only remove what they could and she would keep her faculties as long as possible. Aunt Dee Dee (the oldest of the three girls and my namesake) came to move in with Aunt Gay and Uncle Haskell to help care for her in her final months.

Uncle Haskell *adored* Aunt Gay, but he was not capable of doing all the things necessary to keep her comfortable or tend to her basic needs. He was devastated by her diagnosis, and we all speculated about how losing her would impact him, since they were both so dependent on each other.

Both Aunt Gay and Uncle Haskell smoked Camel cigarettes, unfiltered. They were hard-core smokers, and many an argument ensued about Aunt Gay stopping smoking because it was bad for her health. Aunt Dee Dee wanted her to quit so badly, but the case was made that the cancer was going to kill her before the cigarettes would so what was the harm if they brought her pleasure? She was on so many medications to reduce the swelling in her brain that she blew up like a balloon with the round, puffy face that drugs like prednisone deliver. She was always super thin and athletic, so seeing her in this state was really hard. I stayed away from visiting more than I should, but it was just so hard to see her like that and to feel the heavy energy in the house. As a self-centered teenager, I wasn't aware of the importance of putting my level of discomfort aside to bring whatever happiness I could by visiting my favorite aunt in her final months.

Mom was particularly stressed, having just lost her mother, and now her sister was ill. The last time any of us had dealt with death in the family was when I was four and Baboo's mom, Nanny, had died. Tootie was the matriarch of the family, so losing her was like losing our anchor—the lynchpin that kept the family machine together. Aunt Gay was the fun-loving and joyful member of the family. She lived life to the fullest, and she and Uncle Haskell were so kookie that losing her was like losing the laughter of the family. I didn't realize what these two women meant to me until I was faced with losing them. I spent a lot of time anesthetized with beer and sex during those years, just trying to get through the sadness and pain and finding something that felt good.

Aunt Gay's battle with cancer ended during my freshman year at college. I remember being in my dorm room, sitting on my twin bed with my posters of Rob Lowe and Shaun Cassidy on my wall, when the phone in the hall rang and someone shouted my name to come get the call. Some of the girls had phones in their rooms, but most of us didn't want to pay the extra money, so the hall phone was the only way for folks to get ahold of us.

I picked up the receiver that was stretched to the floor, waiting for me.

"Hello?" No one called me except family, and that was rare. This couldn't be good.

"Hi, Dee, it's Mom. Aunt Gay is gone, sweetie." Her voice trailed off, and I could tell she was trying not to be buried in her tears.

I couldn't respond to the announcement. I knew this was coming, had even practiced hearing the statement in my head, but hearing the actual words and knowing it was here hit me harder than I ever anticipated. She had been sick for ten months, and we all knew it was coming, but I was not prepared for how the sadness of her loss overwhelmed me when I heard Mom's words. In two years, I had lost two significant members of my family, and the pain was something I did not have the tools to handle.

The only thing I had in my toolbox was to "check out," which I did in routine fashion, evidenced by the Budweiser labels on my cement dorm room wall that started to look like wallpaper above my bed. The typical weekend shenanigans began to bleed into the week, with parties and clubbing that resulted in blackouts and "hooking up" with anyone who would look my way. Partying with my more beautiful hall mates meant that they would get the good-looking guys, and I would get the less attractive friend. I didn't care, as long as I was being accepted and wanted by the opposite sex. If I ran hard enough from the pain in my heart, it didn't have to consume me.

Going home for Aunt Gay's funeral was an experience. She and Uncle Haskell were highly revered in the Baptist Church, and I couldn't believe how full the church was! It was standing room only, and I think there were even folks who didn't make it inside the walls of the sanctuary. There was a beautiful painting of her and Uncle Haskell at the front of the church, and I stared at her image, reconnecting with the Aunt Gay that I remember from my childhood: healthy, skinny, and full of mischief in her eyes! I was touched to see how many people loved her and wanted to honor her on this day. I got to see another side of her through the eyes of her friends and church family, and my heart was filled with the love that this community obviously had for her.

Mom was struggling. Not only had she lost two immediate family members in as many years; we realized that Aunt Gay was fifty-two years old when she died, the same as my grandfather who also died when he was fifty-two. Not only that, but Aunt Gay had been the one to find him dead in his bed. From that realization forward, the fifty-second year for any of us became the one to dread. Mom got diagnosed with breast cancer when she was fifty-one and was going through treatment when she turned fifty-two. I was pretty checked out during that time, but I remember Mom being particularly stressed during that year. Not only was she facing a health crisis herself, but she was not sure she would make it through the dreaded fifty-second year. We all breathed a sigh of relief when she turned fifty-three, still breathing and on the road to recovery. In a family of three generations of women, each dying from a different form of cancer, we count our blessings every day that she is still with us.

Later that same year, Bertha was diagnosed with lung cancer. This was the third member of my family diagnosed and dying in a three-year span, and I was beside myself. When Mom told me Bertha was sick, I remember having a sort of out-of-body experience. The news went into a storage bin in my psyche, and the anguish of what was to come was more than I had the tools to handle. I was drinking every day, and to excess each time, in order to block out the pain of my reality. Of all the deaths, Bertha's was the hardest for me. She was my touchstone, and even though I rarely talked with her since going to college, I couldn't imagine life on this earth without her.

More than Tootie and Aunt Gay, there were feelings between Bertha and me that needed to be spoken out loud. Before she left me, I wanted her to know how much she meant to me and how much she had affected my life. I wrote her a long letter, expressing my love for her and thanking her for being the only stable force in my life growing up. I had mauve stationary that I had been given for Christmas one year that had my name embossed at the top of the page. The letter was so long that I had to use scotch tape to keep it closed as the envelope seams stretched to maintain their shape. I had never written this kind of letter before. Come to think of it, I had never loved anyone like I did Bertha, so this type of expression of my feelings for another person was unfamiliar territory, but I had to let her know.

I remember the last time I saw her alive. I went home from college to visit her because Mom told me how sick she was and that she might not be with us much longer. I remember the smell of her home; it was different than anything I had experienced anywhere else. She was raising her grandchildren, and I remember playing with them many hours at her house. This day, the mood in the house was quiet and somber.

I walked into her darkened room, where the curtains were drawn, and found her lying in the bed. A bowl of soup and a cup of water were near her bed on a tray untouched. As I walked into the room, there was a tall dresser in front of me, and on top of that dresser was my letter, out of the envelope and partially unfolded. She had read it. I sat on the side of her bed, and I held her hand. She was so weak that we really didn't talk with each other but just stared deeply into each other's eyes. She knew how much I loved her and how much I owed her for showing me unconditional love at a time when no other was capable of such a feeling. I was so grateful I had told her how I felt, and I left with a full heart because there was nothing left to say between us.

When she died, I didn't go to the funeral. I couldn't bear to say goodbye to her after three years of funerals. I was overwhelmed and couldn't do it again, especially with Bertha. It is the biggest regret of my life. I heard it was standing room only, with many who weren't even able to get into the church, and Mom and Dad were honored to be ushered to the front of the church to sit with the family. I think of this day each time I have the urge to skip an opportunity to honor and pay my respects to a loved one who has passed. I hear her voice in my ear telling me, "Go."

Years later, I wanted to visit her grave and pay my respects. I was home for the holidays, and Mom, Mary, CC, and I all wanted to go find her grave. I called her grandson to ask about directions, because it had been so many years that Mom couldn't remember how to get to the cemetery.

"Hey, Chris, this is Dee. Do you remember me?"

We had played with Chris and his sister Kim our whole childhoods, but I hadn't spoken to him in over twenty years.

"Of course, I remember you! How are you? Where are you living now?"

We fell into easy conversation, catching up and getting to know our adult selves.

"We really want to go visit your grandmother and pay our respects. It's been so long that Mom isn't sure where she was buried. Can you give me directions?"

It was out in the middle of nowhere, and the directions Chris gave me were so vague we were not sure if we would be successful. It was one of those forgotten cemeteries that didn't have a church nearby and except for the families of those interred there, no one would even know it existed. We drove and drove, looking for the sign that Chris said he *thought* might still be up. When we finally saw it, covered with vines and overbrush, we couldn't believe we had found it. We drove down the dirt road, passing run-down country houses with cars on blocks in the yard, and then there it was. The cemetery had not been well cared for, and there was no fence or real boundaries to the space at all.

We spread out, looking for her last name, the four of us walking all over the place, looking for Leach. CC was the one who found her. She exclaimed, "I FOUND IT!" We all ran over to see. There she was, Bertha Ann Leach. I was finally here to pay my respects after almost twenty years. And then…I saw it.

I don't know if I knew what her birthday was while I was growing up. I don't remember ever celebrating it or honoring her on her special day, even though she was such an integral part of our family system. The reality is, as I look at the situation with clearer eyes, she only enjoyed membership into our "club" to the extent that her employment status afforded. It breaks my heart to know that I might never have wished her happy birthday on her special day. She gave me love every minute, but I now know my gifts to her were limited as they often are in a white household to those who see the home as work rather than life.

As I gazed at her tombstone, I was speechless when I saw her birthday: July 20. I started to cry, feeling such a deep connection to her once again as I realized that her birthday was the same day as my sobriety date eight years after her death. This woman who helped shape and protect me during the first eighteen years of my life shared a day with me that was of her birth and my rebirth. I truly believe there are no coincidences, and if I was ever thinking about blowing my sobriety, this is the best reason ever to honor that day as sacred. She continues to guide and lift me up to stay clear and present to the current moment, living one day at a time in sobriety as we share such an important day.

"We" Remains Unbroken

Where do I end
and you begin?
Maybe here,
maybe nowhere.

How do our molecules
connect across space?

It is your light
that connects to mine,
imperceptible to the eye.

Our energetic fingers intertwine
for a grasp
that is unbreakable.

I know my light.
I know your light.
We are one.

Chapter 5

There is nothing permanent except change.
—Heraclitus

I was in my little black Honda CRV, driving to a part of Greensboro I'd never visited before. I had her address on a slip of paper and was trying to navigate the unfamiliar streets (this was before the days of GPS). My heart was racing, and my mouth was dry. I had taken a step that felt like the most adult choice I had made in my life up to this point. I had gotten the name of a therapist and was going to see her for the first time.

She lived at the end of her street, and I felt relieved when I saw the house number on her mailbox. I had found it, and I was fifteen minutes early! I was always chronically early to everything. We used to joke that Mom would be late to her own funeral, so I had gone in the opposite direction and was always early. I would sit in the car to kill time. I didn't want to ring the doorbell and possibly interrupt another client's session. My head was swimming with questions: What would I tell her? What if she tells me I don't need a therapist? What if she tells me I need something more than she could give?

I didn't have the language yet to identify the most obvious behavior patterns I was exhibiting, but I knew, deep down, that I was self-destructing and I needed to do something before I got myself into a situation I couldn't recover from. My drinking had increased to every day and always ended in drunkenness. I had quit smoking cigarettes several times but always started back, as drinking and smoking went hand-in-hand for me. Blackouts were more common, and decisions were being made that routinely put me in dangerous situations. I was lucky to have escaped from them intact.

I had integrated the Crazy into my own eyes, taking it with me when I left home to make sure that my existence stayed as familiar as it could. Even though it was chaos, familiar was safer than the unknown. I was transitioning into an adult who didn't know how to function without the Crazy, so I packed it in my suitcases and took it with me to college. This Crazy was running out of room on my dorm wall for the Budweiser beer labels from empty beer bottles, missed classes, and missed assignments because of hangovers, going home with strangers so drunk that I had little hope of protecting myself when the Crazy showed up in their eyes, and waking up in a puddle of my own piss and shit because I had blacked out and hadn't gotten up to go to the bathroom.

This prompted me to try to clean my mattress and drag it to the open window in my room to try to get it to dry and aired out before my roommate came home. I was terrified she would walk in and find me standing at the window, mattress upright, with a huge yellow and brown circle in the center. This was the first time I considered moving off campus.

I was finding it harder to get along with the other young women on my hall in the dorm. My relationships with women had always been full of strife, whether it was with my sisters, girlfriends in high school, or now in the dorm. I had always felt protected and loved around guys, even if they were taking advantage of me under the guise of "protecting" me, but with girls, I had struggled. I had a "best girlfriend" in high school, but given the choice, I always preferred hanging out with guys. I had never felt accepted by women.

There were always conditions placed by them, whether real or imagined by me, that I seemed unable to fulfill. I interacted with my dorm mates as if they had a rulebook for "girlfriend" relationships that I had never received. I was always trying to "read the room" and figure out how to navigate among these women, and I often missed the mark.

I had established early on that I would be the one to pay for all the pizza and beer if they would just let me hang around them.

Toward the end of my freshman year, I started to experiment with saying no when asked to pay for things. I was met with resistance and anger at the audacity of my refusal. My behavior was growing problematic enough for them that even my money didn't pave the way for acceptance. I was more and more aware of being unwanted in this space and decided that moving out of the dorm to an apartment would be a good idea. In my quest to rationalize this next transition, I decided I would become "cool" again if I had a place where they all wanted to come hang out and party, out from under the watchful eye of the RAs and dorm monitors. This move would be the start of many "geographical fixes" that manifested throughout my adulthood in the quest for happiness and fulfillment. If life wasn't working where my feet were, surely moving to another location would make it all better.

I found an apartment off campus and enjoyed decorating and furnishing it as my own for the first time. Much to my surprise, the parties and hangouts in my new place never materialized. The excuses were always that they were too busy or that I lived too far away from campus. No matter how hard I tried, I couldn't get the girls from my dorm to come fulfill the dreamscape I had created in my head. I would still visit them to make sure they hadn't forgotten who I was, even joining them on the town, which worked for them because I paid for all the drinks as admission to their "club." The cycle of partying, blacking out, and trying to maintain my grades had become more than I could manage. Something had to give.

It was my sophomore year, and I needed help. I had talked with one or two therapists in my teenage years, but they had been woefully unqualified to scratch the surface of my deeper wounds. It was time to do a deeper dive. I asked the school student center if they had any recommendations and got a few names. I didn't know I would find her on the very first try.

Rachel Howard was a single mother in her thirties with two boys, who had a private practice that she conducted out of her home. She lived in one of the older homes of Greensboro with tall ceilings and beautiful wood trim in all the rooms, and I felt completely comfortable from the first moment I sat down. She was a tall, thin white woman with permed curly hair, pronounced cheekbones, and extremely kind eyes.

I remember sitting on her cream-colored couch the first day, rubbing my hands nervously on the smooth fabric while she closed the double pocket doors to give us privacy. There was something soothing about being in her home. Over the years, I came to feel like this space was a second home to me. It was a place where my deepest secrets had been uttered into the walls, and I always knew she would keep them safe for me.

While the Crazy had been—and continues to be—a prominent character in my journey, Rachel was the "anticrazy" in this story. She introduced words into my vocabulary like codependency and boundaries and helped me unpack how these and other behavior patterns factored into my everyday choices. I still remember the day she suggested that I not look at every guy I meet as a possible husband.

I was telling her about a guy I was "dating," having just met him in a bar the weekend before. "He's cute and funny, but he doesn't seem to know what he wants to do when he gets out of school. I don't want to be with a man I have to take care of. I don't know. Maybe he's not the one," I said, hanging my head in disappointment.

"You only just met him, right?" she asked in her cool, steady voice.

"Yes, but I don't want to waste my time! If he's not the one, I want to move on!" I said with incredulity.

"Maybe it's not about 'forever.' Maybe it's just about right now? Is there anything you can learn from him that can be helpful in future relationships?"

I would jump to "forever" with each guy I dated, only to be truly devastated when it ended. Rachel taught me that each relationship was going to end, either through death or breakup, and that I needed to be prepared for that. If I approached each experience with the intention to learn whatever I was to learn, for whatever time I was to have with this person, I didn't have to fall apart each time it was over. She taught me to see the gift in whatever experience I have with people, whether it was the cashier at the grocery store or someone with whom I was in deep relationship. I wanted to know how long each relationship was going to last from the moment of our first meeting.

Looking back on it, I think it was all about control. I was dreading the inevitable pain that I would feel when they left me—because they always did—so I would begin to obsess about it right from the start. That way, if I figured it out before they did, I could beat them to the punch or at least not hurt so bad when they dumped me. It was the old "waiting for the other shoe to drop" scenario. I was really good at it because, in my experience, the other shoe had *always* dropped. I could take what I liked and leave the rest. This concept would factor greatly into my sobriety in later years, but for now, it was access to a freedom that I had not allowed myself to have up to that point. It was my first attempt at living in the moment.

I realized I wasn't taught that change could and *would* happen and that it didn't mean all would crumble in my hands. The house I lived in as a child never changed, the school I attended never grew, and the town I grew up in took great pride in always staying the same. In therapy, I explored why I would move the furniture around in my room every other month, always loving the first night sleeping in my new room arrangement because waking up would feel different. The room I would see as I opened my eyes would have a different perspective, the light would be coming through the window landing on different pieces of furniture, and somehow that would mean everything was going to be alright. The same thrill held true when my teacher would move our assigned desks in our classroom. I was craving new vision in a world where the shadows persisted, almost by design.

I hunkered down and did the work. With Rachel's guidance, I made the dean's List; cultivated relationships with my best friend, Cheryl, and my boyfriend, Jimmy; and saw a light at the end of my college tunnel. I was still drinking to excess and was hopelessly codependent with my friendships and family, but I had hope for the first time in my adult life that maybe I wasn't completely useless and that I could find happiness as an adult in spite of all the chaos.

When graduation was approaching and they asked us to choose one person who affected us the most during our college years to "cap" us during a baccalaureate ceremony, I knew immediately that Rachel was the only person I could choose. She had listened to me, let me cry on her shoulder, and had shown me a measure of love and respect that I hadn't felt since Bertha. I owe her a deep debt of gratitude for her wisdom during those years, for laying the foundation I so desperately needed on which to build a life going forward.

Jimmy and I had met at a bar in Greensboro when I was out with the girls from the dorm. He was a white man with a sweet disposition, wrapped in a thick Southern accent from small-town Virginia. He was in his early twenties but had already lost most of his hair, which he shared made him feel much older than he was. Jimmy wasn't much taller than I was and was slight of build, not necessarily remarkable on first glance. What drew me to him from our first meeting were his electric smile and his kind and laughing eyes. There wasn't anything dark in his energy, like a happy dog who only wanted everyone in the room to love him.

He was in town, visiting his brother, and we hit it off immediately. What was unique about this relationship was that, different from my previous boyfriends, it had the long-distance element. He lived about an hour away from me, just over the state line in Virginia, and had to return home at the end of each weekend. Our courtship flourished quickly with the guidance of my therapist, making it the healthiest interpersonal relationship I had had at this point in my life. Even with all the thriving aspects of our young love, Jimmy was insecure and often wanted sex as a reaffirmation of my love for him.

I remember describing him as a walking hormone, because it felt like anytime we were in proximity to each other, his hips automatically began moving as if they were on automatic pilot. In the beginning, this made me so happy because I equated sexual desire with love, so I felt completely "loved" by him as a result. But there came a time where I felt irritated by his never-ending advances, and we began to have discussions and fights about this cycle. He would indicate his intention to have sex, and I would come up with creative ways why that couldn't happen, such as my back hurting or the old stand-by, a splitting headache. He would feel rejected, which would increase his need for affirmation that I loved him through more sexual contact, which would get rejected...again. This cycle became exhausting quickly.

After I graduated from college, Jimmy and I decided to move to Atlanta together. He had moved out of his family home and lived with roommates for a few months before I graduated, and we were ready for new adventures. We were both ready to live in the same city together, taking our relationship to the next level from the "permanent vacation" we had been existing within. When you are in a long-distance relationship, time spent together is always exciting, and everyone is often on their best behavior for the visit. Everyday issues, such as laundry and house cleaning, don't get addressed together because we would handle those things when we were apart, leaving our time together focused on each other. As a result, many of our trouble points didn't get addressed, and destructive patterns were allowed to fester.

Despite the issues, we had begun to discuss getting engaged and had gone so far as to go window shopping in jewelry stores so that I could make sure Jimmy knew what kind of ring I wanted. After many weeks of not finding the "perfect" ring, a jeweler suggested we could design a ring set that would be unique to my tastes. We picked out the stones, and I met with the designer to sketch out my ideal wedding ring set. No one would have the same rings as I did, and I felt as special as I had ever felt in this process. Growing up in the shadow of an older sister, whose hand-me-downs were always in my closet, the idea of having a ring set that I would never see on the hand of another was intoxicating.

The ring was finished and in Jimmy's hands before we moved to Atlanta, but he was determined to decide when he would pop the question. It killed me to have this part out of my control, but it was also exhilarating to be with a man who wanted to surprise me! As much as I was irritated by his control of the situation, I was equally swooning by the love he was demonstrating he had for me by wanting to make this moment as special as he could.

Mary had attended Emory University and had stayed in Atlanta after she graduated. When I visited her, I always felt energized by the big city vibes and felt like I could take this step because she was already there and Jimmy would be with me. We got separate apartments, as we didn't have a full commitment to each other yet and his family was deeply religious, but we spent most of our time together. It was so exciting to live in the same city, but we understood it was going to be an adjustment from the long-distance relationship we had been living within up to this point. I started learning things about him that I resisted, like when he asked me if I could iron his pants.

"I can, but I would rather teach you how to do it so you don't have to rely on me for it," I replied.

This response began a heated discussion about doing for the other as a couple. What I was resisting was his *assumption* that I would do these types of chores for him. There was an archaic sense to it, and I wasn't down for that. His mother used to iron his boxer shorts for him up to the time he moved to Atlanta with me, so I needed to set him straight about what I was and was not willing to do. It was the beginning of many conversations that would reveal areas where we did not see eye to eye on the roles of women and men in a relationship.

I came from a family ruled by women. Tootie was the matriarch who had never had a male partner during my lifetime. Mom clearly had Dad by the balls and made all the decisions that mattered in our household. Every time we had a full family dinner, there were only two men at the table, Dad and Uncle Haskell, and neither of them made demands to be heard, except Uncle Haskell's insistence on having white bread with dinner.

As kids, we loved it when Aunt Gay and Uncle Haskell would be with us for dinner, because we knew white bread would be on the table. He once held up dinner for us at a local restaurant because they were out of white bread; we waited until one of the busboys ran to the store to purchase a loaf. Living in such a small, predominantly white town where everyone knows you, these types of expectations were not unusual. Except for these small idiosyncrasies, women made all the decisions in my family of origin. As a result, I grew up with a subliminal understanding that men weren't capable of managing most decisions about family life. I don't ever remember hearing

"Just wait until your father gets home" as a precursor to punishment. Mom took care of most consequences swiftly and told Dad all about the outcomes when he came home.

Jimmy and I needed to establish these boundaries and his experience growing up was very different from mine. He grew up in a traditional household, where it was the woman's responsibility to make sure her family had everything they needed, doing all her chores with a smile. He didn't know what to do with my independent beliefs, but his kindness and good Southern gentleman charm allowed him to be manipulated into a similar power structure to my upbringing. He would push back more than my father ever did, which made for some pretty big fights.

What I thought of as independent behavior was really all about control. I did not trust men, especially those who could be led around by the nose. What to others might have looked like a Southern gentlemanly way looked weak and familiar to me. The relationship between Jimmy and me began to look very much like the dynamic between my parents. I called the shots, and he complied until his resentment had built up enough to give him the energy to explode for whatever reason, and we would have a big fight to clear the air.

Even though I knew he was going to ask me to marry him, the moment was *so exciting*—not necessarily because I was looking toward a future with the man I loved, but because someone had asked me to marry him. He'd had the ring for quite some time, and I waited with bated breath, wondering when he would pop the question. He ended up asking me at the kitchen table in my apartment, probably because I was pressuring him to get it over with!

I called Mom immediately, "Mom, I'm *engaged!*"

This statement always seems so telling to me. I didn't say, "Jimmy asked me to marry him" or "Jimmy and I are getting married." It was all about getting engaged; it didn't matter as much about whom it was with. I loved Jimmy as best as I could at that time, but this step of getting engaged was a big transition for me. I had a feeling of accomplishment that I had never felt before. Someone was committed to me enough to ask me to share a life with them. As a young woman who deep down did not believe I was worthy of that kind of commitment, hearing those words come out of his mouth as he slipped the ring on my finger was the biggest dose of outside validation I'd had in my adult life. I had found a sweet man who loved me and would put up with my Crazy. I was over the moon!

Now that Jimmy had shown his commitment to me, a feeling of safety came over me that I had not known I needed. Up until the proposal, I had *always* been drunk (or at least heavily buzzed) during sex as a coping mechanism for the fear and anxiety it produced. The alcohol created the "check out" I needed to let go of my inhibitions, but it also created some of the most dangerous experiences I had ever found myself in. Once Jimmy and I were engaged, there was a comfort level for me that I had not experienced before. I began to allow myself to be intimate with him without alcohol, which was an exhilarating experience on many levels. It was almost as if I were a virgin again and was learning about the sensations, sights, and smells associated with this act of intimacy for the first time.

I felt everything more deeply having sex in a relatively sober state. His whisper in my ear was louder, and his touch was more intense on my skin. Not long after allowing myself to encounter sex sober, I began to feel something other than the now more familiar sensations of sexual pleasure. Panic was becoming a more common state that I didn't know how to identify nor control. At first, I would blame Jimmy for wanting sex too much—an old trope that was easy to fall into. Excuses why we couldn't be intimate were often and repetitive, unless I had been drinking. Then I was willingly cloaked in the familiar warm blanket of numbness that alcohol provided.

One late afternoon, Jimmy and I were on the couch in my apartment, and things were getting quite intense. We were both largely disrobed, and I was completely engaged, until the familiar panic began to rise in my throat. My heart was racing, and my head was filled with this noise that was all encompassing. Next thing I knew, I was pushing him away and yelling for him to stop! I couldn't breathe, and I had no idea what was happening to me. Jimmy was frustrated and confused, as I was clearly interested in having sex just a few minutes ago. He began asking me what was wrong with me, and his frustration sounded like anger as he questioned why I was so hot and cold with him lately.

I didn't know what to tell him. I was just as confused as he was, and when his questions became more and more persistent, I yelled at him, "I THINK I'VE BEEN ABUSED!" I had never said that before that I knew of, and I had no idea where it came from. I started crying, and he put his arms around me to comfort me. I felt like an earthquake had just struck, shifting the very foundation on which my house was built. I had no sense of ownership of the words that came out of my mouth but I knew I would never be the same.

This first full panic attack was a horrifying turning point in my life. Jimmy and I were equally confused, and no one knew what the next step might be. What did I mean when I said I think I had been abused? Where did that come from, and what did it look like? Sexual abuse wasn't as commonly talked about then as it is now. Today, people are more familiar with the difference between a pedophile and a rapist, between a domestic-violence situation and a bad marriage. But I didn't know these things in the living room of my Atlanta apartment on a sunny afternoon with the love of my life. All I knew was that my body was telling me to run, a coping mechanism established long before this afternoon, one that was as old as I was.

The panic attacks began happening more and more, and the stop and go of our sex life was not compatible with Jimmy's high sex drive. It became an even bigger place for us to argue, and the difference with these arguments was that I was increasingly feeling like an open wound and I could not get my bearings. Every time we fought, I felt assaulted, as if I had opened this Pandora's box of feelings that I had no idea existed and didn't know how to process.

After some time of this cycle, we decided going to a couple's therapist was the only solution. How I wished Rachel lived in Atlanta so we could go see her. I trusted her and knew she would not steer me wrong. But all that time I saw Rachel in Greensboro, she never hinted that she had any suspicion of sexual abuse in my story. Maybe it was best to see someone new; besides, I don't think Rachel would travel all the way to Atlanta to work with Jimmy and me.

When we went for our initial session, I had decided I was not going to mention to our new therapist Helen what my suspicions were to see if she came to a similar conclusion after listening to my story. I wanted to see if she corroborated my story by hearing my symptoms. I still couldn't believe this was happening, and I was hoping she would say I was imagining things. If it didn't occur to her that I had been abused, that would be the confirmation that I was making all this up in my head.

Jimmy and I arrived in her office waiting room both very nervous and anxious about taking this step. I had spent a fair amount of time in therapist's offices, but this was new for Jimmy, and he was obviously uncomfortable in this unknown territory. The waiting room was quiet with a few couples there waiting just like us for other therapists who used the office. We sat next to each other, staring straight ahead at the opposite wall, feeling as far apart as two people could feel who were sitting next to each other. The time waiting was not long at all, but it felt like an eternity as the seconds ticked away on the clock.

Helen's office was comfortably furnished but sterile. After being in a lovely room in Rachel's home all those years, this office with its matching end tables and drab upholstered couch and chair looked more like the showroom at a Rooms to Go than someone's living room. As in most things in our relationship, I did most of the talking, sharing my story and his, leading us to this moment with a few interjections of his along the way. She listened patiently, taking notes on her notepad and asking a few clarifying questions.

After about forty-five minutes, she asked me, "Do you think there is a possibility that you were sexually abused?"

I remember feeling like a bomb had exploded in my head. She said it; she came to her own conclusion, and I hadn't fed her the thought. I confessed that I had already had that thought but that I wanted to see if she agreed without any prompting from me. I was a swirl of emotions. I had been validated and horrified at the same time. The questions that entered my head were *who, what, where, when, and how?* I didn't have answers yet, but there was a strange relief in knowing that I might be on a path of discovery that could result in a peace I had yet to know.

Her prescription for Jimmy and me was to not engage in *any* sexual contact until further notice. She was concerned I was being retraumatized every time we engaged. The scab had been ripped off my wound, exposing it to risk of infection if I didn't keep the field clean. It was imperative that my intimate relationships maintained the highest level of safety so that I could unpack what had been hidden away for so long. Jimmy found this boundary less than ideal.

"You know you're safe with me," he would say as he slid his hands up under my shirt as I cleaned the kitchen after dinner. "I would never hurt you. I love you!"

"Jimmy, Helen has said we need to wait. Why can't you listen to her and leave me alone?" As I said this, I felt terribly guilty and deeply angry at the same time. Why couldn't he follow directions and stop putting me in the position of rejecting him? It was just making things worse, and I was scared he would leave me.

"If you love me, why can't I touch you? I'm a man, and I have needs. Why are your needs always more important than mine?"

He just didn't want to accept that I needed this time to begin to process what was bubbling up from deep inside my psyche. These discussions became exhausting. The retraumatization that our therapist wanted me to avoid was happening anyway, as I had to explain to him over and over why I needed him to leave me alone! I needed his love, but not his touch right now, and he did not want to hear that from me.

It was just a few months after the therapy started when we decided to end our engagement. I was such a hot mess that I couldn't be the girlfriend and fiancée he needed, and he became more and more frustrated by our therapist telling him no sexual contact. It just wasn't moving fast enough for him, and he didn't understand the process. His frustration led to him to cheat on me, which broke my heart. I was very sad that we had to break up, but I was so exhausted emotionally by my therapy that disconnecting from him offered some degree of relief.

We loved each other, and we were both sad to separate. But there was no telling how long my healing would take, and he was not down for a journey with no end in sight. We were young, and in the end, it was the right decision for both of us. But it broke my heart just the same. He became a Methodist minister, which always made me laugh because he would have never gotten a congregation being married to me since I didn't really subscribe to religious beliefs at the time. It was the universe taking care of me when I couldn't do it for myself—the first of many interventions.

I had plenty to do with the extra time I now had in my life. I decided that I didn't need to go to therapy anymore since Jimmy and I had broken up and our relationship was the reason we got into it in the first place. Even though I had uncovered a huge detail about my life that I had yet to fully excavate, I allowed the Crazy to convince me that I didn't need the discomfort that going to therapy created right now. I just needed to be alone and work through my "stuff" on my own. Of course, being numb during this was super important, so that pattern did a lot to keep me stuck in this in-between world of knowing my truth without knowing any details of my truth. I was an abuse survivor but wasn't sure who the perpetrator was, nor did I know the details of that abuse. It was a dangerous place to be.

I began to dream about the abuse. I had always been a vivid dreamer and often remembered minute details of those dreams. I began to dream about experiences that were full of fear and panic. After waking up with a start, I would remember a faceless man on top of me but not have any more details than that. Details like the color of the carpet and the layout of the house began to seep into my recollections, which led me to a conclusion that my father's best friend, Uncle Mark, had abused me.

It made sense. The Phillips and our family spent almost every day together. When Amy wasn't at my house, I was over at her place. Uncle Mark would have had ample access to me, and he was always a little *off*. He fit the stereotype I had in my mind of someone who would be capable of this act. He laughed a lot when he'd been drinking, and his cheeks and eyes would scrunch up like Santa Claus's, giving him a pleasing and welcoming look to a child; but I had also seen him in a darker place. My child mind didn't understand what depression was, so when Uncle Mark would disappear during a low, I didn't give it a lot of thought. I had seen him angry, but in their house, Aunt Maria was the rager. Their relationship structure was very similar to my mom and dad's, with the woman as the outward aggressor. I think this is why their house felt so much like home to me. The map of this minefield was engraved on my soul. I didn't have a working understanding of what kind of man would sexually abuse a child, but with my familiarity of the setting and my knowledge of Uncle Mark's moodiness, he seemed a likely culprit.

Domestic Violence

What an odd set of terms,
Domestic violence.

As if there is anything
domestic about
rage and
slicing and
the dismembering of souls.

"Domestic" conjures thoughts
of homemaking
and baking
and lovemaking,
where the joys of togetherness
weave a brightly colored tapestry
of connection and sharing
and touch.

How can homemaking
be violent?

When the home you make
unravels your threads
with tongue lashings
and esteem crushing
and hate wrapped in promises,
never to do it again.

When the lovemaking
is more about bruise making
as he's careful to offend
where they won't see.

Where his statements of regret
are cloaked in descriptions
of your instigations
because he wouldn't do it
if you didn't make him so mad.

I see you, Mother,
who can't possibly leave him
because he's convinced you
of your inability to
breathe
without him.

Because you're too stupid
to go out on your own,
but you're wise because
you've chosen him to be your king.

He's got you so tangled up
you don't even know
that, to me, you are a
Domestic goddess.

A soul so divine
that even in the darkness
your light shines brighter than
the shiner on your eye.

You've lost your way
listening to lies
and fists
and slaps,
but I see you…

Know that when you are ready
for domestic peace,
I am here.

When you know that leaving
Is the only way to remain sane,
I am here.

And you are worth that wait in gold.

Part Two

Mom and Dad had a small private plane for a time, sharing the expenses with Mom's brother-in-law Uncle Haskell, and boy, was that a luxury! Instead of driving to Raleigh an hour and a half away to catch a commercial flight, we only had to drive to the small airport in our hometown to walk a short red carpet and board the plane. I felt like a rock star each time I flew, and the thrill of it never got old. No one asked us to look through our bags or to go through screening. We simply walked through the small terminal and boarded the plane while others took care of our luggage.

This time, I got picked up from the small airport just outside the St. Augustine city limits. The family was already on the plane, and we were off to Jupiter, Florida. Mom and I had been seeing a therapist named Susan, who was willing to have us all to her place for this difficult discussion. It was definitely a point of privilege to be flying all the way to south Florida for a therapy session—on a private plane—but that privilege was not on my mind. I was more focused on what we were traveling to do and how it was all going to go down.

As I stared out the window, watching St. Augustine disappear, I felt a deep sense of dread. I was happy that we had a safe place to have this discussion, led by someone who I felt like was on "my team." I also had to work really hard to feel my feet on the floor. I didn't realize at the time that some level of disassociation was a tactic of my psyche to protect myself. I slipped into it effortlessly, with little awareness of the out-of-body experience I was having.

We had agreed to be at Susan's house at 9:00 a.m. She and her husband lived in a classic south Florida home colored with sea-foam green and coral, and a private pool with privacy fence surrounding it just outside the wall of windows that were designed to let the perpetual sunshine flood the space. I had been to this house many times leading up to this meeting, spending long week-ends with Susan doing very deep therapy work. Susan specialized in hypnotherapy, taking her clients deep into hypnosis to retrieve memories long buried. She created an environment of true safety to allow her patients to fully feel their feelings, no matter how scary they got.

On this morning, Dad, Mom, Mary, and I stepped into Susan's home and found our seats in the living room. Dad and I were each in individual chairs, while Mom and Mary sat on the couch together. The initial conversation was mostly small-talk: "How was our trip down?" "Did you find the hotel comfortable?" It was similar to the initial assent on the roller coaster for that first drop as you hear the *click, click, click* of the wheels on the track. I was full of anticipation but deeply regretting that I had gotten on this ride.

Mom had a closet outside of the big room in our childhood home that we called the secret closet. It had a pocket door and a counter with cabinets above and below on the left when you entered but couldn't have been more than three or four feet across and maybe eight feet deep. It was where she kept all our Christmas and birthday presents, so we were not to go in there under any circumstances. During my therapy with Susan, I had a dream that included that closet. I was maybe five years old standing outside the closed door. Pocket doors have those metal squares where the latching mechanism was housed, and as I stood in front of the door, I could hear my voice coming from inside the closet. I reached up to the metal plate to slide the door open, and it was so hot to the touch that I jumped back, feeling the heat on my fingers. I could hear myself inside pleading to get out, but the outside "me" couldn't open the door. I was trapped and powerless to free myself at the same time. In this moment, I was living out the fear that dream had always held for me.

After some initial pleasantries, Susan began the conversation welcoming us to the space with the intention of getting to the truth. My heart was pounding as I turned to my notes to provide comfort and grounding. I didn't want to float away in this moment that would change the course of my life. Relationships and family dynamics were going to change forever. I wasn't sure of what this transformation would look like in the end, but I knew it was coming, ready or not. It was time for me to open the pocket door and set myself free.

Chapter 6

My coworker Ron and I made a date to go out on the town one Friday night. I had been feeling down since my break up with Jimmy, and we decided he was in charge of cheering me up. He was going to show me the gay scene of Atlanta, and I was down for the ride! We hopped from bar to bar, laughing, drinking, and dancing all the way through the evening. Around 1:00 a.m., the bars in Atlanta were beginning to close, but I wanted to keep going. Ron suggested we go check out The Cove.

The Cove was a members-only club that charged you a $1 membership fee when you entered. It was a loophole in Georgia at the time for bars to stay open twenty-four hours. If they were membership only clubs, they could make their own rules. The Cove had no windows, and when I walked in, it was as if I had entered the Twilight Zone. There were all walks of life here: gay, straight, punkers, transgender, drag queens, druggies, and all others who didn't even fit into a category. It was where Atlanta went to party when all other bars closed down for the night.

I was wearing a black miniskirt with small white polka dots and a fuchsia off-the-shoulder sweater—very early '90s. As soon as we got inside, I needed to go to the bathroom. The place was so dark and smoky you could barely see your hand in front of your face. Ron said there was a bathroom that had multiple stalls and then there was a single bathroom that I should use, with a lock on the door. (It was that kind of place!) We went around the bar and found the line for the single bathroom. As I approached, I saw Ron run up to a guy waiting in line for the bathroom. He ran up behind him, sticking his hands up under his shirt, and began playing with his chest hair. I figured Ron knew who he was by his familiar greeting, but the look on this guy's face when he swung around told a different story.

"WHAT THE FUCK ARE YOU DOING!" the guy screamed at Ron, and that's when I noticed the three very large men descending on Ron with very angry and determined looks on their faces. It was like a movie was being played out in front of me, and I thought Ron was going to die. Ron immediately began pleading for mercy as the three men grabbed his shirt and lifted him off the ground.

"I didn't mean it!" screamed Ron. "I thought you were someone else! I'm sorry!"

The guy looked past Ron, and our gaze locked. He was a white man, about five foot nine, with blonde hair, intriguing green eyes, a very thin face, and a nice body. He was wearing a white tank top and jeans and looked just like all the others in this den of iniquity, but his energy was suddenly focused on me, and it sent a charge of electricity through my body. He assessed me up and down and asked, "Are you with him?"

I must have looked terrified! I couldn't speak at this point but could only nod my head to say yes. I was in a strange place with strange people, and I wasn't sure Ron would get out of there without a serious rearranging of his face. Talk about a buzzkill. I was suddenly completely sober.

The guy motioned to his goons to let him go, and they dropped Ron to the floor. He told Ron that he should keep his hands to himself and not make assumptions going forward. All Ron could do was say yes, and he went scampering off—leaving me there.

"Hi, my name is Adam," he said, so close I could feel his breath on my cheek.

The starting bell rang, and we were off to the races!

*****

I had really been struggling since Jimmy and I had broken up. Life had the peculiar sense of being untethered, and I was drifting through most days. I had no fiancé and was not busy planning a wedding as I thought I would be at this point. I had a job in the leasing office of the building I lived in, which sometimes meant I didn't go outside for a week at a time. I got up, went to work downstairs, went back home after work, ordered pizza, and went to bed. Going out to show a prospective renter the pool was often my only chance to get fresh air. Buried deep in this cycle, the Crazy settled in as the committee in my head, weighing in on every decision with multiple opinions that never seemed to reconcile.

Then there was the shadow of my truth as an abuse survivor that was lingering in the wings while I did everything I could to avoid dealing with it. Most nights, with six to eight beers on board, I started going to that dark reality where imaging the world without me in it seemed to make sense. I lived on the eleventh floor of my building and had a balcony off the living room. I would sit on my couch and stare at the railing of my balcony visualizing myself going over and falling silently to my death. Would anyone miss me? It seemed like the only way to get the committee to quiet down in my head. Spending time alone in my apartment was dangerous, and I was doing it regularly.

Mary had lived across the street from me, but she had moved into the same building some months before. We joked about finally becoming friends when I moved to Atlanta and marveled at how long it took us to get there. It was wonderful to have a big sister who not only *liked* me but wanted to be around me. Of course, in my excitement to have her fully in my life, I went too far and became enmeshed, not establishing boundaries that allowed for us to be two separate people with two separate lives. I told her everything. She had unlimited amounts of advice on all topics, including what to wear, how much to drink, and whom to date. I was reveling in having an older sister to consult with on life, so much so that losing myself in the relationship didn't come with a warning sign.

When I began to discover my truth about the abuse, she was right there. She didn't know the details, for that matter neither did I; but she listened to me talk it through, and she held my hand while I cried. When the suicidal ideation began, I was afraid to tell her at first. What would she think of me, and would she truly care to stop me from ending my life? We had been in each other's lives for more than twenty years at this point, but friends for only one. Connections between us were still fragile, and the fear of losing what I had so longed to have was almost worse than discovering the layers of trauma I was desperately trying to keep buried.

One evening, after getting off work and going upstairs to change into comfy clothes and order dinner, I was sitting on the couch in the silence. I had painted the wall behind the couch with a feather in a light green color as an accent wall and had painted other walls the same solid green color to offset, which was my feeble attempt at interior decorating. The apartment was a two bedroom and two baths with an open floor plan for the "dining" area and living room. The carpet was a neutral beige color and the sliding glass door to the balcony was in the far left corner of the living room when you entered the apartment. I had started to accumulate furniture that actually matched—somewhat—and was beginning to appreciate an actual "grown up" living space. I didn't like dark wood furniture, probably from growing up around it all my life. So the shelving I got for the living room was made of pressboard and was a light color, looking almost white-washed. The couch I had gotten at a thrift store had big mauve flowers on it, and I purchased a mauve wing chair to round out the seating. This night, I was curled up in a ball on the couch, crying, all alone. The sense that my life was spiraling out of control was intense, and I did not have a remedy for the Crazy that was standing in the middle of my living room, showing me the way to the balcony railing—with a smile. I picked up the phone and called Mary.

"Hello?" she said. Her voice was full of anticipation; this was before caller ID existed.

I couldn't do much more than breathe in the phone. "It's me."

"Are you okay?" she asked with increased worry in her voice.

"No" was all I could muster before the tears started flowing again.

"I'll be right there!" And she hung up.

When she let herself in the apartment (we had shared keys because we were sharing everything right now), she found me in the same fetal position on the couch I had been in for a couple of hours.

She bundled me up into her arms and began rocking me in silence while I fell deep into the ugly cry. I don't ever remember any member of my family holding me like this while I moved through the landscape of hell before or since. We didn't have to talk about what was going on, except that I was able to say I was seriously looking at the balcony after I had cried for about an hour. I was grateful she was so close, and I truly believe she saved my life that night. I was deep in my despair. Having a family member with me to remind me that I mattered was the only thing that kept the Crazy from winning that night, and I could feel it returning to the shadows while she soothed my tears.

*****

Of course, what I needed was an unhealthy relationship to take my mind off my troubles. That night in the Cove while Ron was trying to escape with his face intact, I found the perfect candidate. Adam and I found a couple of bar stools to sit down; actually, his goons told someone to get up so we could sit down, and we talked about everything. He called me Legs, bought me drinks, and wanted to know everything about me. Each time I would ask him questions about himself, he would redirect to me. I thought he was being attentive, but he was really just avoiding telling me anything about himself. He offered me drugs and flashed around a large wad of bills each time he paid for a drink, and he was intrigued that I didn't want his money or his drugs.

"I don't do drugs, and I have my own money, so you can put that all away," I said to him with immense pride. I wasn't going to tell him I was a Rockefeller after a lifetime of training of how to keep that close to the chest. He probably wouldn't have believed me anyway.

It was like we were both drugs for each other. He was the bad boy who seemed to have the whole place under his thumb, treating me like a princess, and I was the independent rich girl who didn't want him for anything other than himself.

We danced and drank and laughed until the sun came up. I was completely hooked by all the excitement of the night, but I was very aware of something. His goons kept coming up to him and whispering in his ear throughout the night. He would brush them off and tell them to get lost, but they were clearly not happy about it. Finally, he confided to me that he worked for a big drug dealer in Atlanta, and his boss was not happy that he had not been selling any product since I walked in the door. He told me that they had already run my license plate, and he knew more about me than I did at that point. I was completely intrigued by all this. I had never met anyone like him before, and he had my head spinning.

I finally realized what time it was and that in just three hours, I had to be at work. I told him I had to go, and he insisted on walking me to my car. When we walked outside, the sun was coming up, and I felt like a mole coming out of my underground den blinking my eyes, willing them to adjust so I could see where I was going. He walked me to my car, but not without showing me his car, a beautiful silver Porsche. I had another chance to tell him it didn't impress me and see his reaction again at my indifference to his shiny objects. We said our goodbyes, and I somehow made it home with just enough time to shower, change, and get to work still very, very drunk. I was working at another building from where I lived, in the leasing office. This building only showed apartments by appointment, so as long as no one called, all I had to do was maintain for just a few hours until I could go home and sleep it off. It was all I could do to keep my shit together, drinking coffee and water, hoping to get a little clear-headed before someone needed me to be coherent.

I couldn't stop thinking about Adam! This bad boy had completely stolen my heart, but there was *no way* in hell I could see him again. What would I tell my family? He was a drug dealer! I was a good little rich girl from small-town North Carolina. There was no way I could bring him home to that. But he was sexy and different, and he made me feel things I had never felt before. It was intoxicating...or maybe that was just the leftover drunk I was dealing with.

After three excruciating hours, the phone rang. I answered with my pat. "Good morning, this is the Ashley Terrace. How may I help you?"

"Hi, Legs, what cha doin'?"

Oh. My. God! I couldn't catch my breath! He called! I didn't give him this number. How did he find me? Oh yeah, he knew more about me than I did.

He wanted to see me again that night. I hemmed and hawed since I had determined I couldn't see him again. But oh, how I wanted to. I decided we could meet at a pool hall just down the street from my apartment. We'd play a few games, have a few beers, and then that would be it. I swear.

Well, it was another glorious night of him making me feel like the center of the universe, which was one of my drugs of choice at the time. But this time he came alone, no goons. I asked about them, and he said tonight he wasn't working, he wanted to spend the evening alone with me.

We ended up at my place that night in a drunken swirl of sex and beer. The next morning, as we lay in bed, hungover and spent from a night of lovemaking, the fisherman landed his hook.

"I'm going to quit the business. I want to be with you. I know you can't be with a drug dealer, so I am going to call my boss and quit!"

Friends, have you ever heard such sweet words spoken to you before? I tell you, to a codependent alcoholic, he couldn't have cast that line any better. He was going to give it all up for *me*! He was going to walk away from the horrible life he was leading to be devoted to me. I followed in my mother's footsteps of falling for the sob story of the twisted soul who was looking for redemption and love. When I think back on how beautifully he orchestrated this play, I can only shake my head at the depth of my stupidity.

He left the apartment for several hours and returned with three cardboard boxes full of stuff and a couple of large garbage bags of clothes. He had told his boss he was done and had promptly lost his car, apartment, and all his belongings except what he came with. I felt so sorry for him, as he seemed completely deflated at the realization of his new existence. At the same time, however, I was further hooked by the fact that he gave this all up for me. He had proven his love for me in the most powerful way, and I was ready to start our new life together.

One of Adam's superpowers was his charm. He was a *fantastic* storyteller, and boy, did he have stories to tell! What I didn't realize was that he was spinning a web of lies that I had no idea I was caught up in until it was too late. He spun wonderful stories about his exploits in the underworld of drug dealing that had me riveted. I had never been around anyone like him and wouldn't have the slightest idea if what he was telling me was truthful or not. It wasn't until we went to dinner at a cute little middle-eastern restaurant in Buckhead that I began to hear the deeper stories about his origins.

We sat at a small table and started looking at the menu. Many of the names of the dishes were in Arabic, and he began to pronounce them and tell me how they were prepared. I was surprised at his ability to speak Arabic so fluently, but I wasn't more surprised than our waiter when he came to the table.

"As-salamu alaykum," Adam offers to the waiter when he approaches.

The waiter's eyes got really big, and he answered in the traditional way with a tone of shock in his response. This white boy with blond hair and green eyes did not look like anyone who should be speaking Arabic fluently.

They had a little back and forth with each other before Adam ordered for me, and when the waiter left, I must have had a quizzical look on my face, so he felt compelled to fill in the gaps.

"What was that?" I asked.

"Oh, I speak Arabic," he replied.

"And how in the world do you speak Arabic?"

"Well, I grew up in Saudi Arabia, so I spoke Arabic growing up. I also speak French, some Spanish, and Italian."

"How is it you speak all those languages?" I knew there were stories, and I couldn't wait to hear all about it.

He told me he was born in Rota, Spain, on the navy base, that his father was a chief petty officer and his mom was a buy-me-a-drink girl in Morocco when they met. He told me the story of how his mother spoke very little English and when his father told her he was a chief petty officer, she just heard "chief" and thought he was good to marry. On the day of the wedding in Casablanca, she walked down the aisle and took one look at his medals and knew he wasn't the kind of chief she thought he was. The wedding almost didn't happen, but Don was able to convince her that he would give her a good life (his son got his charm from him). They traveled all over the world while his dad was in the Navy. Then when he retired, his dad was hired by the Saudi Air Force to teach them how to fly C-130 airplanes (since the US had sold their old fleet to the Saudi government). Adam told me about the compound that they lived in, surrounded by other American families who lived in Saudi Arabia for various reasons. His mom was French-Moroccan, so she spoke French in the home.

"Are you an only child?"

"No, I have two older cousins whose parents were killed in an earthquake, and they came to live with us right after. My parents ended up adopting them, so they are my brothers, but technically, they are my cousins. I have a twin sister, too, but we are the only two biological children."

We ate our dinner as he told story after story about his time growing up in Saudi Arabia, like the fact that alcohol is illegal there so his father would get some kind of homemade moonshine that the fellow compound mates would make, or the story of the time the air conditioner went on the fritz.

"We couldn't figure out why the air conditioner wasn't coming out of one of the vents in the hallway. Dad thought something was blocking the vent, so he got the broom and stuck the handle into the vent and shoved it into whatever the blockage was to try to dislodge it. The handle began to shake and jerk, and he heard this horrible sound like a wood chipper was eating the handle! Dad pulled the handle out of the hole—he had had his arm in there all the way up to his shoulder as well—and most of the handle was gone! Something really big was in that hole, and none of us knew what it was.

Then out of the hole comes a five-foot-long lizard! It worked its way out of the hole, looked up and down the hall at the screaming people who were now on the countertops to get away from it, and ambled its way out the door with its enormous tail swishing the width of the hallway with each step. I had climbed onto the counter in the kitchen, and Mom began to yell at me to open the door so it would walk right out of the house. The good news was that the air conditioning was cooling the house again. The bad news was that they needed to get a new broom."

Stories like this began to flow out of him every time he had an audience. He was fun and exciting, and there was never a dull moment with him around. We went everywhere together and partied like there was no tomorrow. There was a fun side to our lives, but there was also a dark side that few knew about at the time.

Adam rarely left the apartment without me, but when he did, he often came home hours or days later with a black eye or busted lip. He would tell me stories of how his old boss would take him and try to get him back in the business, and he would point out suspicious vehicles outside our building and say they were watching us. I fell for all these stories and was terrified that one time he would go out and not come back. I would try to convince him not to leave when he wanted to venture out alone, but I often would not win the argument.

Looking back on these times, it is clear that he was still using (meth or cocaine were his drugs of choice) and would score when he went out without me so I wouldn't know. He had sworn to me that he was no longer using hard drugs, and I believed him, as I believed most things he told me. I was so naive about drugs, being just a drunk myself, that I hadn't clued into the fact that he could drink me under the table most nights and when I was falling asleep, he was full of energy. We did have one experience when we were out at a bar together one night. We were sitting there enjoying our drinks when a sketchy-looking skinny white dude with spiky bleach-blond hair, dressed all in black, sat down next to him at the bar and quickly engaged him in conversation.

"Hey, aren't you the cooker everyone talks about?"

"No, man, you got the wrong guy," Adam said dismissively.

"Yeah, yeah, it is you! You the best cooker around, man, you the best! You got any stuff on ya, man? You got anything you can give me, man?"

Adam started to get agitated. He insisted he was out of the business and told the guy to fuck off. This dude wasn't taking no for an answer, but I was more focused on the fact that all the stories he had been telling me about people trying to get him back in the business must be true! Here was proof that seemed completely unsolicited. I have no idea if he paid the guy to say all those things, but it further set the hook.

After some months of financially supporting both of us, I was ready for him to get a job. He had every excuse in the world why he couldn't get a job, except the real reason: that he had no real forms of ID to prove who he was. He did get a job at a nightclub for a while, and I was so happy to have him earning some money to contribute. I'm not sure how he even got it for the brief time he had it, but it might be that he had a friend who worked there who could slide him in without all the documentation most people needed. He was keeping many secrets on many levels, and I am not sure how he didn't lose his mind during this time.

We finally concluded that we needed to move from Atlanta. As much as we loved the city, he couldn't function here without someone trying to get him "back into the business," and my nerves were shot! We decided St. Augustine, Florida, would be a great place to move to. A beautiful and quaint town with so much charm, St. Augustine seemed like a great place to start our new life. We started the process to go, finding a place to live in an over one-hundred-year-old house that needed to be refurbished. I had never been to St. Augustine, but Adam convinced me that it was the next step in our journey, and I readily agreed. I dreamed of being in a town where he could move about without me worrying about his safety, and this move seemed to fill that need.

Adam didn't have a birth certificate, and he was concerned he wouldn't be able to get proper identification in Florida once we established residency. He told me the story of how he had been born in Rota, Spain, and had dual citizenship so he had to fill out a complicated form to request a new copy. One day, when he was not at home, a large manila envelope came in the mail. It wasn't addressed to me, but having no discernable boundaries, it seemed absolutely logical to open that which wasn't mine. I broke the seal and pulled out the contents.

It was a birth certificate for someone named David Christopher Franklin Boudreaux with the same birthdate as Adam but two years older.

I looked at the completed paperwork that they had returned with the certificate and read the details of "David's" family history, all written in Adam's handwriting. His mom had died in 1983, but his dad was alive and living in Smyrna, Georgia, only a forty-five-minute drive from where we lived. He was the youngest of four siblings, with no twin sister. His sister was the next oldest to him, then his two brothers, who went by the same names of those Adam told me were his cousins.

I couldn't breathe. The details I was reading were an amalgam of all he had told me, lies and truth. My head was spinning, and I felt the anger well up in me from deep inside. WHO WAS THIS PERSON! What else had he told me that was a lie? I was about to move my entire life for this man in two weeks, and now I was suddenly finding out that he wasn't who he said he was. What was I going to do?

Next to his father's name, there was an address and phone number. This man, whom I had always believed was dead, was in fact very much alive and just a short drive away. The next thing I knew, I was dialing the phone number. When the voice answered on the other end, he sounded just like Adam, but older.

"Hi, I'm looking for Donald Boudreaux?" I said, my voice shaking.

"You got him! This is Don," he said. I could tell he was smiling. You know how you can hear that over the phone? I began to describe who I was, that I was living with his son, and we were about to move to St. Augustine, Florida, together. He knew who I was, and I could tell that Adam/David had told him about me, but he was surprised to find out why we hadn't met.

"He told me you were dead," I said hesitantly.

"Oh, well, that would make it hard for us to meet, wouldn't it?"

I was sitting in the living room when Adam/David came home. I was so angry, and I didn't even know how to begin this conversation. He knew something was wrong immediately when he entered the apartment. I handed him the envelope with the birth certificate and other papers.

"I talked to your dad," I said.

The next twelve hours are something of a blur. There was screaming and yelling, pleading and crying. He had been caught in his web of lies, and all the walls he had constructed to protect himself came crumbling down.

"I couldn't tell you who I was," he said almost in tears. "If you ever kicked me out and I had to go back to dealing, I had to make sure you couldn't find me."

"I wouldn't kick you out if you were just fucking honest with me!" I said, feeling the hook set in my heart. He always had a way of making me work twice as hard as he to keep him exactly where he wanted to be.

"I was scared! I love you, and I love our life. I didn't want to screw that up," he said. "my boss made up the whole identity. Adam is my nephew's name, and he got me all the identification cards I needed to function in this new identity."

"Did you tell me anything that was real?" I asked between the tears.

"Yes, the stories about my upbringing, boarding school in Rome, breaking both my collarbones in the desert—they were all real."

And the revelations continued… His mother had died as he had told me. His father wasn't dead but was living in Smyrna and didn't agree with his chosen profession. His oldest brother James lived in Atlanta, next brother Stephen lived in California, and sister Abby lived outside of Atlanta. Perhaps one of the biggest truths came a few hours into the confession, when I thought I had heard it all.

"Is there anything else you haven't shared with me that I need to know?" I asked with silent trepidation.

"Yes," he paused. "I've been married before."

The explosion in my head was so loud, I was sure he had heard it. What the fuck was he talking about? Married! I was scared to hear the answer, but I couldn't turn away at this point. I had to hear the whole truth.

"Do you remember when I told you about my friend in the navy whose wife was raped in their bed while he was in the bathroom, taking a shower?" he asked.

"Yes. I remember when you told me that story. We were over at Mary's house for dinner."

"Yeah, well, the guy wasn't a friend of mine. He was me, and my wife's name was Betsy."

We were on the patio at Mary's when he told this horrific story with such detachment I had no problem believing he was speaking about someone else. I recalled the story so clearly.

"*My friend* lived on the navy base with his wife in Norfolk, and he worked in communications, which required he be up and out of the apartment very early every day. One day, he got up at 4:00 a.m. and got in the shower, careful not to wake his wife. When he stepped out of the bathroom to sneak out of the house, she was lying in bed with her underwear around her ankles, crying, and she told him she had just been raped.

"The assailant had come in through the kitchen, grabbed a knife out of the counter block on his way through, and put it to her throat as she woke out of slumber and told her not to make a sound. The water running in the shower ensured *my friend* would not hear any unusual noises coming from the bedroom, and the rapist was done and out of the house by the time he came out, ready for work. The room was dark, but she had felt a beard on his face, and since they lived on base, it had to be another sailor. African American naval men were the only ones allowed to wear facial hair, so that narrowed the search down for the authorities.

"They found the guy, and he stood trial for his crimes. He had been casing their apartment for weeks, and he knew the routine to a T, so he knew exactly when to enter the apartment and how much time he would have before he came out of the bathroom. The trial got a lot of publicity as it was an African American enlisted man who raped the wife of a white officer. He was convicted for his crime and sentenced to Leavenworth, but not before it was a media circus."

I remember being deeply moved by this story when David told me the first time, and I remember feeling sorry for his friend and his wife that they had to go through such a terrible ordeal. Now, I had to deal with the fact that this friend was sitting in front of me and that he had an ex-wife.

"Do you have any children?" I asked, not sure if I would believe the answer.

"No," he responded.

I didn't know what to do. We were supposed to be moving to St. Augustine in ten days to begin our new lives together. I had just learned that he has a different name, birthdate, family history, and an ex-wife. There was no way in hell I was moving with him! How was I going to explain to my family? How could I trust anything that came out of his mouth again? I cried so hard that afternoon that my body was exhausted. I insisted he leave and that he find somewhere else to stay that night.

Mary came over immediately, and I told her everything I could remember. She was *livid* and had much to say about how I should never speak to him again and I should pack up his things that night. I realized while my sister was processing what she had just learned that I was softening to my new reality. As angry as I was at him, I loved him, and I understood on a crazy level why he lied to me and kept the truth of his life a secret. It was another piece of the underworld puzzle that was a constant source of intrigue for me.

He called later that night and asked if we could talk. I told him I would meet him in the parking lot of the restaurant where he worked. He was contrite and remorseful and begged me to stay with him. He promised he had told me all the details and that he was holding nothing else back from me. Mary drove me to meet him, and I remember her sitting in the car watching us and listening to me give in to his promises. I insisted that we go meet his dad before we left for St. Augustine, that he'd introduce me to his family, which on some level was proof to me that he was being truthful. He agreed, and after two hours of standing in the parking lot, I gave in. I would move to St. Augustine with him if he met my demands.

Untethered

Abandonment.
When breath
is caught
in my gut,
festering,
bubbling,
like peroxide
that kills infection.

Loneliness.
When memory
of him
floats away,
making it harder
to smell his voice
or hear his sweat.

Craving.
When each moment
fills with
anticipation
of the next moment,
I will crave
your soul.

Insanity.
When the knowing
of you
makes me question
the knowing of me
since I don't know me
without you.

My untethered heart
beats for you,
always.

Chapter 7

When we moved to St. Augustine, we rented a one-hundred-year-old house on St. George Street in the heart of the city that needed a lot of work. There were at least three inches of dirt on the floors, as no one had lived in it for a long time. There were several layers of extremely old and ugly wallpaper on the walls, and the last tenants had painted primary colors throughout the house, but the color was on the trim in each room, not on the walls. It was blood red in the kitchen, mustard yellow in the dining room, a mauve color in the front foyer and living room, and blue upstairs.

The spindles on the stair railing were beautiful, ornate, and delicate, and the trim on the soffit of the front porch was something straight out of a storybook. The outside of the house was yellow with white trim, and what used to be a white picket fence out front (that looked like it would fall down if you blew on it). When you wound up the stairs inside, you came to a landing with a bathroom straight across from the stairs and four bedrooms, one in each corner.

The house smelled like stale air, dust, and mouse poop. We agreed with the owners to do all the work to clean it up and restore it if they paid for the materials and gave us a super low rent of $650/ month. It took us two months of working every day to get the house to a livable state. First order of business was to strip the wallpaper, which had been on the walls for decades and did not want to come down.

The night we arrived in town, we knew our furniture wouldn't arrive for a day or two, and we were going to have to make do. We had my two cats, Teddy and Gizmo, who were loopy from the cat tranquilizer we gave each of them for the four-hour car ride that day.

Teddy got very anxious during car rides, and Gizmo was claustro-phobic, so he would bang his nose into the door of the cat carrier until it bled if he wasn't sedated. The two were quite the pair when we arrived to this very dark and dirty house. They needed to be let out of their carriers, but I was worried about their safety. Between the sedation, which caused both of their third eyelids to be half closed, and the state of the house, we had no idea if there were holes in the walls or dangerous nooks they could get stuck in.

I did a quick look in each room to see if I saw any glaring issues before letting them out of their carriers. I set up a cat box for them in the sunroom downstairs, but the two of them roamed all around the house crouched as cats do when they are in a new space, howling to each other no matter where they went. Their paws were filthy with all the dirt they were tracking through, and David was getting very irritated by the incessant meowing they were doing, which continued all night long. At one point, the cat's screaming was joined by David's screaming at them to shut up. It was going to be a long night.

We had brought blankets and sleeping bags to set up on the floor for that first night since the furniture wouldn't arrive until the next day. There was just one problem. We didn't have a clean spot anywhere on the floor to make our palette. We found a broom and dustpan in the closet off the kitchen and swept a square the size of a king-size bed on the floor in the foyer because it was the only room that had an overhead light. After setting up the blankets and pillows, it looked like an island in a sea of dirt. After venturing downtown for a little food and some cold adult beverages, we did a lot of laughing when we returned to this incredibly dark and dirty house with two screaming cats, not expecting to get any sleep that night.

It was quite a sense of accomplishment to restore this old house to some semblance of its glory. We would work all day, shower, and walk down to the Tradewinds to drink the night away. We made fast friends at the local bar, something David did anywhere he went. His charm and willingness to buy drinks for all won him an instant clan. The Tradewinds bar was right downtown, across from the Bridge of Lions, which was St. Augustine's crowning glory. It was one of those bars that had regulars who stayed day and night.

Everyone knew everyone, and there was a stage where live music was played almost every night. The walls were lined with grass paper to give it a "tiki hut" feel along with old license plates, notes from patrons professing undying love to the bar, and old drum cymbals from bands long gone. We became quick friends with the owners, and each band that came in to play became our new best friends. From the Alligator Cowboys to Fiasco, classic rock and roll, and some kickass guitar—these could always be found at the Tradewinds. The best part about Tradewinds was its proximity to our house. We could have walked easily, but that would have taken too much time and energy. I was always the designated driver, which in those days meant I was designated to be the *least drunk* of the group so I could navigate the cobblestone roads and find our way home. Those years were filled with lots of laughter, lots of hangovers, and not many memories that could be recalled due to the consumption. To the outside world, we were the couple that had it all!

One thing that David made sure was always present was his community. He made quick work of befriending those who would make sure the environment was always revolving around him so that he could feel safe. Bartenders and servers always knew his name, which at times felt like the crowd yelling "Norm!" every time he entered *Cheers*. It wasn't enough that he could feel like he belonged somewhere. The environment had to revolve around him for it to be satisfactory. He wasn't cool with just feeling a part of the group, he had to feel like he invented the group and that the majority of the oxygen in any room he entered belonged to him. For those of us who traveled through life with him, we were at a constant state of oxygen deprivation. Many times I was happy to let him take center stage, telling his stories about life in Saudi Arabia or high school in Rome, Italy. What you learn quickly about being in an "energy sucker's" orbit is to breath shallow, don't over exert yourself, and you just might survive.

One night, there was a couple in the Tradewinds who clearly were not from the US. David was immediately taken with the woman because she reminded him so much of his mother when she was young. Allen and Elsa were from Spain and were living on a thirty-eight-foot sailboat in the St. Augustine marina. They were funny and loved to party just like us. We were fast friends, and that first night, you would have never known we had just met. The beers were flowing, as well as the shots. I stayed away from the tequila and left that to Allen, David, and Elsa to consume. We drank the night away, telling stories and dancing. David was born in Spain, so he and Allen seemingly had a lot to talk about. Really, they didn't have any stories in common, but when you've had enough to drink, everyone seems to know all the same people and have had all the same experiences.

David and I drove home that night, and as we were getting settled in for the night, I looked out the front window to see a car driving very slowly in front of our house. It came to an abrupt stop, and I saw a woman jump out and begin to hurl in our front yard! I went running out to find Elsa tossing her cookies in our bushes. Allen and Elsa had gotten turned around when they left the Tradewinds and had ended up in front of our house, with no idea how to get to the marina. Allen was in no shape to drive, and Elsa looked like death warmed over, so we took them inside and told them they would stay the night. We got them tucked in to bed, and all went to sleep.

The next morning, they invited us out to see their sailboat. This was exciting to meet two young adventurers who were planning on sailing from St. Augustine to the island of Bimini in the Bahamas when they got their sailboat ready to go. They had some repairs to do and small jobs to ready her for the trip, so they anticipated being in St. Augustine for another few weeks until they would be ready to go. We were thrilled they would be staying for a while and anticipated a great party for the next several weeks while they were here.

As we got closer to the time for Allen and Elsa to leave, they asked us to sail to Bimini with them so the party could continue. I had never sailed on an extended trip like that and was thrilled at the prospect but also a little scared. We really didn't know these two that well, and we certainly didn't know if they knew what they were doing on a sailboat to take us that far away.

Despite my fears, the trip down to Bimini was amazing! Allen played the guitar at night and sang to us, the alcohol was always flowing (along with other substances I chose to turn a blind eye to), and the nights were incredible sitting up on deck, watching the stars. We made it to Bimini in just a few days, intact and without incident.

I don't remember if we had a plan for getting back to St. Augustine. We had made arrangements for someone to take care of our cats while we were gone, but this was before cell phones, so we had no real way to contact anyone. Once we got to Bimini, David and Allen's partying increased, and the cocaine seemed to be ever present. I had gotten very good by this time of ignoring the drug use that was happening right under my nose. Cocaine scared me. I had never done it, nor did I know what to do to get him to stop. The money that we brought with us could cover food for a time, but with David's drug purchases, it disappeared quickly.

The nights were wild, and our days we spent recovering, only to turn around at night and do it again. Something seemed to be broken on the boat every day, and Allen was very frustrated about the state of repairs. After about ten days, I began to ask anyone who would listen: what is the plan for getting us home? I didn't seem to get any answers. No one but me was concerned at all about our return to St. Augustine.

I tried to make phone calls to get money wired to us, and that didn't seem to work. I couldn't get my bank in the states to talk to the bank in Bimini, and we had no way of getting any money. This was 1992 and the technology was not well developed to have banks speak to each other internationally. I didn't have anyone in St. Augustine I could ask to wire us money, and I didn't want to let my family know that we had gone all the way to Bimini with no contingency plan or way to get cash if we needed it. One night, I lost my shit on David, screaming and yelling that I wanted to go home before we were stranded on this God-forsaken island. We were standing on the rocks with the crystal blue water lapping at our feet, screaming at the top of our lungs at each other.

"I have done *everything* I can think of to get money. We have only a couple hundred dollars left, and we have to buy two plane tickets with that, or we will be stuck here!" I screamed at him.

"What's wrong with being *stuck* here? We don't have anything to get back to since you don't fucking work! Why can't you live a little and fucking relax? Jesus, you are so fucking uptight! I used to travel all around Europe with no idea when I was gonna go back to school. Why do you have to be such a buzzkill?" he fired back at me. It was always my fault.

"I'm tired of being here, and I don't know what we are going to do when we don't have any money for *food*! Allen and Elsa are not going to pay for anything. What are you gonna do, *get a job?*"

"Why the fuck can't you get any money? You family is fucking loaded. You're a goddamn Rockefeller, for Christ's sake! Have you never traveled like this and dealt with this before? Why the fuck don't you know how to do this?"

This argument got louder and louder, and I started to worry that someone would call the authorities. His insults just kept coming, and there was nothing I could say to get him to accept any responsibility for the predicament we found ourselves in. I don't know why I thought this time would be any different than any of the times before. Allen and Elsa didn't know when the repairs would be finished, nor were they even sure if they were going back to St. Augustine, as their original plan was to sail south. Decisions had to be made, and he wasn't gonna make them. I had to take control.

I got us two tickets out of Bimini on a small pontoon plane with the last of our money. Allen and Elsa were sad we were leaving, and David was not happy with me for dragging him away from his party, but we had to go. I was not about to stay on Bimini indefinitely, and David must have realized that without money, his party was going to be severely hampered. It was time.

The day our flight was to depart, the weather was terrible! The wind was incredible, and I remember standing at the "airport," which was really just a small building about the size of a mobile home and a dock where we would get on the plane. We said our goodbyes to Allen and Elsa and got on the plane as they stood watching and waving.

The pilot aborted the takeoff *twice* before we finally got in the air! On our first attempt, the plane moved away from the dock and pointed itself away from the shore to have enough water to use as a runway. The propellers picked up speed, and we began to shoot across the water to raise into the sky. Just as I felt we might be going fast enough to take off, a gust of wind took the right wing and tipped it down so hard that it went under water.

"ABORT, ABORT, ABORT!" I heard from the cockpit, and we heard the engines power down until he could get the wing to resurface from the water. My heart was in my throat! We were going to die, all because I wanted to get home so bad. As the pilot turned the plane around to go back to our original starting point to try again, David was yelling at me about this being a bad idea and how it was my fault that we were going to die, but I didn't hear him over the ringing in my ears. We gained speed as the small plane shook violently due to the wind gusts, and just as we thought we were going to lift up again I hear it again...

"Abort, abort, abort!"

Jesus! I could see Allen and Elsa standing on the dock, watching, and all I could think was we were going to die, in front of our friends, and they would never recover. Even though they were far away, I could see how big their eyes were, and the terrified looks on their faces. This was excruciating. As much as I wanted to go home, I was almost ready to demand they let me off this plane. Maybe it wouldn't be so bad to stay a few more days...

Third time's the charm, right? The pilot returned to our original starting place, turned the plane around to face out to the ocean, and tried one more time. The engines roared, the plane picked up speed, and suddenly, we were in the air! I have never prayed so hard in my life! We were climbing, and I could see the crystal blue water pulling away from us as we leapt into the sky. The wings of the plane were at the mercy of the wind gusts, and the plane was pitching and rolling back and forth while we climbed to a safe altitude above the fray. Finally, success! Everyone on the plane began to clap and cheer for the pilots as we realized we were going to survive, and we were going home. We never saw Allen and Elsa again, and it was a long time before David stopped telling the story about how I almost got us both killed because I just *had* to come home.

*****

Each day was a crap shoot with David. I never knew when the day began whether it was going to be a good day or a bad one. And even if the day started full of love and laughter, in just a few hours or a few minutes, all hell could break loose. The smallest things would set him off, and I developed my own system for determining in my head how bad any particular fight was going to be. It's funny how the psyche works to find the smallest detail it can predict within a tidal wave of uncertainty.

It was called the tornado scale. When he would "spin out" over the cat box not being cleaned often enough, the laundry not being done, or the trash can in the living room not being emptied of it's one ball of paper fast enough, the scale with which I measured how long the fight would last was the tornado scale. I imagined him standing in front of me with a tornado spinning around his head, a dark-gray mass of swirling energy. If the tornado was see-through, the fight might only last a couple of hours or maybe a day. If the tornado was completely opaque, the fight could last multiple days, followed by several days of recovery for me after the storm passed. On the days when the tornado was opaque, I rationalized in my head that he just couldn't see me through the dirt and debris.

During these fights, which sometimes went on for three or more days, I would move from room to room trying to find a safe space to hide, in the hopes that he would forget that I was the object of his anger and the storm would pass. I would go into our bedroom and shut the door, but he would come bursting in within minutes, screaming at the top of his lungs about how incompetent I was because I couldn't keep a clean house, how we were living in a pigsty, and that though that might be okay for *me*, he wasn't going to put up with it. I would answer his accusations with logical answers, trying desperately to get him to see how his frustration was unfounded.

The problem with all this is that logic never seemed to work inside the swirling chaos of the tornado. I could talk until I was blue in the face—and often I did—but he could not hear how he was wrong in his assessment of me. I thought if I could just find the right sentence, this would all end, but that magical sentence never came. At any given moment, the tornado would disperse. I could see the clarity return to his eyes, his shoulders would drop and relax, and I knew he could see me again. He would often be fine at the end of these rows, whereas I would collapse into my bed, completely exhausted. It sometimes took a week for me to recover, and all I could hope was that recovery would happen before another storm began.

David acted much differently in public, of course. When your partner in life is usually filled with laughter and stories, is the life of the party, and is the person everyone wants to be around, personal disbelief at the circumstances of your story runs deep. I struggled to convince any of our friends of the reality of our lives together, mainly because I wouldn't have believed it myself. Others occasionally saw David's ability to explode and blame me for everything, but those moments when he allowed the world to see his true self were fleeting and usually cloaked in a heavy fog of alcohol.

If anyone spent any time the next morning, considering what they might have witnessed the night before, they might have questioned their memory and supposed it wasn't as bad as they thought because they were plastered. He had an innate ability to work the room in such a way that all came away with an undying love for him, even changing the details of events in their minds to fit the overall vision they had of his gloriousness.

David was dynamic, tortured, funny, illuminated, smart, devious, and a pathological liar. He had lived a life that was beyond anyone's comprehension, and we were enraptured by his stories of intrigue and danger. Most gatherings culminated in everyone sitting on any surface available in the living room, faces upturned, as he held court and spun tales of his childhood in Saudi Arabia and Rome.

"Sparky and I were bored one day and were hanging out on top of one of the buildings that overlooked the busiest road near our compound." So many of these tales began with Sparky and he being bored. I don't know how Jeddah survived the two of them.

"We decided to throw eggs at the cars below to see if we could hit any of them," David continued. "The way the building was structured, the 'thrower' had to launch the egg from a position where they couldn't see what was going on below. Someone had to be the lookout and let the other know when to let the egg fly."

David's arms would mimic the launch maneuver to show the arc needed to get the egg where you wanted it to go. Sparky was the thrower, so he had to rely on David to give him the launch sequence at just the right time.

They had practiced a couple of times but had missed their targets. They talked about adjustment of trajectory and that Sparky had to put more into it if he was gonna get this right! "COME ON, MAN!" David chided his weak-ass throws and berated him until Sparky worked up the fire necessary to get the egg to its intended target.

In the next moment, David heard cars coming and was ready to give Sparky the countdown. "Get ready...get ready... Thr—NO, DON'T THROW, DON'T THROW!"

But it was too late. Sparky had already let the projectile go, and it was on its way to the unsuspecting vehicles below. What Sparky didn't realize was this set of vehicles came with flags, indicating their occupant.

The black limousines stopped abruptly as the egg went splat on the windshield. Large men with machine guns jumped out of the cars and began scanning the rooftops for the culprits. David ducked just in time to avoid detection. He ran over to Sparky, who was firing one hundred questions at him trying to figure out what just happened. All David could say was "RUN!" The boys didn't stop until they were far away from the rooftop and back in the safety of the family compound. It was then that David told Sparky about whose car he had hit—the Chinese ambassador! It was a cautionary tale of two boys who almost caused an international incident because they were bored.

His stories were always full of palace intrigue and international escapades: like the time he and the son of the US ambassador climbed over the embassy wall because they couldn't be bothered to walk all the way around to the gate. When their feet hit the ground, they were met by Marines with machine guns. Or the time when he got an impromptu haircut at the hands of the "prayer police" in the market because they began to attack his mother for showing her forearm in public and he came to her defense, losing his hat in the scuffle and allowing his long blond hair to fall. Long hair on a boy wasn't against the law, but it was a great way for them to teach him a lesson about attacking the authorities in this country where he was clearly a visitor.

Or the time he rode his motorcycle out into the dessert to practice his tricks, miscalculated a sand dune, and flew off his bike, only to land on his head. The helmet was too big for him, as that kind of equipment was hard to find in Saudi Arabia, and when he landed on his head, it was violently pushed into his body, breaking both collarbones simultaneously. He lay in the sand until his bike ran out of gas, and he passed out, waking up to a group of Bedouins, who had picked him up and were taking him to their village so the medicine man could "heal" him. When he finally got them away from the mirrors on his bike (which they had never seen before) and could convince them to take him back to the city, he ended up with casts on both arms, immobilized for eight weeks, and *mortified* because his mom had to wipe his thirteen-year-old ass until the casts came off!

When David was weaving his stories to a captive audience, he became this conduit for all of us who had never experienced life outside of our privileged bubbles. We got to travel without a passport, seeing the mysteries of foreign cultures and lands through his lens. This David superseded any of the Crazy he embodied in the dark moments. All was forgiven as we traveled to far-off lands through the enthusiasm of this charming storyteller.

I've often heard people who have had near-death experiences describe floating up to the corner of the room, either operating room or crash site, and looking down on their body and the activity around it while they determined if they would live or pass on to the light. As I reflect on the early years of my relationship with David, I've had a similar "out of body" experience of rising up to the corner of the room and looking down on my friends and family as they are drawn into the mystical world of David.

What I see is a group of people mesmerized by his tales, willingly allowing their attention to be held while atrocities were happening all around them. In this group, I am the most taken of them all. I see myself sitting with my chin resting in my hand as my eyes gaze up to his face, eagerly awaiting the next story, not realizing that the oxygen was being slowly sucked from the room and we were all in danger of suffocation. This is often the most dangerous part of loving a narcissist: the precision with which they can captivate and spellbind their audience while almost surgically dismembering them—unbeknownst to them until it is too late to save themselves.

He was also full of quirks that only I got to fully experience. David lived with the torture of obsessive-compulsive disorder (OCD). This manifested in many ways, usually around cleanliness. Arguments often began with something not being cleaned fast enough or to his satisfaction. It was a full-time job to keep up. The good news was that I always had clean clothes, as he did at least one load of laundry every day. The bad news was, there was never a moment where I wasn't on guard about what cleanliness shortcoming I might have overlooked, which might result in an F4 storm.

After living as a drug dealer for a time in his life, he had an acute sense of safety radar that had been honored. He never sat in a public place with his back to the door, and I learned very quickly during our time in Atlanta that I needed to be aware and supportive of this compulsion or he would not hesitate to remind me of my place, no matter how many eyes were watching. His routine included checking door locks multiple times before sleep could come and most of the time I think he slept with one eye open. He was convinced that he was important enough to be followed, investigated, and observed by authorities and could not be reasoned with to the contrary. I didn't see this at the time as the narcissism that it was. I had become so accustomed to the navigation of it all that I became a coconspirator in the story he was writing on perpetual loop in his mind.

The Crazy found all of this hilariously funny. Not only had I taken it with me into adulthood; I had now found the *perfect* vessel for it to reside in on a daily basis. In many ways, having the Crazy live outside of myself was a relief. The familiar was always better than the unfamiliar, and I was an expert on how to look into another person's eyes and render a diagnosis of the depth of Crazy I was dealing with and how I was going to get it to end. I had been raised to believe I possessed these powers by a mother who embodied the Crazy on a daily basis, and I felt fully equipped to ride this roller coaster every day.

In fact, I prided myself on it. I thought I knew every nuance of this Crazy and felt more able to breathe in the chaos than when I was out of it. When the Crazy lived within my own mind, I couldn't escape it like I could when it resided in another. My drug of choice was the Crazy wrapped in the package of this man who was unbelievably broken and who needed me to fix him.

Anxiety Dance

My brain says stop
then gives
a thousand reasons
why listening to it
makes me weak.

My heart beats
a mile a minute,
making me feel
like it will
exit my chest
to do the merengue
on the table
between my utensils.

My breath gets shallow,
depriving me of oxygen
at the very moment
I need it the most.

My brain
whispers to me
with little foundation
in fact
yet I swear
it's the gospel
that only I can hear.

All movement stops,
all knowing of strength
and wisdom
and power
go the way of the bird,
and I am left panting.

Grasping for a hold
on the railing
to break my fall
as my knees give way
and the floor disappears.

You tell me
that I am strong,
that my fall
is only imagined,
and I am standing
feet planted firmly
on quicksand.

You say I am in control
of my breath,
but I know that your lungs
work differently than mine.

When will you see me?
When will you understand
that my world looks
wholly different than yours?

I wish I didn't have
this kind of brain,
but I do...

I wish I could
make you understand,
but I can't...

I can only focus
on the next step forward
and hope you will
still be there
when I fall again.

Chapter 8

The daily routine of hangover recovery, household chores, and decisions about where the next party would be was a full-time job. We were living off my trust money, but it never occurred to me that this was a problem. One of the most hurtful statements my father ever made to me was "You will never have to worry about money." I was not raised with any awareness of monetary stress and was reminded of how foolish my worrying was by David if I ever tried to express concern. I was the one who paid the bills, largely because he couldn't sit still long enough to write all those checks and make sure the checkbook balanced.

Looking back on it, however, I know it was also because he was the king of denial, and if he didn't have to be conscious of how the money was spent, he didn't have to be held accountable for any of the consequences. It worked for him to have me managing all this, but it also put me in the position of being the monitor. I was often "the bad guy" in conversations around finances, a pattern I would recreate again in future relationships. If I was in charge of the bills, I thought I was also in control of the money spent, a fact that could not have been further from the truth. The structure simply put me in charge of orchestrating reasons for him to verbally abuse me for being too controlling or just your average nag. Conversations like this always ended in how I was torturing him with my bullshit. All I heard deep down in my heart was that he cared enough about me to be bothered by my behavior.

When I form a picture in my head depicting my place in space through my childhood and into my adulthood, I see myself standing in a fog bank. If you've ever been in thick fog—either driving over a bridge, feeling like you are floating in nothingness because you can't see the world past the guardrail, or walking in a field and the only thing you can see is the grass beneath your feet—you know that feeling of total isolation. It's as if you are the only human in the world, and the sounds of life beyond your vantage point are muffled and disconnected from their source. Some days the fog around me was thick enough to see the actual molecules of water that blurred out the world; other days, it was thin but served as a shield that made my reality fuzzy enough to withstand without breaking me into a thousand pieces. If you asked me then how I was, I would have launched into a diatribe of "fine" and "great." To the best of my understanding, I was fine and great. I didn't know what I didn't know; and I didn't know that I didn't know. It was suspended animation without the awareness of being suspended.

There was a big part of my story that had been put on hold. I had successfully cocreated a reality so distracting that I rarely thought about the fact that I had been sexually abused as a child. I was still in a place in my life where there was safety in the fog bank. Subconsciously I had decided to stay in the fog and do what I could to maintain the fog because stepping out of it was too scary. It was a part of who I was, but I had settled into a comfortable state of "checking out" and had enough on my plate without further excavation.

Because I wasn't working, I was able to continue my habit of watching *The Oprah Winfrey Show* every day. Oprah was fearless, and she had revealed to her audience that she was an abuse survivor, often having topics and guests on her show who were discussing aspects of sexual abuse as she processed her own journey in front of all of us. I had a VHS tape dedicated to her shows and would record them every day in case I couldn't watch it live. She featured psychologists and psychiatrists giving support and guidance for those who were processing abuse at every level and interviewed guests like Trudi Chase, who had almost one hundred personalities as a result of severe sexual abuse during her childhood.

I remember watching the show with Trudi with deep awe of her struggle and being completely fascinated with her journey into Dissociative Identity Disorder (which was then called multiple personality disorder). I couldn't believe the mysteries of the psyche, that a person's brain could split into separate awareness in order to keep the main personality from going completely insane. The survival instinct of the brain is strong, and Trudi was an example of true heroism. I only knew that I "got her" and I couldn't get enough.

Along the way, there were two movies that had captured my attention growing up—*Sybil* starring Sally Field and *Nuts* starring Barbara Streisand. *Sybil* was released in 1976, and I remember watching it for the first time while sitting on the floor of our den, cross-legged, in front of the enormous cathode-ray TV in my childhood home. It tells the story of a young woman who discovers she has Dissociative Identity Disorder through the guidance of a therapist. They uncover the darkest memories of the abuse she suffered during childhood, which her personalities had worked to keep hidden from her.

I am not sure how many times I watched this movie, but I remember having such resonance with it and being completely engrossed with the whole process of uncovering repressed memories and identifying the truth of what this young woman suffered. I had no idea when I first watched the film of the parallels to my story; it would be years later before the truth of why this film touched my soul was revealed to me.

Nuts was released in 1987 and tells the story of a call girl (played by Barbra Streisand) standing trial for the murder of one of her clients. Richard Dreyfuss plays her lawyer, who is desperately trying to get her to plead guilty by reason of insanity to spare her any jail time, but she refuses to condemn herself to an institution because she maintains that she was not insane when she killed him. As the storyline progresses, we learn that she had been triggered by her client's behavior that put her into a blind fury. During the course of the trial, her lawyer uncovers that she had survived sexual abuse by her father, which is why she was triggered that night by her client, resulting in his death. She does not want this fact revealed because it is the family secret and she wants to protect her mom. In the end (spoiler alert), the lawyer does go after her father on the stand, and the abuse comes to light, making her more pitiful in the eyes of the judge and allowing her to not serve time for the crime. The moment her mother realizes what has just been brought to light, she looks at her daughter with horror, and a sensation of unknown origin pierced my heart.

My "fog" was so thick at the time of seeing these movies, even though they were years apart, that I was completely unaware of why I was drawn to the storylines. They were speaking to a version of me deep inside the fog that I was not ready to acknowledge.

The one thing I did know, now that I knew sexual abuse was a part of my story, was that I didn't want to become an abuser myself. I had watched enough Oprah shows on adults who had been sexually abused as children, and the general consensus was that those who were victims as children and didn't do the work to heal often became perpetrators when they grew up. I did not want this to be my reality, yet I was having very active dreams that made me sick to my stomach when I woke up in a start and realized what I was dreaming about.

Looking back on this time in my life, I realize that I was not "fantasizing" about abusing children as much as I was processing what my child psyche knew as "normal" behavior. But these dreams scared and sickened me, and I made a quiet pledge to myself to stay away from children until I got a handle on this piece of my puzzle, even though I had a special education teacher's certificate and I missed working around children immensely. I never shared my fears with David. I imagined him maybe showing empathy at first, but the minute we got into a fight about anything, I felt sure the details of my darkest fears would become ammunition for his weaponry. I couldn't take the risk that he would blurt out my secret struggle after having a few beers or shots at the Tradewinds to amuse his audience. I was often the brunt of his jokes without me contributing to his extensive arsenal.

There was a lot of discussion in the media about sexual abuse and repressed memory syndrome. Even if I wanted to completely ignore this part of my story, there was a lot of buzz around me that kept it close to the surface. I believe it was watching an Oprah show that highlighted the authors of a book titled *The Courage to Heal* that was a turning point for me. Ellen Bass and Laura Davies had written a book whose tagline was "A Guide for Women Survivors of Child Sexual Abuse." It spoke directly to my core. This book was different than some of the others I had looked through in that it was full of first-person accounts of the journeys of other survivors, along with expert advice on how to navigate the minefield of uncovering repressed memories and then learning to live with the aftermath of what is revealed. There had been other books I had read that were full of expert advice, but this one had the words of fellow survivors—women who had walked and were walking a similar path. These women were feeling all the same feelings of abandonment, disgust, repulsion, fear, and loathing of what was becoming our story as the fog lifted and the details became clearer.

I did not think I was as bad off as the women quoted in this book because my abuser was my father's best friend. He wasn't a parent. Although the abuse was just as impactful, there was some solace in knowing it wasn't my own flesh and blood who had touched me inappropriately. In my experience, the rationalization my mind did to minimize or diminish the impact of what had been done to me never ceases to astound me. Abuse is destructive, no matter at whose hand; it seems the psyche never misses an opportunity to alleviate the stress of its person by making the reality a little less real. I read *Courage to Heal* in short sittings, trying to digest it in very small bites. I would sit in my room, on my four-poster king size bed with the door closed for privacy, and read the accounts of women who had experienced every possible scenario of abuse that you could imagine. I was not under the care of a therapist at the time, so I was left to process what I was reading with the often-broken psyche that was already reeling from the awareness I had uncovered in the past year and a half. In hindsight, I am surprised I wasn't opening my first beer in the morning of each day. I had plenty to anesthetize from, but I saved all the intake to the evenings where it manifested with a vengeance. At the time, I thought checking out was actually checking in. I had convinced myself that I was more in touch with my feelings and my authentic self when I was drunk, which could not have been further from the truth.

David had little empathy for what I was going through because it hindered his ability to live his life without compromise. As with Jimmy before him, my growing awareness about my history directly influenced my sex drive and what I was willing to do with my partner. David had introduced me to a darker world of sex than I had ever experienced including attending "swinger" parties when we lived in Atlanta and incorporating porn into our repertoire, largely because he had trouble getting aroused without outside help, chemically or visually. I had gone along with this in the past because he would berate me for being a prude if I didn't. It became more important to avoid conflict than to honor my feelings about this aspect of our intimate life. But this was changing as I began to dive deeper into my memories of sexual abuse.

Reading books and articles and watching shows about repressed memories and sexual abuse survivors were waking me up to the idea that I could have a say in what I participate in within my sexual life. It never occurred to me that I could be aware of how a sexual experience might feel to me and then set boundaries about what I was and was *not* willing to do in the bedroom. When children are sexualized early, the foundation of healthy boundaries is grossly inadequate and can lead to troubling adult sexual encounters within their own intimate partnerships or—God forbid—the blurring of lines between themselves and others too young to know any better. Thank goodness I never participated in the latter, but the former was definitely in play with David, and I didn't know how to stop it once I let him cross those lines.

When I did have the courage to say no to a suggestion of his about something we could do in the bedroom, he was relentless in his insults. I was cold, a prude, boring, and he even called me sick that I would say no to him rather than yes to any and all deviant suggestions he had. If I tried to express to him what I was going through instead of wrapping his arms around me in expressions of patience and love, he would chastise me and call me names until I relented or he got so drunk that he passed out. I got to the point where I stopped sharing with him any details of what I was feeling, hoping he would go out to the Tradewinds every night, with or without me, and drink so much that us being intimate was not an option. I got really good at pretending to be asleep when he stumbled into the bedroom after St. Augustine had closed down for the night, to avoid the inevitable clumsy attempt to "turn me on" and the rage that followed if I had the courage to turn him down.

One day, I was tucked up in our room, reading my current dose of *Courage to Heal*, when I read a line by a survivor that knocked the wind out of my lungs. She was telling her story about what had happened to her, and the last line of her quote contained a hidden explosive. I immediately couldn't breathe. It was as if someone had punched me in the gut as hard as they could and both my lungs were empty.

I felt dizzy as her words reverberated in my head: "The person who had taken my virginity was my father."

As soon as I read the words, I knew it was true with every molecule in my body. In all the soul searching I had done over the course of the past couple of years, I had second-guessed myself and entertained the possibility that I was crazy and didn't know my truth at all, but this statement resonated to the core of my being.

As the tears began to flow and the room began to spin, my thoughts returned to that day sitting in the pool house with Mom, Dad, and Mark as I had accused Mark of molesting me and destroyed his life. Dad had invited Mark to the house under the guise of watching the game on TV, knowing what I was going to say to him, and he knew it wasn't true. We had met up in the pool house to avoid anyone overhearing our conversation, and I remember Mom sitting on the couch with her knitting needles, furiously clicking together as she tried desperately to bear witness and yet be as far away from this turmoil as she could while sitting in the same room.

I had told Mom and Dad that Mark had abused me, and the arrangements had been made for this confrontation. I don't remember what we thought the outcome was going to be, and it breaks my heart to think that I was responsible for hurting this man who had been a second father to me all my life with no real "memories" to reflect on or validation of the same. I had dreamed that he was the abuser, and since I wasn't under the watchful eye of a therapist at the time, I made very poor decisions about how to move forward.

One of the ugliest parts of this debacle is that Mark, being bipolar and unstable for most of his adult life, walked away from that meeting, thinking maybe he had molested me! He didn't have any recollection of touching me, but he had been struggling so hard with his own demons at this time that he left the pool house that day, questioning his own innocence of this crime.

After becoming fully aware of the real memories of abuse by my father's hand, I did apologize to Mark for my disgusting accusations, but the damage was done. He was so gracious during that conversation, accepting my apology and excusing my mistake by acknowledging how hard it must be to navigate recovery from sexual abuse and showing great empathy for what I was going through. I was blessed enough to gain his forgiveness, but it would be a very long time before I could give it to myself.

Perhaps the sickest piece of this puzzle is that my true rapist sat in that room, puffing on his pipe with his legs crossed one knee over the other, listening to me destroy his best friend's life to keep his guilt a secret. He orchestrated this sacrifice, knowing full well what the truth was, and he never blinked. As the reality of these details began to sink into my brain and heart, the flood of pain threatened to consume me and whisk me off to a hell from which I did not know if I would return. I couldn't even *get* to the next questions that you might expect would surface after this sort of revelation.

How many times had it happened?

What were the details?

Did Mom know?

I was in a fetal position in the middle of my king-size bed, struggling to breathe on the day that the truth of my being was brought up from the depths and into the sunshine and I could no longer pretend not to see.

*****

Everything was different, and nothing was different. I was still an abuse victim. I was still learning how to be with this new yet old facet of my history revealed to me when I was marginally ready to receive it. But now there was a difference I could not ignore. My father—the man whom I had championed my whole life as the long-suffering, poor, put-upon man by the bipolar and unpredictable wife—was a monster. He wasn't even the kind of monster that I had grown up fearing, one that comes bursting into your home with arms flailing, making horrible noises as you run for your life. He was the silent monster. The monster who lurked in shadows, a monster everyone was so convinced was the victim, someone who could molest his daughter without detection.

After the initial shock subsided enough for my committee to start gabbing, questions started resurfacing, questions like *what really happened, how many times it happened, if he just touched me or if penetration happened, and if so, how often...* They were swirling around in my brain most waking hours. I didn't have any clear recollection of these details at the moment, and I knew I needed to do a deeper dive to try to clear some of the fog that I had previously found solace within. I was having nightmares that sat me up in bed screaming in the middle of the night, with no clear understanding of what I had dreamed. My subconscious was in turmoil, and I needed to create a safe space for the work to be done so I could get to the end of this wild ride and find a peaceful existence, maybe for the first time in my life.

One of the first steps I needed to take was to talk to Mom. She had been present when I sat down with Mark and accused him of such atrocities. Now, I was going to tell her that the man she was married to, the man she had built a life with, had done something to her daughter. I was nervous to have this conversation because I didn't know what her reaction would be. Would she believe me? Would this be the end of our relationship? Would she leave him? This was unfamiliar and unknown territory that did not have an obvious path through. The risk I took when I sat in the pool house with Mark didn't feel the same as this. This conversation could have an effect on my life that could, and would, last until its conclusion.

As seemed to be my pattern, I closed myself up in our bedroom, sitting in the middle of our four-poster bed with the phone in my hand. As I dialed the numbers that were so familiar to my fingers that they knew where they were on the keypad without me looking, my heart began to race, and my breath got shallow. We exchanged pleasantries to check in with each other, but she knew me so well that she could tell from my voice that I had called for more than just to say hi.

"Hey, how's it goin'?" I said in almost a whisper.

"I'm doin okay. How are you?"

"I'm okay..." My voice trailed off, and I was aware of standing at the edge of a cliff. Would I have the courage to step off?

Looking back on this conversation has been challenging. I am aware of having another of those moments where I floated up to the corner of the room and looked down on myself while we were talking. I can see my posture on the bed: sitting up but slouched in such a way that my body was essentially in a ball, with my arm wrapped around my knees, pulling them close, hugging myself through the experience. Memory plays such a curious game of hide-and-seek sometimes. To someone who has not experienced the kind of trauma I have, not remembering dialogue details might seem implausible. How could you forget the words you used when you told your mother that your father, her husband, had raped you?

But that is precisely when the protection skills got deployed by my psyche. I was experiencing another traumatic experience by telling my mother my truth, and the age-old practices resurfaced without me having to summon them. As I observed this experience from the upper corner of the bedroom, I was slowly absorbing one very important feeling. She wasn't fighting me. I was explaining my reaction to reading that one very powerful line in *Courage to Heal*, and she was accepting what I was saying.

She wasn't capable of corroborating my story at that point, but she knew in her heart, as I did in mine, that this was the dark secret of our family finally come to light. Everyone knew about *her* bipolar, *her* crazy, *her* yelling and screaming, and the predictability of *her* unpredictability. In all of that knowing, however, there was always an element about our family dynamic that seemed just out of reach, just beyond the fingertips of an outstretched hand.

There was no great reveal that day of details or evidence or stories to bring everything into focus. But on that day, the woman whom I had looked to for protection and comfort during my child-hood finally delivered on her promise made to me as I grew in her womb. She listened without judgment and offered what help she could. She had been seeing a therapist down in Florida for quite some time working on recovering *her own* childhood memories that had been wiped away by abuse, and it was working.

"What would you say to me sending you down to work with Susan?" she asked. "I'll get you down there and pay for her sessions."

"Thank you," I said through the childhood tears that were finally allowed to flow.

Rape Culture

You stride through the bar,
taking inventory of your prey,
like a lion on the Serengeti.
Lips, breasts, thighs, hips,
all for your amusement
at a moment's glance.

They're here, right?
They know they are
on the menu, right?

They know they better be smart,
be quick to block your hands
from entering their treasure chest
with your skeleton key.

You were raised to know
that all goddess energy
is yours to consume
and abuse and devour
until your appetite is satisfied,
and their no
just makes you more ravenous.

Their no means yes, right?

Because we're here,
we're dressed to please,
and we're incomplete
until your essence
drips from our loins.

We must want it, right?
We must need it, right?

Because boys will be boys
and all the locker room talk
only serves to make us
want you more, because
nothing makes me hotter
than being
objectified and
marginalized and
patronized
while I sit in my own living room
and my father gazes
across the room,
waiting for bedtime
to arrive.

Mom, can you put me to bed?
Mom, can you sleep outside my door?
Mommy, can you protect me?

She can't
because she's too busy
fighting the nightmares
her father forced inside
her soul.

See, my body is my temple,
and I have learned
that only the *new* version
of king can enter.

He is humble and strong
and not afraid to use his power
to shield me more
than abuse me.
He worships my temple
as the Holy Land

and never misses a chance
to remind me
of my sovereignty, because
he does not rape my body,
he does not wound my soul.

He uses his tongue
to educate others
on their misuse of power
instead of pleasuring me,
unless I ask him to.

He uses his body
to stand between me
and those who would take
without permission
instead of driving me
to peaks of ecstasy,
unless I ask him to.

He uses his hands
to hold back those
in his tribe who think
my essence belongs to them
instead of softly caressing
the shallows of my curves
as I quiver,
unless I ask him to.

This new king
enters with the key
that only I can give him.

And I can sleep in peace.

Chapter 9

This was not the first time I was going to meet a new therapist, but this was the first time I had to fly on a plane to get there. Susan lived in Florida, specializing in deep, intensive therapy and hosted her clients at her home for an extended weekend or sometimes longer. I had been in and out of therapy since my teenage years, but this was the first time I had experienced staying in a self-contained setting where I had nothing else to do except be in a space of vulnerability and safety as I took a deep dive into my memory bank. I was nervous about how it would go, worrying about things like whether she would believe me or think I was crazy. It helped that Mom had been seeing her and was able to vouch for the experience. Looking back, I think my nerves were more about the content of what I would uncover rather than who would help me do the recovery.

Her house was very comfortable and inviting. She had a therapy room, which was filled with a couch and overstuffed chair that you could sink into, increasing the feeling of safety. We spent the first day getting to know each other as I shared with her the details of my journey up to that point. It did give me some hesitation that she was also working with Mom, as I wondered about confidentiality and how she would keep our sessions separate from her work with her. But to her credit, she was open to my caution and was happy to explore my concerns thoroughly, answering every question I had while offering details of how she had handled this kind of proximity within family members before in her practice. She had worked with many families around abuse and so had very clear boundaries established to help everyone feel heard and protected.

One of the advantages of staying where you are doing your work is the ability to take breaks when needed, without having to dive back into the distractions of everyday life. Susan had a beautiful outdoor pool that made great use of the Florida sun, so I would often take breaks sitting out in the sunshine to rejuvenate and replenish between sessions. She cooked loving and nutritious meals for me throughout the day and didn't put any expectations on me to interact with her and her husband when I wasn't in session with her. I could sleep or read to my heart's content and not feel like I had to be social if I wasn't up for it. It was the first time in my life I had ever experienced this type of freedom from obligation to others whom I was sharing space with, and that, in and of itself, was a great healing to me. It never occurred to me that you could be in relationship with someone and yet still keep your sense of agency and privacy. The exposure to this concept, and the opportunity to practice this boundary was as big of a gift as the therapy itself.

Looking back on my time at Susan's, I am so aware of how privileged I was to be able to receive this opportunity to fully explore my trauma, which had been locked in the deepest recesses of my subconscious for almost twenty-five years. Throughout the course of this work with Susan and even after I had finished meeting with her, I still had a great deal of unprocessed anger toward my mom for not protecting me when I was a child. Having her provide this opportunity for me was such a gift that I am not sure I was fully in touch with until many years later. I carried an attitude of entitlement, which surfaced as "It's about *time!*" for the help she offered for many of those first years in recovery from childhood trauma. I was still moving through space, using anger as my accelerant, and it would take many years before I was able to transmute that to love and gratitude toward Mom and others.

Susan offered two aspects of therapy that were new to me: hypnosis and sensory deprivation. Since I knew I had memories that had been buried by my psyche for my own protection, it stood to reason that I would need something unconventional to bring them to the surface. Mom had been utilizing hypnosis to uncover her repressed memories and had many good things to say about the experience.

Experts describe hypnotherapy as a form of "guided meditation" or "trance-like state" that allows for the practitioner to go deep into the recesses of their mind to adjust behaviors, heal old wounds, and/or gain a deeper understanding of themselves.[2] I am not a doctor, and can only speak to my own experience and how the practice helped me. As always, it is recommended to work with a licensed psychologist who is trained in administering any method you chose to explore for this kind of work.

Susan had a special room in her home with a large hot tub in it that I came to call "the womb". The warm water in the tub was soothing to my skin, not too hot and not too cold, and provided an opportunity to float with no other sensory cues. At first, my "committee" in my head spun out thinking about the water, the room, my bathing suit, and any other *thing* I could focus on outside of myself. With some time, I started to let go of the compulsive thoughts and relax into what I began to regard as comfort within this womb-like space. It was my introduction to meditation—the practice of quieting the mind, observing the thoughts as they surface, and returning to the space of no thought without internal judgment.

I was ready to do this work. I was ready to know what this part of my story was and walked willingly into the darkness to turn on the light. Susan and I discussed how much I needed to unearth for clarity without re-traumatization. Our goal was to learn answers to the most prominent questions: *How long did it last, how old was I when it started, and how far did he go?* I recall one of the guided paths she took me on during hypnosis was through doors. I would approach a door which might feel locked to me at first, then we would spend some time getting centered and in touch with a sense of safety to get the courage to unlock the door and step through. On the other side might be another door, or I might walk into a memory which she would help me speak out loud when I was ready to reveal its truth. This metaphor of a door which opened to reveal truth was a main theme in one of my recurring nightmares I had as a child.

---

[2] Psychology Today website—https://www.psychologytoday.com/us/therapy-types/hypnotherapy

In the dream, I was a newspaper reporter who had been assigned to a story about a serial killer. People had been going into the house of this man and not coming out, so the paper sent me in to find out why. The suspect lived in a house positioned where Tootie's house was in my childhood with the surrounding horse farm land feeling and looking very familiar. I approached the door and hit the enormous brass knocker three times. *Bam! Bam! Bam!* He opened the door and welcomed me in. To this day, I do not recall his face, but we stood in the hallway, exchanging pleasantries for a minute or two. As my eyes adjusted to being inside, I realized that the house was nothing but long hallways lined with closets; all the doors were closed.

As we were talking, the phone rang somewhere in a far-off room. He left me to go answer the phone, and I could not resist knowing what was in the closets. I approached the first door and very slowly turned the knob and pulled the door open to reveal one of the missing persons murdered in a grotesque fashion, standing in the closet that was about three feet by three feet square, holding its severed head. As I opened each closet, I found another victim, killed in another gruesome way. After two or three closets, I knew I had to get out of there as I heard his footsteps approaching down the hall.

Tootie's house and my childhood home were about a block away from each other. The area was nothing but horse farms with dirt roads, so they weren't the same distance as a city block, but if you drew a square around her house and ours, it would resemble the same. After realizing I had to get out of the house, I found myself running down the dirt road from the corner where the entrance to Tootie's barn was toward my childhood home, the suspect in hot pursuit with a machete held high above his head, screaming at me that he was going to kill me. Knives of any kind always played a starring role in my nightmares throughout my childhood and into my young adult years.

As I am running for my life, I see my mom, Tootie, and the police down at the corner, screaming for me to *run* and waving their arms to encourage me to run faster. I am never caught by the serial killer, but I also never make it to the safety of my family because I always wake up before the conclusion, in a state of full panic. I cannot tell you how many times I had this dream throughout the years, and now doors are in my life again, revealing gruesome scenes if I have the courage to open them.

I would settle in on the couch in her therapy room, and she would guide me into a deep state of meditation through guided imagery. When I was feeling ready, she would ask me to approach the first door, taking me through the steps needed to gain the courage to open the door. Sometimes I would stand in front of the closed door for some time, mustering up the courage to put my hand on the doorknob. There were times when I never got past this point as the panic of what might lie on the other side would consume me, causing my heart to race and my breathing to quicken. Susan would gauge these situations and talk me through the feelings, reminding me that I was safe and that I was only watching the experience, not living it. Her voice would come from a distance offering comfort and reassurance that I was in control of my surroundings and I was safe.

When I did have the courage to turn the doorknob and open the door, what I saw on the other side was a piece of my life that had been hidden deep in the shadows. It didn't act like a movie where you would watch a scene from beginning to end with full fluid movement of the characters; it manifested for me as a series of snapshots—still frames of action that allowed for an understanding of the event without the realness of a live-action short. When I opened the door on this day, it was the door to my childhood bedroom—the yellow room. Mary and I had twin beds, each in opposite corners of the room with a desk in the window in between.

My bed was the first bed you saw when you opened the door, and in this memory, I saw his back hovering over my bed. My father's body was fully overtop of something on my bed, and he was fully engaged. As my grown-up self moved into the room, I got a snapshot of what he was engaged in doing. I saw my little body on my back on the bed with his lanky body draped over me like a giant spider engulfing its prey. His forearm was over my neck to keep me still and quiet. This particular memory was crucial because it answered the question of whether or not penetration occurred. It was a major breakthrough in my progress and required time out of hypnosis processing the feelings of disgust, dirtiness, and rage I was feeling when that particular section of fog had been lifted.

Through the course of my work with Susan, I gained a deeper understanding of the framework of these events in my life, uncovering a timeline of occurrences and some pivotal moments that would allow me to know what he did to me so I could begin to heal. One of the gifts of sharing my story with you is the conversations I have had with key members of my family and others to remember the nuances of these times.

When I called Susan to ask for her recollections of that time, she offered an interesting description of whom she met when I arrived at her home. She recalls me being intensely frightened of making a mistake—and the punishment that would follow. When I pressed her further, she clarified that the mistake could have been about what drink to order at dinner, or what fork to pick up to eat. I was in such a state of survival mode that I did not have confidence in any decisions I might make about anything in my life. She described me as flat, colorless, without dimension or depth and likened my sensibility to a child's drawing.

How many times have you seen a young child draw a stick figure of a person next to a house and tree, and the person is taller than the house and taller still than the tree? She remembers that I didn't have any idea of my place in space or of my dimensions related to others, just like a child's drawing. I found her description to be so ironic because I used to say all the time that I couldn't draw a stick figure right. Now I am painting, and I am creating scenes that I never thought I would be able to do. The use of these descriptors, compared to how my life is now, is not lost on me. I consider this an indicator of how far I have come, and I am grateful for the progress.

Not only did that time with Susan give me back a part of my life that my psyche had buried deep in the recesses of my mind for protection, but it also gave me tools for moving further forward through my journey. We determined that a full confrontation with Dad would need to happen, and Susan was willing to host that event in her home where I felt the safest. The date for this confrontation was set for April 24, 1993 and plans were made to travel back to

Jupiter, FL for that weekend. I remember having conversations about logistics, but I think Mom planned most of the trip, making hotel reservations and arranging for the plane to get us down there. Dad would not fly with us, nor would he stay at the same hotel. He must have known on some level what was due to take place, but I was so focused on the feelings I was having leading up to confronting him that I did not allow any of the space in my head for any of the details of what he did and did not know.

I had worked with Susan on what questions I was going to ask and what details I felt comfortable saying to his face. We would sit in Susan's living room, which helped with my anxiety as her space had become a place of healing for me. It felt like my "safe space," like being wrapped in a warm blanket while a storm raged around me. She had a lovely Floridian home with white furniture, pastel-colored walls, and a lap pool just outside a wall of glass, surrounded by a privacy wall covered in greenery. When I can picture the scene in my mind's eye, it is as if he is this tall dark figure among a sea of white.

He arrived at almost the same time we did, and we all entered Susan's home and sat down. I remember not being able to look at him in his eyes and the feeling of something punching me in the stomach by just being that close to him. Every grown-up molecule reverted to their childlike version within my body in an instant. I had to work very hard to stay present and not float up to the corner of the room as was my default in scary situations. He took a yellow legal pad out of his briefcase and sat it on his lap, presumably to take notes. He was a mathematician and a banker, so he moved through space with precision and always took a business-like posture in all events. While I was at Camp Yonahlossee as a child or later in college, his letters to me were always typed with only his signature handwritten. He did not know how to be casual with those he loved.

Susan thanked all of us for being there and gave just the barest hint of ground rules for the exchange. When she completed her welcome, she looked at me and indicated I could begin whenever I was ready.

"My first memory of you touching me was in my crib. You were masturbating while touching me between my legs," I said, looking him straight in the eyes.

My breathing was shallow, and my muscles were equal parts rock and liquid. I was *terrified!* I relayed the memory of penetration in the kid's bedroom across the hall from our parents' room, where he held me down on the bed with his forearm across my throat to keep me still and quiet. I was two years old... I still can't handle anyone putting their hands or pressure on my throat.

As I spoke, he wrote notes on his legal pad. His demeanor was calm, as if he was sitting in a board meeting, taking notes about the next merger. I spoke without interruption for what seemed like an eternity, but really, it was probably fifteen to twenty minutes. When I was done, my whole body was shaking with adrenaline, and I thought I might shimmy myself right out of the chair if I wasn't careful. I had asked him questions during the retelling of my story, and he had not provided answers to those questions. Susan asked him if he would please address the questions we had all heard.

"On the advice of counsel, I will not be answering any questions," he said. The room fell silent. "I do have some questions for you," he said to me and Susan.

As he was beginning to form these questions, Susan spoke up and said, "Why do you think it is fair for you to ask questions when you have already refused to answer any of hers?"

He repeated, "On the advice of counsel, I will not be answering any questions."

Susan replied, "Well then, you do not get to ask any questions if you refuse to answer any."

My father, whom I had protected and defended for twenty-five years, who always seemed to be the victim within his life and marriage, looked at me in the eye and simply stated, "Well then, there is nothing more to talk about."

He got up and walked out of my life.

*****

As the door closed behind him, Mom, Mary, Susan, and I sat in complete and heavy silence. What just happened? One minute, we were in this life-changing moment in all our lives, and the next it was done—done with no completion, no answers, no remorse, no claiming of responsibility. But with all the results that we didn't see, what did happen was the three of us saw each other in a way that we had never previously. Mom, Mary, and I had—and continue to have—a unique bond. Sometimes, we are as thick as thieves. Other times, we are each other's worst enemies. We went through more together than even my younger sister understands, and we were now sitting in this room, feeling like all the oxygen had been sucked out as he left the room.

Where do we go now? We made our way out by the pool, sitting at a lovely table overlooking the water, and began to talk—I mean *really* talk—about what life was like growing up in that house, what our biggest fears were, and how the reality of our story was completely different than what we had thought all these years. We began to peel back the layers of the narrative we had told ourselves about Mom being the source of all crazy when Dad had been at the root of an evil so deep none of us could bear to look at it until now. We cried and laughed and spoke truths into the air that had never seen the light. I had never felt supported by these two women as much as I did in this moment.

I was so surprised by Mom's pain, and I had moments where I was afraid she would stay with him when divorce was clearly what was indicated. She talked in the beginning as if there was no other recourse than divorce, but then as the conversation went on, I could tell she was conflicted about what it would mean for her life. She had never lived on her own. She had gone straight from her mother's house to his, and they had been married for thirty years at this time. I could tell she was afraid, but I was equally afraid that she wouldn't follow through. Mary and I both picked up on her hesitation. We urged her to stay the course and make the decision to finally support her children the way a mother should—by rejecting the abuser and choosing the love of her children over the stability of a marriage that had died long ago.

In the following months, Mom would have moments where she considered reuniting with Dad out of fear. She really had no idea how to be alone, and it was all-consuming for her at times. I always went to the place of feeling rejected again when I knew she was consider-ing reconciliation. My "awakened" self was so new and fragile that it could be rocked at any time. I would come out verbally swinging at whatever I thought was compromising my sense of peace. I was fight-ing *hard* for this new normal, and I would be damned if I would let her go back on the promise she made to me to support me—finally.

I had lessened the fog that existed around me through the exer-cise of confrontation, but there was still much to do. At each phase of my life, I've done the work I can do that is in front of me with little awareness of how much further I have to go. If you had asked me at this time if I was completely "cured," I would have said yes with no hesitation. One of the complicating pieces of an awakening journey is the constant state of not knowing what you don't know. Earth-shifting awareness had been revealed to me, and I had processed them in a way that helped me to feel empowered in my life, but I had no idea how much more needed to be brought to the surface.

In many ways, it was another example of my psyche protecting me, as it had been doing all my life. If you had an honest conversation with me at that time about all the other pieces of my life that had yet to be dealt with, I would likely have imploded or would have been so overwhelmed that a complete shutdown was imminent. There is a saying: "God gives you only what you can handle." I believe this with all my heart, because it has always been true for me throughout this walk on the earth.

Carousel Song

In the past,
I chose the horse
with the prettiest colors
and the kindest eye.

The rhythm and motion
lulled me into a state
of trance,
seeing the world pass by
in a blur,
never focusing on a point
of origin
or transformation.

Today I am on
a merry-go-square,
where the cycles persist
of pattern.
But the sides are finite,
and choices to turn a corner
are mine to grasp.

No longer can I blindly move
around
and around
and around,
blaming the physics
that keep me in place.

I have options now.
I have purpose now.

And I move in gratitude
for the journey.

Chapter 10

Because I didn't have enough change going on in my life, I figured getting married just six months after confronting Dad was a good idea. David was so proud of himself for buying a wedding ring set at a local pawnshop, and we went to our favorite Chinese restaurant in St. Augustine the night he popped the question. I knew it was coming, as he didn't do anything big without dropping hints and sometimes outright asking so that he wouldn't risk being rejected. I was excited nonetheless. The whole restaurant knew what he was doing, and they all stopped their intimate conversations to clap for us, making me feel special and giving David the audience he so craved. It was the culmination of a now repeat pattern—the act of being proposed to was more important than who was doing the proposing. Even with all the red flags, sleepless nights, and tears shed, I was practically *running* into the arms of a man who was the perfect personification of the Crazy! I had perfected the process of ensuring that I would always be the calm in the middle of the storm and, in so doing, solidified my place as the saint in a land full of sinners.

I was now planning a wedding at lightning speed, and my father would not be walking me down the aisle. I remember floating through my life during that time, with my feet rarely touching the ground. It is probably an odd time to decide to plan a wedding when I have just blown up my family, but I think I was searching for some small happiness in the middle of the biggest storm of my life. I could lose myself in the dress and the details, the food, and the music and forget about the bombshell that had just detonated in my family of origin. I felt a sense of connectedness to my mother and older sister that I hadn't felt before. For one of the first times in my life, they were concerned for me and wanted to support me through the planning of this magical day with an excitement that I didn't often experience from them. I felt like the center of attention for once, and I relished in the limelight, if even for a moment.

The guest list got shorter, as I was now not going to be inviting any of Dad's side of the family, and I felt like I had "control" over my life for the first time *in* my life. Funny how that sense of control is so relative. If I compare it to the sense of "control" I have now, I was still very trapped in the fog bank of my life. All I knew was I had told my father what he had done to me, I was seeing my mother stand up for me and with me for the first time in my life, and I was only inviting people to our wedding that I wanted to be there. To me, these boundaries felt monumental as I mapped out what my new life looked like.

The wedding would be at the small park down the street from our house. This park was attached to the Llambias House; the oldest house in St. Augustine. The ceremony would take place in the park in front of a beautiful trellis that was covered in ivy, and the reception would be next door in the courtyard of the house. I think we invited about 150 people, and Mom was going to walk me down the aisle since Dad was out of the picture. There was a part of me that longed for the tradition of my father walking me down the aisle. When I found myself pining for what I couldn't have, I realized I was missing the "idea" of him as a father, not his actual presence. It occurred to me that I had wished for a father for a long time, but had never really identified that longing until now. He had always been in the background, only coming to the forefront when he was angry or inappropriate. As a child I had tried to get him to engage as a father to no avail, feeling different levels of rejection when he couldn't be bothered or repulsion when he crossed into the dark side. Now, he was out of my life, and I no longer had to work harder than he did to keep that connection between us. It was liberating, but also carried a certain level of embarrassment. The "father of the bride" fulfills a pivotal role at a young woman's wedding. His absence would be felt; and while no one would ask me to explain why he wasn't there, it felt like a bit of a dark cloud hanging over what should have been a bright sunny day.

I made all the important decisions about who would be with us in the ceremony, where it would be, and who would officiate. Mary, CC, and my best friend Cheryl would all be my maids of honor since I didn't want to make a choice and risk hurting anyone's feelings, and David asked Ronald, Benny, and Bryan (the rock-and-roll bass player, the gay neighbor, and the biker) to be his best men. The pictures would look like something straight out of a movie, and I was thrilled by how out of the box my wedding party would be.

Ronald was one of the first people we met when we moved to St. Augustine because he was a regular at the Tradewinds and he played bass in a band that we often went to hear at the local watering hole. Ronald and David hit it off immediately, and he was engaged to a woman named Liza, whom I connected with. Ronald and Liza were a young, white couple, with dynamic personalities and incredibly curly hair! At our second time partying with them at the Tradewinds, we began telling Ronald where we were living, and he quickly realized we were living in the house he grew up in! He came over the next day and showed us the growth marks on the doorjamb of his room that we had not painted over when redoing the house because we thought they might be important. What a small world! As we talked further, we came to discover that he and I were both related to well-known newspaper editor from Atlanta. WE WERE COUSINS! That realization sealed our friendship, and the four of us were inseparable from then on.

Bryan was a biker who pressure-washed houses for a living. We also met him at Tradewinds, and he and David connected over their love of motorcycles. Bryan looked like Rip Van Winkle with long hair and an even longer beard. He was very skinny and tall white man who was incredibly soft-spoken, which did not fit his biker persona at all. But he quietly hung around and partied with us, fitting into our growing group just fine.

Benny was our neighbor across the street. As we were furiously working on our house, I would marvel at how often the house across the street would change colors! The house I grew up in *never changed* one day of the nineteen years I lived there. It never occurred to me that you could change the color of the outside or inside of your house on a whim, but this is what I kept seeing happening across the street. The outside of the house was hunter green, and he even painted the shutters red for Christmas the first year we were there!

One day, I needed to borrow some milk, and I walked across the street and knocked on the door. A clean-cut white man in his late twenties or early thirties answered the door.

"Can I help you?" he asked as he opened the door. His smile was warm, and his eyes were dancing as he welcomed me into the house. The home smelled of baking, and it was impeccably furnished. He ushered me into his kitchen, launching into an explanation of his decorating style as if he was giving a *Better Homes and Gardens* tour.

"Ah, well...I'm so glad to finally meet you!" he said with a flourish of his hand. "I've been meaning to come over and introduce myself, but I have been so busy redoing this house, and I just finished the kitchen, and...you know, it can be so tedious and time consuming to redo a kitchen!"

We hit it off right away! He was a pharmacist and loved to travel and redecorate his home. I could tell this was the beginning of a beautiful friendship. After living in Atlanta for a time, I felt right at home with him, even though I did not know anyone who identified as gay growing up. He was the perfect friend for us as a couple. He would go to strip clubs with David to hit on the bouncers, and he would bring the Spiegel catalog over so we could sit on the porch and decide how to redecorate our houses. It was a win-win for both of us.

The day before the wedding, I went down the street to check on the progress. There was a center fountain in the park where the ceremony would take place; it had been capped for many years, and my florist had created a massive flower arrangement to go on top of the cap. Lilies and roses and all kinds of beautifully fragrant flowers were cascading down bringing the fountain back to life. There were flowers all along the opening of the trellis, and everything smelled amazing. I was so excited to see all the planning coming to fruition, there was only one problem. They were calling for rain.

And did it rain! Torrential Florida rain started the night before the wedding and continued into the big day. There were many issues with rain for an outdoor wedding with an outdoor reception, but one that was particular to St. Augustine was street flooding. St. Augustine's beautiful cobblestone streets flooded quickly during this kind of rain, and this day was no exception. We had arranged for the bridal party to dress at our house, and the groomsmen would dress at the Llambias House. There were to be two horse-drawn carriages to pick up the bridal party, and we would arrive for the wedding at the park with all guests in attendance. We kept the carriages largely because our street was so flooded that it might be the only way we could get to the park, which was just down the street from the house.

Everyone looked so beautiful! I had someone come to the house to do all our hair and makeup, and we all felt like princesses for a day! We had the photographer there to take pictures of us getting ready and then took some staged photos on the stairs of the house. I was panicked for two reasons that day. The first was looking at the rain as it did not look like it was going to let up, and the second was the fact that my flower girl and ring bearer were not in St. Augustine just hours before the ceremony. I had asked my cousin Samantha (Aunt Dee Dee's daughter) if her twins would be my flower girl and ring bearer, which she had graciously accepted.

The trouble was they lived in Ohio and were traveling to St. Augustine for the big day, but they had not arrived in town yet. I had been calling them nonstop that morning to find out their estimated time of arrival, and for a while, they weren't answering their phone. Then, when I got Samantha on the phone, she basically told me she would arrive when she got there and I should relax about the fact that I had no control over their speed. She even suggested at one point that we should just go on without them. I was so irritated by her attitude and couldn't understand why she was acting this way. I never really got an explanation, and we haven't spoken since that day.

They did end up arriving just in time to get the kids in their outfits and get a few pictures with the full bridal party before it was time to get in the carriages to go down the street, but we never resolved why they seemed so cavalier about possibly derailing my special day. Thinking back on it, it may have had something to do with the situation with Dad, but Samantha and I never spoke about it. It remains an unresolved conversation to this day.

The day before, we had ordered large tents to cover the bar, tables, and food stations at the Llambias House so there would at least be a dry area for folks to be under. Finally, I made the decision that we would not use the park at all since it did not look like it was going to stop. It was decided that I would walk down the aisle into the courtyard of the Llambias House and have the ceremony under the tent that covered the bar, which, in retrospect, was God having a sense of humor.

Mom and I rode in our own carriage, and my three attendants rode in a separate carriage. We rode through the two feet deep water to the Llambias House, and I was apologizing to Mom the whole way there.

"I am so sorry we've wasted all this money, Mom," I said with such sadness. She had spent so much money on the flowers and chairs in the park, and we weren't going to touch them.

"It's okay, sweetie. There isn't anything we can do about it now. We just have to make the best of this day."

"If it lets up at all, we'll take pictures in the park to try to get the most out of the flower arrangements," I said, trying to find the bright side.

We arrived at the Llambias House, and the music began. The rain was still coming down, so Tommy, my wedding coordinator, covered each of us with an umbrella as we walked down the aisle to the ceremony. As I came through the gate with Mom at my side, I saw David standing in front of the bar with Bryan, Benny and Ronald by his side. A dear friend of ours named Pete had agreed to officiate the ceremony. When he wasn't marrying people, he was the lead guitar player for the Alligator Cowboys, our favorite band at the Tradewinds. Pete was dressed in his finest jeans and a navy-blue sport coat with a Grateful Dead tie on. I couldn't believe he wore a tie!

I finished my procession to join David, and Mom quickly made her way over to the big tent where all the tables were. This was where all our guests were standing, those who were able to make it to the ceremony. The flooding downtown was so bad that at least fifty people did not make it in. Thankfully, most of the family was staying at a bed and breakfast across the street from the Llambias House, so they were able to walk over. Flooding didn't keep them away!

The rain continued and got even harder during the ceremony! Pete opened the ceremony, talking about life and marriage and how important it was to love each other every day. David and I wrote our own vows and promised to honor and love each other with no mention of the word "obey." The rain was coming down so hard on the tents that it drowned out our vows, and the guests told me later that the only way they knew we were married was because they saw us kiss.

When Pete declared "I now pronounce you man and wife, you may kiss the bride!" and David planted a big kiss on me, I burst out with "I need a beer!" as soon as the kiss was done.

While we were in the park, taking pictures when the rain let up enough for us to try, my lawyer came up to David and me to seal the deal.

"Do you take this man in marriage?" she asked me.

"I do," I replied.

"Do you take this woman in marriage?" she asked him.

"I do," he replied.

"Okay, you're married," she said.

Since Pete didn't have the authority by Florida standards to officially marry us, she had to take care of it after having witnessed the ceremony. It seemed fine to us, but I would find out thirteen years later that my mother had thought the whole ceremony was a sham and that we had gone to the courthouse when we left for the airport to *really* get married. She resented us all that time because of what she thought she knew and never bothered to ask me about it for the entire marriage.

When it came time to throw the garter and the bouquet, we were well intoxicated and having a lot of fun between the raindrops. I lined up all the single ladies to throw the bouquet and insisted Benny be in that group since he was single and there were so many handsome eligible bachelors working the reception. He needed his chance too! Since most of the women had dresses on that made it tough for them to reach high in the air, Benny came down with the bouquet. Now it was time for the garter. David made a big deal out of going up my leg under my dress to find the garter, and everyone was hooting and hollering as he dramatized this part. When the garter emerged, he had all the eligible bachelors line up to catch it…and Bryan caught the garter!

Everyone cheered, and I promptly said at the top of my lungs, "The person who caught the bouquet and the person who caught the garter have to dance!"

Resounding cheers went up from the guests, and Benny and Bryan, in their tuxedo finery, came arm in arm to the center of the dance floor for their dance. Benny put the bouquet in his teeth, and Bryan had his top hat on as they swirled and twirled. It wasn't until I watched the wedding video after returning from the honeymoon that I saw my Aunt Dee Dee (my mother's oldest sister) dart across the dance floor behind Benny and Bryan and *leave the reception*! She went back to the hotel and never returned. I guess watching Bryan and Benny in that embrace was just too much for her Christian sensibilities.

The bottom of my dress was wet and caked with three inches of mud as I couldn't keep it off the rain-soaked ground, and I was worried it would never come clean. I changed into a dress at the Llambias House to leave the reception, so that I could leave my dress and veil behind and Mom would take them back to the house for me. David had been in and out of the Llambias House all day, which I now know was because he was doing cocaine all day with his buddies. I had been drinking all day, so by the time we got into the limo, I was completely exhausted and he was wired for sound. I remember sitting in the limo, staring out the window, and feeling a special level of numbness come over me.

Wedding days can be so overwhelming, and this one was no exception. I hadn't eaten all day, I had drunk probably six to eight beers, and we were headed to Jacksonville and off to Rome, Italy, the next morning. I had never been to Europe, so I was very excited for

David to show me where he had grown up and experience it through his eyes and memories.

We got to the hotel around 6:00 p.m. and checked in. Our flight was at 7:00 a.m. the next morning, so we thought it would be easier to be closer to the airport for such an early flight. We got our luggage into the room and started to settle in. I got my trousseau out of my suitcase and took it into the bathroom to change and get ready for the wedding night. I had a beautiful ivory silk gown with a matching robe that had lace on the cuffs and lapel. I got changed and made myself all pretty for our special night and then came out of the bathroom.

"Why are you dressed?" I said, realizing that he had changed out of his tux but was in regular clothes. He did not look like he was getting ready for an early night.

"Oh, I'm going out. I'm not tired, and I wanna keep celebrating." He hesitated and stared at me. "You want to come?" he asked sheepishly, like you do when you really don't want the person to say yes; you just asked because you thought you should.

"You're going out? But this is our wedding night," I said, standing there in my silk nightgown and robe, feeling rejected.

"Yeah, you can come with me, but you look tired, and we have a big day tomorrow. I won't be gone long. You get some sleep."

I was dumbstruck. He turned and walked out of the hotel room, closing the door behind him with a loud *click* as the latch found its resting space. I walked over to the bed and sat down, staring at the door in disbelief.

He left me. It was our wedding night, and he just left me.

*****

I sat on the bed, staring at the wall for an hour. I was wearing a beautiful off-white lace silk nightgown with a matching robe that any woman would love to spend their wedding night in (and out of). My face was streaked with tears. The loneliness of being left by my new husband on my wedding night was numbing, like you feel when you hyperventilate and your hands get tingly and your mind starts to get fuzzy. When I did crawl into bed, I lay there for hours, allowing the tears to fall and soak my pillow. It crossed my mind that I was just an hour away from home, and I could get a taxi to take me there and not go across the Atlantic with him tomorrow. He would return to the hotel to find me gone.

I fantasized about what his face would look like when he realized I wasn't in the bed—and further, when he saw my luggage gone. Imagining how my choices might impact him was a favorite pastime, but it rarely yielded action that would affect change in our lives. I was so focused on how my choice would affect him that I rarely got to the point of the fantasy where I could imagine how it would affect me.

So many thoughts were circulating through my mind, but the distance from my head to my feet seemed immeasurable. This moment could have been a time for me to set a clear boundary and refuse to go start a life with a man who left me alone on our wedding night to go party. I could wait up for him and tell him when he returned that I was not going to go all the way to Italy with someone who clearly disrespected me and our newly enjoined marriage. I saw myself standing with my spine erect, telling him he could go without me because I was returning to St. Augustine and calling my lawyer.

None of these choices, of course, won out in the end. I had already lost the other most important man in my life that year and was not willing to go through that disruption again. That level of failure was incomprehensible to me. I did not have the self-respect or self-knowledge to navigate a path to wellness by refusing to continue the farce of this marriage we had just created. Every breath I took was about survival. I existed based on my proximity to others, and my breath only delivered oxygen that was provided by those around me. I did not know how to do this on my own.

The next morning, we got up, showered, and made it to the airport in time for our early flight to Rome. It is another clear example of waking up the next morning and pretending like whatever took place the night before didn't happen, similar to my childhood. I don't even remember having any residual feelings about him leaving me on our wedding night. It was like it didn't happen or that it just didn't matter. Since the norm of our relationship was gaslighting and pretending, it was not a big deal for me to move the reality of my experience to the far corners of my mind, where they would likely not be seen or heard from again.

The flight was long, and we were thankful that we got upgraded at the last minute to Business class seats so we had more leg room and better service. The universe was taking care of me in this situation because David did not handle being uncomfortable very well. When we landed in Rome, I remember feeling like a wide-eyed girl in a new land. I viewed David as the adult in this situation because he had lived in Rome during his high school days and knew the city like the back of his hand. My first indication that I "wasn't in Kansas anymore" was seeing the heavily armed military men with automatic rifles lined throughout the airport concourse. I had never seen anything like that in the US, and I'm sure it was obvious to anyone around that I had not been out of my country before.

We stayed at the Hotel Forum, which is the hotel where David remembered his parents staying when they came to visit him during his high school years. It was a beautiful hotel nestled in between two larger buildings, so much so that when you got to the third floor, you had to walk down the hall around the corner of one of the neighboring buildings to get to the staircase again to continue ascending. The hotel was essentially wrapped around another building! Our balcony looked out at the Coliseum, and we could see the sex workers who stood on the street corners outside the structure looking for work. The room was lovely! I have never felt such soft sheets before, and they were super white! The bathroom didn't have a showerhead, so I was introduced to taking a shower with a handheld sprinkler. And why was there an extra toilet in the bathroom? Oh, that's a bidet! I made just a couple of observations out loud before I realized that he was mocking me for my ignorance of European features and quickly went quiet with my amazement.

There was so much that was new for me, but for David, it was like coming home. His stories were now coming to life as he could walk me around the city and show me the places in person—the Spanish steps where he used to hang out and the exact spot where he threw up on John Keats's house, the Trevi Fountain where he'd stripped naked and swam across on a bet for a beer, the columns at the Vatican where he used to skateboard because they made such good slalom courses! All of it was exciting and reinforced the awe I felt over the life he had led compared to my simple and untraveled existence. But his patience quickly waned for my awe and splendor.

"Don't you want to go out anywhere by yourself? I'm getting tired of leading you around by the nose like a scared child!"

"I'm going out to play pool. It's in a rough part of town, so you don't need to go. I'll be back later."

"You're so clingy! Jesus, it's like you've never been anywhere before!"

It took only a couple of hours for the insults to begin. At each turn, he reminded me how ignorant I was to the ways of the world. I had been out of the US before, but only to the Caribbean islands and always with my parents. I thought he wanted to show me around and take care of me. I was wrong.

We did have some good moments. We found the school he had attended, which was closed down. He was so sad that he couldn't go in and try to find the lunch lady who treated him like he was her son. We ate great food and drank as much as we could handle. We stayed in Rome for seven days, and then it was time to ride the train through France to Torremolinos, Spain. He was getting restless, and I was happy to have this next leg of our journey to take the focus off how much of a country bumpkin I was.

The morning we left the Hotel Forum, we hadn't even gotten out of the room before he was berating me for bringing so much luggage.

"If you bring it, you're gonna carry it" was what I heard *all the way to Spain.*

I had brought just the right amount for seven days in Rome in one hotel, but for traveling on a train through two more countries, I had way too much. Just getting from the hotel to the train station was an indicator of how hard this part of the journey was going to be, because he would not help me with anything! I had a big suitcase (no rollers in that day and age), a hanging bag, and a small square toiletry bag. He reminded me every chance he could that I had brought too much stuff.

We arrived at the Roma Termini (train station) and got our tickets. We were riding the train to Nice, France, this first day and would spend a couple of nights in Nice before making our way to Torremolinos, Spain. Train stations in Europe are like airports in the US. They are huge and grand, with trains that look like something out of a movie with their bright colors and pointed noses. There were close to twenty tracks outside of the station and many people milling about. Managing my luggage was already proving to be a challenge, but I was *not* going to prove him right by complaining, so I sucked it up and figured out how to move the three pieces all by myself.

We got into the train, found our space, and stowed our luggage. Now I could relax for a bit. We found the club car, because that's what you do, and began drinking. It wasn't long before we met two guys from Canada in the club car who seemed to have the same lust for drink that we had. They were backpacking across Europe and were headed to Nice just like us. We became fast comrades after a beer—or two or three!

I remember seeing Nice for the first time as we approached. What a stunning city! The French Riviera! We stopped briefly in Monte Carlo before arriving at the Nice train station, and it all looked just like it did in the magazines. The stunning white beaches, the colors of the buildings and homes dotting the coastline, and the beautiful blue water were just as I imagined it. David had talked our Canadian friends into hanging with us in Nice, joking they could be our roadies because I had brought too much luggage (there he goes again).

I think they felt sorry for me because of all the insults he was hurling my way, but they knew they hadn't paid for a drink since meeting us, so why not? We had made reservations at a hotel for one night and made our way there, settling in and quickly going back out to find the nearest watering hole and adventures with our "roadies." As we walked down beautiful cobblestone streets, lined with open cafes that had umbrella covered tables full of patrons, the sun was going down, and each restaurant seemed to have small white twinkle lights surrounding each doorway. It was magical!

The next morning, we packed up and headed back to the train station for our final leg to Torremolinos, Spain. We arrived at the station about an hour early and got our things onto the train in the car we were assigned. The Canadians were a *huge* help to me, and I cannot imagine hauling all that gear without their assistance. They were willing to help, but not my new husband. Oh, the signs were endless...

After we got settled on the train, David decided he needed beer and pizza for the trip. We didn't have much time before the train was going to leave, and I didn't want him to go for fear he wouldn't get back in time. We argued briefly, but in the end, he always did what he wanted to do, and off he went to find beer and pizza. The time was ticking by, and I was getting nervous! I walked through our car and through the next to the platform in between two cars to await his arrival. Somehow, I felt if I watched for him extra hard, he would get there quicker. What was I going to do if the train left without him? I didn't know where I was going or where our hotel was in Torremolinos. The committee in my brain started working overtime with what-ifs of how this could turn out.

The train blew its whistle, announcing it would leave in three minutes, and we had no David. I was looking at my watch every two seconds, praying to see him come around the corner. Remember, this was before anyone had cell phones, so I had no way of reaching him! Should I get our luggage off so that we would stay if the train left and we could catch the next one? What would his reaction be if he got here in time and all our stuff was off the train and we missed it? I had no time to make this decision, and it felt like life or death.

The final whistle blew, and the train *began to move*! I was standing between two cars, and the train was leaving him behind. Just at that moment, he came running on to the platform with two pizza boxes and a six-pack of beer in his hand.

"I'M COMING, I'M COMING!" he screamed as he leaped onto the small platform I was standing on without dropping the pizzas or the beer.

Whew! He made it, and we were on our way! I was berating him for scaring me like that when we moved onto the next dilemma—we are locked out of the train car! Once the train began to move, the doors at each end of the train cars locked automatically. I did not know this, but we quickly realized what a big deal this was.

"Where is our stuff? Where are our passports?" he screamed at me over the sounds of the train leaving the station and the whistle blowing long and loud.

"They are in the car!" I said, realizing that we were two cars over from where our belongings were, with no way to get to them.

"YOU STUPID BITCH! If someone steals our passports, we are *fucked*! I can't believe you left our shit unattended, and now we can't get to it because the doors are *fucking locked*!"

Cue the full-blown meltdown! The pizza boxes and six-pack were now a distant memory as we have gone to DEFCON 1 to get back to our stuff. Each door going into the car had an oval glass window in it, and he thought it was a good idea to kick it in so we could get inside. I stood in shock and tears, managing the movement of the train on this "in-between" platform as he braced his upper body while kicking with all his might at the oval window while verbally attacking me for being the stupid shit who let this happen.

"Why the *fuck* didn't you stay with the stuff!" *Kick.* "You are so fucking stupid!" *Kick.* "Our passports are gonna get stolen, and we are going to be stuck here. You are gonna have to figure out how to get yourself home!" *Kick.*

Three kicks in, it finally gave way and popped out of its space, leaving a hole in the door. As it fell to the floor, I remember feeling relief that it hadn't broken and thinking that maybe we wouldn't get into too much trouble for kicking it in. They would understand, right? The oval glass was now lying on the platform, and he crawled through the hole to make his way to our belongings, leaving me holding the pizza boxes and beer to follow if I felt like it, which I didn't, because I thought we had just sealed our fate and that we were getting a divorce.

Tears were rolling down my face as I stood in confusion, anger, and pain for what had just happened. I finally gathered my wits and crawled through the hole to follow and return to our stuff. When I got back to the car, all our items were untouched, and he grabbed the beer and pizza from me, exclaiming how hungry he was after all that bullshit. I sat down, shell-shocked, and tried to compose myself.

We arrived in Torremolinos, Spain, that same day. We got ourselves to the hotel, and I was glad that part of the train journey was over. We would stay here for four days, and I was ready to be in one place for a time.

Torremolinos is a lovely coastal city that looks like something straight out of a magazine. The beach was deep with rows and rows of colored umbrellas to give shade to the tourists. There were more touristy areas with high-rise hotels, and then there were the back-walking streets lined with small shops and cafes where you could amble for hours to shop or stop for a coffee or a snack.

The first night we were in Torremolinos, I was exhausted from the journey and ran out of steam early. David was still eager to party, so I went back to the hotel room without him, ready to go to bed and get some good sleep. He was going to stay out with the Canadians and party, so I figured I would wake up sometime during the night and find him in bed next to me.

The next morning, he was nowhere to be found. He had not come home. This was not terribly unusual at this point, but in a strange city, I was concerned. Where would I even begin to try to find him? I didn't even know how to get ahold of our roadies, the Canadians, so checking to see if he was with them wasn't even an option. I stayed in the hotel room all day in case he returned, with each passing moment "the committee" in my head getting louder, fearing that he was dead somewhere, lying in a ditch, and no one knew who he was or where he belonged. I didn't even speak the language to call the police. The day passed with my panic increasing. Around 3:00 p.m., he walked in. His eyes were so dilated they looked black, and he was completely oblivious to the fact that he had me frantic with worry.

"WHERE THE HELL HAVE YOU BEEN?" I was so distraught by this time that all he was gonna get from me was anger.

"I've been partying with some Morrocans who wanted to party when they found out my mom was from Morocco. We had a blast! I don't even know where they took me, but we went everywhere!"

"I've been worried sick! How could you leave me again to worry you were in a ditch somewhere?"

"You know me better than that! I would never end up in a ditch. I know how to handle myself in any country I'm in."

I caught myself looking at his wrist. I had given him a gold bracelet as a wedding present that he had worn ever since receiving it. Looking at his wrist now, it was gone.

"Where's your bracelet?"

"Oh, I must have lost it somewhere. No biggie."

He cared so little for my wedding present to him that he hadn't even noticed it was gone. It meant nothing to him, and I was numb, again. He exclaimed that he was exhausted and needed to get some sleep. He flopped on the bed with his clothes on and was quickly snoring. I picked up my purse and slipped out of the room so as not to disturb his rest. My anger transformed to relief that he was safe.

I spent the afternoon wandering the streets while he slept. Regardless of how he lost it, my mission was to find another bracelet for him that looked like the original, because it was my wedding present to him and I wanted him to have it back. In retrospect, he likely sold it to get money to party with the Moroccans he hung out with the night before, but I didn't allow myself to see that part of the story. After searching for a couple of hours, I found a replacement and bought it to give to him that night when I went back to the hotel. I remember there being some "committee speak" going on in my head, suggesting I wasn't being "fun enough" for him to want to keep me with him while he went on these adventures. I would do anything to make sure he didn't leave me behind.

That night, David, the Canadians, and I smoked hash together until we were all in a complete stupor in our hotel room. I had to go to the bathroom at one point and fell asleep while on the toilet. I fell to the floor at some point and slept on the floor of the bathroom all night, with my pants around my ankles. This was how they found me the next morning. Oh, the lengths I would go to keep someone toxic around.

Baboo died while we were on our honeymoon. I called my older sister while we were in Malaga before we flew back, and she told me she was gone. I hadn't visited Baboo since confronting Dad. I was worried that she might ask me about him or that she might have heard something about our split and want to talk about it and I would have no idea how to have that conversation with her. I was also actively avoiding any opportunity to run into him, and I couldn't predict when he might show up at her house, so I stayed away. It was hard to not see her, and I didn't know she would die before I found the courage to go see her again, but there we were. She had been sick for such a long time, and she often didn't recognize visitors when they were there. I convinced myself that she wouldn't know me anyway, so what was the point in visiting?

The funeral was while we were still out of country, so I wouldn't have been able to go anyway, but I wouldn't have gone had I been home. The break with my father was so fresh, and his side of the family didn't understand what it was all about, so that environment wouldn't have felt safe. I felt a sense of abandonment and deep sadness that she was gone, but I knew she had been suffering since her stroke nine years prior and would be very happy to have that all behind her. The abandonment was more about it happening while I was gone and knowing that no one was going to miss me at the service.

The break with Dad was really still in process, and I hadn't fully dealt with what it meant to me to lose all those family members that went along with breaking with him. Baboo was the gentle and fun grandmother. I had such fond memories of her painting my toes and fingernails and doting on us when we spent the night with her. She was always laughing and dancing, and I will always carry love for her in my heart.

When we returned from the honeymoon, life returned to normal. Partying became the focus of the day—every day—and we were all just trying to make it home in one piece each night. David's partying got more intense, and he was spending more and more evenings out all night. He had gone back to using cocaine and meth, and he needed to use that without me around. He had developed friendships that revolved around what he could supply to those around him, and I was clueless. I had never done anything harder than smoking pot and hard drugs scared the hell out of me, so I was a hindrance to his partying if I got wind of what he was doing.

I began to grow weary of his staying out all night, not necessarily because I was worried he was cheating on me. I knew he had no libido, as evidenced by the lack of sex in our lives, so I never imagined cheating was happening. This was all about his drinking and partying, which I knew, but I somehow was relieved by the break from trying to keep up with him. If I could come up with excuses why I couldn't join him, I could take a break from the Crazy for a brief moment.

This became another recurring pattern between us—me accepting unacceptable behavior like staying out all night, just to get a break from him. I learned how to replenish my soul by creating distance between us. The fog bank I was supporting wasn't as much around me as much as it was *between* him and me. This is an important life pattern that I used for survival as a child, and as an adult, it became a way of escape that I didn't realize I was employing.

Sobriety

The world I see
looks just as different
as it always did.

Colors have edges,
sharper to my eyes,
causing squinting
and wrinkles
and tears.

Flavors linger longer
on my tongue
without the
chaser to
wash them down.

My tongue constricts
from the bitter
and sweet
and savory,
pretty much anything.

Clarity comes as loud
as the train,
running through the living room,
echoing the call
of the horn
blaring its presence
no matter the hour.

I am grateful for
this one more day
of life

even if the rawness
of its figure
makes my skin crawl.

Now I can laugh
at myself
as I cry
with myself
at the slow-moving
twister that threatens
to uproot my tree.

Sobriety was promised
when I put down the glass,
and they all said
this, too, shall pass.

But it doesn't,
because now I feel
every breath,
smell every stench,
and hear every sound
with the repetition of
a caterpillar's footprint.

Each step is a gift
that I wouldn't have gotten
if numb was my drug of choice
today.

Just for today, I will rise.
Just for today, I will breathe.
Just for today, I will look into the eyes
of this stranger
and introduce myself again
to the world.

Chapter 11

David's behavior had gotten so out of control. He was staying out all night several times a week, and I could see how much money he was spending, which confirmed for me that he was using again. Looking back on this time, it is baffling to me how long it took for me to realize he was back to using hard drugs. But the reality was, he never stopped. He had honed his skills of gaslighting to such a degree that I always felt like the crazy one when I heard the whispers that he was using more than alcohol.

I had confronted him several times over the past weeks and months following the wedding, but it seemed to fall on deaf ears. He would give me all kinds of excuses and reasons to explain away his behavior, turning the focus on me and how fucked up *my* behavior was to accuse him. Then he'd go out and do it all again. I walked through every day feeling completely insane while he was having the time of his life.

One day, David and Bryan were out partying at St. Augustine Beach at one of the roadside hangouts they frequented together when his choices caught up to him. When David left the bar and began driving home, he noticed a police car that had been sitting on the side of the road and had now pulled into traffic to fall in line behind him. He knew he had been drinking, and he knew he had other illegal substances in the car that would certainly land him with multiple charges. What did his brain tell him to do? Run! He took off, hoping to put some distance between him and the cop so that he could pull into a bar, jump out of the car, and run inside so the cop couldn't prove he had been driving. Sounds like a reasonable plan, doesn't it?

He was able to do exactly as he intended, pulling into a local watering hole, jumping out of the car, and running inside. When the cop came running into the bar, he had to figure out who was the driver of the car he had been pursuing and arrest him. David was convinced that since the cop did not see him behind the wheel, he couldn't charge him with driving under the influence. The cop did charge him with reckless driving and resisting arrest because he took off when he saw the cop, but the angels were definitely on his side that day. Even though he reeked of alcohol, the cop did not give him a Breathalyzer test.

I had to go bail him out of jail and listen to his ranting about how fucked up the situation was and how the cop had screwed him with the charges. He took *no* responsibility for the situation—of course—and we were now facing court, possible jail time, and legal fees. Something had to give and soon.

One morning, after an all-night disappearance from him, I called the Tradewinds to leave a message that he needed to come home right away. When he walked in through our front door, he looked like he had his tail between his legs. His head was down, and his body language suggested guilt and shame.

I looked him straight in the eye and said, "I know how much money you have been spending and for what. You are out of control, and you need to go to rehab, or this marriage is done."

We had been married for eight months. He had mentioned many times before that if I ever divorced him, he would make my life a living hell. I was feeling strong, and I knew I had him dead to rights, so I had an unfamiliar level of courage. This was the first time I had accused him of using hard drugs since we got together and he supposedly gave them up for me. There was no way he was spending that kind of money without there being cocaine involved. I was feeling powerful.

He gave in much faster than I expected. I took this as a sign that he was ready for it and would be compliant. It reminded me of the morning we woke up together after our second date and told me he was quitting the drug-dealing business to be with me. He cared about me enough to upend his entire life, which gave me a deep sense of worthiness. I felt a similar sense of power in this exchange. His quick acceptance of my ultimatum translated to me that he loved me. It never occurred to me that he had his own ulterior motive that had nothing to do with love for me. He was simply trying to survive, and at the moment, I stood in the way of that survival if he didn't give me what I wanted. Understanding addiction now, I can see that part of this exchange so differently than what I saw then.

I called around to find a placement and found a month-long inpatient spot in Jacksonville. We had the privilege of being able to pay for it out of pocket (since we didn't have health insurance at the time), and we signed him up. I drove him up in two days' time and checked him in. He was quiet and introspective, which was not his norm, and I remember feeling so hopeful that we were finally going to achieve the loving, balanced relationship I had dreamed of. When I drove away from the center, I felt a sense of accomplishment. He was gonna get clean, and I was gonna help save him, which was what I always wanted.

The first couple of days he were gone was pure bliss! The house was quiet, I knew he was in a safe space where he was actually getting help, and I could sleep peacefully. I decided it was important for me to go to Alanon while he was gone. Alanon is for friends and loved ones of alcoholics and addicts, of which I qualified for long before David. I figured while he was getting the help he needed, I would go to meetings to learn how I could continue to fix him after he got home. I decided I would stop drinking, too, so I could be supportive to him. I cleaned out the house of all mind-altering substances, and I went to my first Alanon meeting on July 20, 1994. Little did I know this would become my own sobriety date.

I remember the first meeting. I found one in a church community room, and there were about twenty to thirty people there. I walked into the space, blinded by the fluorescent lights and found hard folding chair to sit on in the circle. The faces came in one by one, greeting each with hugs and smiles as they milled about the room and found their places. It felt like I had walked into a reunion of sorts; everyone seemed so genuinely happy to see one another, and the feeling in the room was warm and inviting even though I was scared to death. I didn't share, but I listened and my "committee" was super busy processing all I was hearing. I was struck by how everyone was quiet while whomever was speaking had the floor. What a novel concept to a person who lived with a narcissist who couldn't allow anyone else to talk for more than a few minutes without turning the attention back toward themselves. They had rules about "cross talk" and not directly responding to what others had shared. It was all new and mind-blowing to me.

After the meeting, there was a group talking, and they motioned me to come over and join them. They welcomed me as a newcomer, and when they lightly prompted me to share why I was there, I began to emotionally throw up on them! After so many years in the program, I have had many newcomers do the same to me, but at the time, I wasn't sure how to shut it off once it began to flow. They stood patiently, listening to my words as they came pouring out of my mouth so fast I couldn't even keep up with them—the details of our marriage, his drug use and drinking, the partying, the staying out all night, and finally, the ultimatum to get sober by going to rehab. All these came tumbling out. I told them I was there to learn how to fix him and keep him sober—words that elicited the small smiles on all their faces. They knew the journey I was embarking on so well, and they knew I had to find my own way through it, in my own time.

One of the gentlemen standing in the group walked over to the table with the books on it and picked up a small blue book. Then he quietly walked back over to where we were standing. I was still spewing my (David's) story and had not missed a beat while watching him. He patiently waited until I took a breath, standing silently with the book in his hand in complete presence to my words.

"Here," he said as he handed me the little blue book. "This is the Alanon ODAT [One Day at a Time]. When he relapses, it will be important for you to have a strong program so you can keep your center. This will help you do that."

WHEN HE RELAPSES? What was he *taking* about! I was so insulted. The look on my face must have been one he had seen many times before.

"When he relapses? Isn't that a self-fulfilling prophecy? If I expect him to relapse, how is that helping him?" I had started to quickly decide that this program or at least this meeting was not going to be for me if this was how they talked about people who were trying to get their lives together.

"No, it's a reality of sobriety. Most people relapse at least once. If you expect him not to relapse, you will be blindsided when it happens. If you accept that it is a possibility—actually, a probability for some—you can focus on *your* emotional health instead of keeping him sober. Get yourself a sponsor, and my business card is inside if you need someone to talk to until you get one. I hope to see you again." He then turned and walked away.

I made my way back to my car, stunned. What had just happened? I had gone to a meeting of a group that I *thought* was going to tell me how to keep him sober, only to be told he will probability relapse and that they don't talk about the alcoholic. When I got in the car, I looked at his business card:

Bill Wilson.

Bill Wilson was one of the founders of Alcoholics Anonymous, along with a man named Dr. Bob. This wasn't *the* Bill Wilson, but it was a significant sign that I was in the right place and I was being helped if I would take it. I still have my ODAT all these years later, and I still have his card inside.

I spent the first two weeks of David's absence getting to know myself again. It had been so long since I had only myself to worry about that it took longer than I expected to acclimate to that space again. I could sleep for as long as I wanted, I could eat anything I wanted for meals, and I could keep the house as clean or as unclean as I wanted it to be without the constant probing from David that I wasn't keeping things up to his impossible standards. I skipped across the street to visit with Benny whenever I wanted, and we talked about whatever I wanted to talk about without waiting for David to burst in and take control of the conversation. It was blissful, and I found myself sleeping more soundly than I had in a very long time.

Halfway through his stay, they invited the spouses and family members to the center for family time. I was going to drive up to the center and visit, take in a meeting or two, spend some time alone with David, and see how he was. I was excited to see him because he was a big part of my addiction and it had been two weeks since I had had a hit. I had convinced myself that I missed him and that I was ready to receive whatever version of my husband would present to me when I arrived.

Had he gained weight? Did he look rested? Would he be happy to see me? Did he miss me? These were the questions swirling in my mind along with one hundred others. The "committee" was very busy, and I could feel a familiar version of the Crazy creeping in as I drove to Jacksonville. As much as I thought I had untangled myself during his absence, just knowing I was moving closer to seeing him began the process of retangling all my energetic wires into familiar patterns.

They brought all the family members to a large room full of couches, chairs, and tables and asked us to have a seat. Our family members would be with us shortly they said. I took a seat and remember feeling out of body, not even noticing the twenty others who were in the room with me. This is what it can feel like when an addict is about to take a hit after two weeks of nothing; all you can focus on is the hit.

He walked in with the others, and I leaped up to hug him! I was sooo happy to see him that my face was going to break with how big my smile was.

"Hi! I love you so much! I'm so happy to see you!" I said as I hugged his neck so hard he was choking.

"Hi, I'm glad to see you too," he responded.

He looked better than he did when he left. I could tell he was sleeping and eating well. His eyes weren't as sunken and hollow, and his skin tone looked good. He was quiet and reserved, which was not a demeanor I would have attributed to him. I definitely had enough enthusiasm for the two of us.

We had a large family meeting in that room. It followed the structure of an AA or Alanon meeting, so I was familiar with the process. Neither one of us shared, but it felt good to be participating in something that was healthy as a couple. After the meeting was over, he suggested we take a walk in a courtyard that wasn't far away.

We walked into the courtyard into the sunlight. It was a warm July Florida day, and we quickly found some shade in an open gazebo that was in the middle of the space. We made some small talk, he asked about the cats and Stanley (our basset hound), and I filled him in on the goings on in St. Augustine. I had stopped drinking when he left, so I didn't have any party stories to share, but if I had, I wouldn't have offered them since we were supposed to be about health now. It felt strangely similar to sharing in a meeting, as he was being quiet and listening to the stories I was weaving without interruption. What I didn't realize was, I had become the oxygen sucker; there wasn't much left for him to have when I was done.

He got real serious all of a sudden and started telling me about some of the counselors who were helping him. They were in recovery too, and he really valued their support and opinion because they had been where he was. There was a counselor who was not in recovery, and he quickly told me how this man was a dick and that he hated him. He didn't know what it was like to want something so bad you'd think about it every moment. He was very bossy, and David didn't listen to him at all. I started to get in his business about listening to everyone, which he very quickly cut off.

"I've been really focused while I am here, and I need you to understand that my sobriety is the most important thing in my life. If I put anything in front of it, I risk losing it. That means it's more important than you or my family or anything else."

"Well, of course, your sobriety is important. I wouldn't dream of suggesting anything else. But I am important as your wife. I have put up with a lot of shit from you, and I am ready for that to change."

"No, my sobriety is more important than even you."

I was *pissed!* How dare he, after all he put me through, after all I sacrificed for him and all the sleepless nights, suggest that I wasn't his top priority. I clearly had not had enough Alanon yet to understand how messed up my feelings were, and I was acting as a "dry drunk" when I look back on the experience. I was dry, but I wasn't sober. I hadn't dealt with my own addiction. I had been focused on his and how I was going to help him get better.

I left the treatment center and fumed all the way back to St. Augustine. How *dare* he not acknowledge the hell he had put me through. I thought his sobriety meant I was going to finally have the doting husband I felt I deserved. This was a symptom of my own disease that had not even begun to become clear to me. I actually recall having moments where I felt lost knowing he would return from rehab and be sober and I wouldn't know what to do with myself. The fear of the unknown began to fester, and it was in full force by the time I got him home a week or so later.

We now had to figure out our "new normal." In Florida, if you don't own a boat or don't drink, there is really very little for you to do. Benny, Ronald, and Bryan tried to be supportive, and they would come over to visit for short times since meeting at a bar was not an option, but it always felt strained and awkward and forced compared to the fun times we used to have.

David's court date for the reckless driving and fleeing the scene was approaching, and he needed to have a job when he went before the judge so that he could ask for work release accommodations. His lawyer described this as him doing some time in jail, but he would be allowed to leave jail every day to go to work then return to lock up at the end of the day. We decided this was the best situation possible, even if he had to sleep every night in custody.

A friend of ours worked for the sightseeing boat that went up and down the intracoastal waterway, and he got David a job just before he had to go to court. The lawyer we had hired did a great job pleading his case for work release, and David cleaned himself up and knew just what to say to the judge. It also helped that he had gone to rehab and was sober now, showing the judge that he had amended his ways and learned from his mistakes.

The judge granted him work release, and he was sentenced to twenty-one days in jail. He was to report to jail in two weeks' time to begin his sentence. He bitched and moaned about the ruling, but it really was such a privileged "slap on the wrist" for his behavior. Those two weeks leading up to his sentence were the longest two weeks that we had lived through in a long time. It just so happened that the day he was to report to jail was the day Cheryl and I had tickets to go see Billy Joel and Elton John in concert in Orlando.

I remember having the conversation with him about whether or not I would go. We went around and around with him telling me to go ahead and go, but I didn't believe that he wouldn't hold it against me for the rest of my days. In the end, I did go to the concert. While Cheryl and I sat in the stadium seats, watching Billy Joel and Sir Elton John pound out "Piano Man" on dueling pianos, David was spending his first night on a cot behind bars. One thing I can say about my life—it was rarely boring.

I began to realize how much I missed drinking. I found myself thinking about it several times a day. I began to fantasize about having a beer and how I would go about getting that without him knowing. I tried to make it all about his drinking and his acclimation, but I was hiding a secret from myself and others. I missed drinking terribly and had begun to think about it all the time. Looking back at it, I had gone from regularly checking out to no mechanism for coping with stressful situations—cold turkey. I poured myself into supporting his recovery, which became my new method of coping, through an old method of codependency. Everything old is new again.

After several months of trying to find our new rhythm to life, we began to think about making a geographical change. Our lives in St. Augustine had been woven completely around drinking, and even though our friends were trying to act enthused about spending time with the new versions of Dee and David, we weren't a whole lot of fun to be around. We decided staying in Florida was not going to work. Not partying made life very dull and challenging. David was not settling into AA meetings in town because so many of the old drunks didn't want to accept him as a drug addict. They would ostracize him because what he did was *illegal* and they believed their drunkenness was better because it was at least *legal*.

I often thought he made up most of this discomfort because he wanted to have a reason not to go to meetings, but I will never know. His sobriety was difficult. He wanted to still be around drinking and act like it didn't bother him, so we still went to bars all the time and he drank non-alcoholic beers to feel like he was still a man about town. Trouble was, he would drink twenty of them in a night, and sometimes I felt like he still had a bit of a buzz.

We started fantasizing about where we might live if we moved. One night, we spread a map of the United States out on the table and essentially closed our eyes and pointed. We ended up in the region of Colorado and began to dream about being near the Rockies. We could go skiing anytime we wanted, and when we looked up images of Colorado, they took our breath away. Doing research on the demographics of the towns around Denver, we thought areas like Longmont would be affordable but still close enough to Denver for the arts and social aspect. We decided to take a trip out to Boulder and check out the surrounding areas to decide which would be the best fit. We got our plane tickets and were there within a week or two.

When I got off the plane, everything looked extra sparkly. I believe it was the lack of humidity in the air, but it was a visually beautiful experience. We stayed in a hotel in Boulder and drove to neighboring towns with the intention of finding a place that appealed to us. We didn't consider Boulder itself because we believed it was too expensive to live there. Each town we visited, however, had reasons why it wouldn't be a good fit. Meanwhile, we had fallen in love with Boulder from the moment we arrived. At the time, we did not practice any restraint in spending, so we quickly convinced ourselves that living in Boulder was the best choice. We found a townhouse to rent before we headed back to St. Augustine and returned home to begin the process of embarking on a new life adventure.

The hard part was saying goodbye to our community. Ronald, Liza, Bryan, Benny, and our gang threw us a going away party that was full of love and support. We were sad to leave everyone, but there were many plans made for them to come out to visit us and go skiing, which was something fun to look forward to. I was so excited to start our new life! I was convinced that being in a new environment with new friends would be just the ticket for keeping David sober, and I had never lived off the East Coast before, so this was completely out of the box for me. It was a true geographical fix, but we were oblivious to the textbook response to discomfort we were falling into. All I knew was that this was an opportunity for a fresh start where we could be in charge of the temptations that surround us for the first time in our marriage.

Transformation (Four Haiku)

Bipolar takes life
to the depths of darkness.
Please show me the light.

Codependency
locks the trap door of my life
Must find an escape.

Recovery breathes
new life where there wasn't one.
Fills my lungs with love.

Wisdom of self calls
all cells to open to love.
Knowing reflection.

Part Three

I was standing at the sink in the kitchen, washing the dinner dishes, when David came in. Our daughter, who was five at the time, was at the kitchen table, writing small words that I prompted her verbally to spell as I praised her accomplishments. It was a classic scene of mommy multitasking, but the energy in the room shifted as his heavy biker boots made their way down the hall and into the kitchen.

When I turned to look at him, I knew it immediately. His face was red, and his lips moved limitedly as he spoke. Someone else might have attributed his slurred speech to being cold, but I knew the real reason—he had been drinking. He was wrapped in black leather, and as he took his gloves off, he began his explanation of the day's events trying to seem lucid to throw me off the scent. It reminded me of the "inspection" days of my youth, except this time I was the inspector instead of the one being inspected.

There is a thing in Alanon called the "Alanon kiss." This is when you determine if you are right about your loved one's drinking by slyly taking a deep breath as you give them a kiss hello. I took a deep drag as I gave him the obligatory kiss on the lips and smelled it right away. It was of a heavier level than usual, and every cell in my body wanted to launch into twenty questions about where, when, and how much he had consumed. I knew better than to approach it in this way, so I let him start talking to see how many details I could get without even uttering a word.

He took me through his day, stop by stop on the bike, and worked in that he had been drinking nonalcoholic beers all day. This was supposed to explain the smell and satisfy my burgeoning interrogation and eventual judgment about his behavior. He was anxious and talking a mile a minute about the day's events, rarely taking a long enough breath to allow me to get a word in edgewise.

Mimi ran up to him with her arms stretched up to the sky, saying, "Dadddddddyyyyy!"

He picked her up with a sweeping motion and cradled her into his arms, telling her that she was his girl and asking her if she had been a good girl today. Seeing her in his arms gave me pause. He wasn't dangling her in any precarious position, nor was she in any noticeable danger. But my sweet little cherub with big cheeks and a button nose was in the arms of her drunk father, and this reality caused me to catch my breath.

I must have looked at him with a look of knowing, and I saw his eyes change. The Crazy had entered, and I knew what was coming next. He started peppering questions at me like "Why don't you believe me?" and "How the fuck do you know anything? You haven't seen me all day!" I didn't even have to say a thing. We both knew exactly where we were going next. It was times like these that my body kicked into a familiar mode that was no longer of my choosing. It wasn't just "fight or flight" but a desperate search for the exit door.

How could I weather the storm that was coming with the least amount of damage to myself or my little one? Since having Mimi, these situations became more intense on the *inside* of my soul. I not only had to protect myself, but I had to do everything I could to minimize the damage to her psyche. After spending so many years in this pattern, the typical "Mama Bear" fight didn't surface in the way it might for someone who is in a new experience and is tasked with protecting their child. When you factor in years of minimizing, degrading, and soul-crushing emotional abuse, the means to achieve the goal look very different.

After a ten-minute barrage of how fucked up I was for questioning his time out with his friends, he concluded he would change and go back out in his car because he wasn't gonna stick around "for this bullshit." He put Mimi down at some point, which allowed me to breathe a little, but he did it because she began to cry, which could trigger further anger directed at her for being too loud and having nothing real to cry about. He'd give her something to cry about, if we weren't careful.

He changed clothes and left with a last-ditch verbal attack as he headed out the door. I don't remember what he said because I was holding my breath until I heard the garage door close behind him. We were safe for the night.

Later that night, Mimi spiked a fever, which had her awake and crying most of the night. She rarely got sick, so I was quite worried and began calling him to tell him she was sick and ask him to come home. He wasn't answering his phone. I sat on the floor of the doorway of her room, listening to her whimpering as we waited for the pain reliever to kick in. Meanwhile, my "committee" was having a knock-down, drag-out argument in my head.

"When he comes home, I am going to tell him to pack his bag and *leave*!" said one member.

"But I can't be the one to break up her family! What kind of mother would I be to do that?" said another.

"He's a *dick* and will never change! I have to do this for *her*!" said yet another member.

These conversations went on and on and on inside my head. I waited until it was a reasonable time in the morning to call my sponsor. I gave voice to all the arguments my committee had been making inside my head all night, along with the awareness that I knew what it was like to be without a father and I didn't want to do that to my little girl.

After listening intently to me, she offered one sentence that has stuck with me the rest of my days: "If you leave him, you will be teaching her not to accept unacceptable behavior. She may not understand now, but she will someday, and that is one of the greatest gifts you can give her as her mother."

I knew what I needed to do, but I wondered if I would have the courage to follow through when he came home. He finally called at 10:00 a.m., and he knew from the tone of my voice that the day of reckoning had arrived. At noon, when I heard the garage door open, I took a deep breath and asked my higher power for the strength to utter the words. It was Super Bowl Sunday, and there was about to be a showdown.

Chapter 12

Settling into Boulder was a new adventure that we got to explore together. Since getting clean, we were both walking around like raw nerves, feeling everything but not knowing how to process the feelings. There was excitement about this new land we were exploring, but not knowing how to move through space without being numb proved challenging.

David remembered how helpful it was for him to have mentors in rehab who had been down the road of addiction, and he turned his sights toward getting a job in the recovery field. He applied in several places and finally got a job at a halfway house in Longmont, which was about thirty minutes away from our home. He hadn't been in recovery long, so it was a challenge to sell himself to potential employers. They knew what new sobriety could look like and were looking for someone with a little more time in recovery. But the one thing that David always possessed was his ability to charm the pants off anyone he encountered, and this job search was no exception.

The shift they were hiring for was graveyard, or overnight shift. We talked about what that would mean for our marriage since he would be gone all night and sleep all day. We determined it could work because I had gotten a job at a preschool in Boulder that required me to be gone all day and the house would be quiet for him to sleep. The graveyard shift would bring other challenges. We would not see each other very often unless our days off coincided. I was also worried about the effects of David flipping his sleep schedule, which can often cause damage to someone's personality. He was eager for the opportunity and was determined to make it work. We ordered blackout blinds for our bedroom so he could sleep during the day, and he accepted the position.

I took great comfort in his working within the recovery community. As what happens with newly sober addicts/alcoholics, David was quick to find fault with the traditions and habits that others formed while on their path to sobriety. He would often chastise the people he met in the "rooms" (a common way to reference meetings) about their substituting one addiction for another. He even took issue with how much coffee people drank and how many cigarettes they smoked, saying that they had replaced their addiction to alcohol and/or drugs with these substances.

He also found fault with the action of going to meetings, which, to him, translated as weakness. These types of justifications for not being involved in program started back in St. Augustine when the old drunks judged him for being an addict, and he used that as an excuse to not go to meetings. It was an ongoing discussion in our house about the merits of working the program by going to meetings, reading the literature, and getting a sponsor who would walk him through the steps.

We met couples and individuals who were in Narcotics Anonymous (which David felt more comfortable in than AA) and began to form friendships within these circles. They welcomed us to their meetings and in their homes for potluck gatherings, which almost always included a meeting. These folks had been sober for some time and took us both under their wings. Slowly but surely, we were building a friend base in this new town that gave us people to call when things got tough, and there were gatherings that we could go to which supported our intention to stay sober. Some of these new friends even vouched for David when he was interviewing for the job at the halfway house and gave assurances that he was surrounded by a strong recovery circle who could support him in his sobriety while he was supporting other addicts at work. I was so happy when he got the job at the halfway house because I knew even if he wasn't saying how much he liked the program when we were home alone, he was surrounding himself with the steps, traditions, and concepts of sobriety that would only serve to help him stay sober longer. I figured he wouldn't admit it, but he was still showing up and doing the work.

It was not lost on me the difference in our lives from even a year before. We went from him attending parties in Atlanta with bowls of cocaine on the counter in the bathroom, going on sailing trips to Bimini with people we just met, and being the liveliest couple in every room we entered to working all the time, attending pot-lucks, and playing Scattegories with this new group of friends. He had found a new group of people who had not heard all his stories about high school in Rome or childhood in Saudi Arabia, and he would come alive with telling the stories. They still hung on David's every word, but there was something different about the experience. David continued to be the most dynamic person in the circle, but in this circle, he also got called on his bullshit. He didn't like that at all. If we got into one of our fights and I called on some of the members of the circle for support, it would eventually get back around to him in a conversation where he wasn't allowed to make it all my fault. While this stroked my ego and helped me feel a stronger sense of sainthood that I had even felt before, it pushed him further away from the group because his narcissism was not being nurtured. He was being asked to be real about what he was contributing or not contributing to our marriage, and that kind of reality check didn't set well with him.

The search for adrenaline was ongoing and harder to secure. One of the things we were excited about doing when we moved to Colorado was skiing. I had gone skiing maybe twice in my life, and always on the East Coast where there was more ice on the slopes than powder. I was not proficient, and expected to spend most of my time on the bunny slopes than anywhere else. David had taken many long weekend trips to the Swiss Alps when in boarding school in Rome. He hadn't skied in a long time, but we went to the store to buy boots, skiis, poles, and the clothes to take up our new hobby.

He decided we were going to go to Breckenridge for the week-end not long after we got settled into our new place. I didn't know anything about the ski mountains of Colorado, so I didn't have an opinion about where we should go first, and if I had one, I likely wouldn't have shared it. We booked a hotel room and loaded up the car to go on our new adventure. I was nervous about not being a good skier, but he assured me they had bunny slopes that I could go on and get stronger in my skills. It was early in the season so the temperatures were not terribly cold yet; in fact, you could wear short sleeves if the sun was out. I sure did love the Colorado weather—the dry air and sunshine were a great combination after growing up in the humidity of the south.

We arrived at Breckenridge and went straight to the slopes. There wasn't any snow on the parking lot which seemed weird, and there seemed to be less people than there might be in full season. I was happy for this, as I didn't want a bunch of good skiers zipping around me while I tried to figure this out. I asked David about the idea of me taking a skiing lesson, but he couldn't be bothered with the time that would take. He would teach me all I needed to know. This type of setup was common in our relationship, and it never ended well for me. But that didn't mean I didn't fall for it every time.

We got our ski passes and our maps of the slopes. Right next to the lodge was an enclosed gondola that would take us up the mountain. I was nervous that this might not drop us off at a slope I could handle, as I had never ridden a gondola up to a bunny slope. But it was the only ski lift we could see, and so we got in line for the adventure. As the gondola ascended the mountain, it was an incredible view. One of my favorite things about living in Colorado was the ability to see for miles and miles. It was such an open and free feeling, and the vistas were always breathtaking. As I looked out over this beautiful vista I could see the open ski slopes off in the distance that looked like they were more my speed. The problem was, I couldn't figure out how to get to them, and the gondola just kept going up… and up…and up.

When we finally approached the station to get off, we had been climbing for almost ten minutes. This was way too high for a bunny slope, and as I got off the lift and looked at the map that showed "You are here," there were nothing but black diamond slopes—in all directions. My heart started racing, and I began to protest to David that we had taken the wrong lift, but he didn't want to hear my whining. We were here, and there was nothing we could do about it now. I would just have to suck it up and ski down. It won't be that hard. He'd help me.

I stepped into my skis and clicked them on my boots. I slowly made my way to the top of the slope and looked down. Experienced skiers were all around us, leaping into the great beyond with confidence. I remembered from my few times skiing growing up about snow plowing and began my descent with the tips of my skis pointed toward each other to control my speed. Each stretch of slope had a plateau in between where you could take a little break and catch your breath, not that anyone else needed to do this but me. When I got to the first plateau, I worked myself over to the side to get out of everyone's way and looked around for David. I remembered what his ski jacket looked like and was desperately trying to find him, but he was nowhere to be found as the more experienced skiers swooshed by me with no fear or hesitation. After waiting for a few minutes, and getting yelled at by the ski patrol for being in the way, I decided I had to keep going. Maybe I would find him at the next plateau.

With each stretch I got more and more tired, and the slope got more and more icy. It was early in the season, and we hadn't had a lot of snow yet, so Breckenridge had been making snow, which often was more icy than powdery. As I made my way down to the lower elevations, I could feel the consistency of the snow becoming more icy, which made my level of control decrease. Between that and how tired my legs were, I was more and more of a danger to myself and others the further down I went. When I got to each plateau, I dreamed of a bench to sit down on, but there was nothing like that available. One time when I was stopped to rest, I looked over to see one of the open ski lifts off in the distance. It was where I belonged, but I could not see a way to get there. I was going to have to continue down this mountain or die trying. I had stopped looking for David, as he had clearly left me to fend for myself, and the people around me were so busy cussing me out as they flew past me that they were not going to be of any service. There were many members of the ski patrol who were yelling at me to get out of the way or to slow down when my legs got so tired that I could no longer control my speed. Instead of asking them for help, I just screamed through my tears that I was trying but that my legs didn't work anymore! I didn't know how to advocate for myself. It never occurred to me to ask for help.

Finally, I got to the last plateau, and I could see the station where we boarded the gondola. I had only one more stretch to go, and I cried with joy when I knew I had made it. I turned my ski tips toward each other and began to go when I stopped. My legs were quaking so hard that I couldn't go any further. I was done. I disconnected my skis from my boots and picked them up to put on my shoulder. Even if I had to slide down on my ass, I was getting down from this fucking mountain!

Just then, a voice came from behind me: "Do you need some help?"

I burst into tears and said, "Yes!"

It was a stranger who had watched me for a bit and knew how exhausted I was. He took my skis off my shoulder and took off down the last stretch, saying he would be waiting for me at the bottom. I walked, step by step, sideways down the last stretch to the bottom. It had taken me two and a half hours to get down that mountain.

I had no idea where my husband was, and I could barely stand up. The lodge was there with plush seats and a warm fire, which looked like just the place to recuperate from my harrowing experience. This was before we carried cell phones on a regular basis, so I had no idea how to get ahold of David or what to do. So I went inside, got a hot chocolate, and found a seat facing a big picture window that looked out at the slopes. I would sit here and wait for David to come down the mountain. Then I would rip him a new one for leaving me alone to die.

I figured he had been up and down a couple of times in the time it took me to get down once, but I had no idea how to find him except to sit here and watch for him as folks came down the mountain. I waited for another hour, looking at all the green ski jackets to see if it was him. When he didn't appear, I started to get concerned. What was my next move if he didn't come down the slope? I finally decided to lug my skis back to the car in the parking lot to see if he was there. He had the keys, so I couldn't get in, but I couldn't think of any other way to figure out where he was.

My boots were open and flopping on my feet, and I had my skis and poles over my shoulder as I worked my way across the half-empty parking lot. As I approached the car, I suddenly heard someone screaming, "LEEEEGGGGSSSSSS! LEEEGGGGSSSSS!" I looked in the direction it was coming from, and there he was, one boot on and one boot off, limping across the parking lot with his skis over his shoulder. I was so relieved to see him, but I was *furious* at the same time!

"WHERE THE FUCK HAVE YOU BEEN!" I screamed at him. "It took me two and a half hours to get down that fucking mountain, and you were *nowhere*! You left me to *die* up there!"

"I yard-saled right after I started skiing down the first time! Some little kid cut me off and took me out, and my skis and poles went flying. I hurt my ankle, and the ski patrol put me on one of those stretchers and took me down the mountain to the first-aid station. I've been stuck there ever since! The fuckers yanked my ski pass and wouldn't let me back on the mountain because they saw me get hurt. I left messages for you at all the ski slopes. Why are you pissed?"

"I NEVER SAW ANY OF THEM! I've been trying to get down that fucking mountain since you left me!" The tears started flowing, and I couldn't stop as I related my horrible experience. "I'm never coming back to this wretched mountain! I can't believe I let you drag me here in the first place."

"It's not my fault! You're the one who can't fucking ski!"

*****

When David was in the rehab center in Florida, they prescribed antidepressants for him to help with the detox and early recovery time. While it seemed obvious to both of us that he needed some support in this area, it didn't seem to be addressing all his issues. He was capable of showing signs of depression, like not being able to get out of bed for days on end, lack of appetite, and a deep sense of melancholy that I couldn't talk him out of no matter how hard I tried. But the other side of him was not needing to sleep for more than four to five hours at night, not being able to sit still through a two-hour movie, or exhibiting obsessive compulsive tendencies around cleanliness of the house or laundry. As we moved deeper into recovery, he began to show more obvious "cycling" behavior where he would move from depression to hyperactivity and back to depression, sometimes during one argument. Growing up in a household ruled by bipolar gave me a familiarity to the disease that triggered my awareness of the cycles. I began to talk more and more about finding a doctor who could diagnose what was truly going on with him.

I started researching local doctors and found a well-renowned psycho-pharmacologist in Denver. David pushed back at first, not wanting to go to another doctor who would remind him he needs to be on medication for the rest of his life. He struggled with this reality when it came to the antidepressants, and I knew this would be an uphill battle. I had learned how to push an issue with him in such a way that he finally grew tired of me asking and relented to an appointment. But I had to do this delicately, or it would take much longer to get to the conclusion I desired. I had been living with this type of person all my life. I had a PhD in "talking people off the ledge," especially those who spend the majority of their time as their own worst enemy.

We went for our appointment, and I liked the doctor right away. He identified the disconnect between David's depression diagnosis and his behavior, noting that not being able to sit still for a two-hour movie or not needing much sleep are typical symptoms of mania more than depression. He ordered blood work to examine David's chemical levels in his brain, something no other doctor had done before, which immediately helped me know we were on a different path to diagnosis than we had been before.

The final question he had of us before we left was the most surprising to me. He gave me a phone number to use, and he gave David a phone number to use. His request was that we each call our numbers twice a week and leave a short message about how we were feeling and/or what behaviors we were seeing. He explained that bipolar is a disease that manifests differently for each person struggling with it and the perception of the person's life who *has* the disease is going to be different than the perception of the person *living with* the person who has the disease.

In order for him to get as complete a picture as possible of how David might be reacting to any drug changes he undergoes as we carefully walked the path of determining the right medications and correct dosages, Dr. Woodman would need an account from both the brain that is experiencing the disease and the brain that is living outside of the diseased brain. No one had ever suggested this approach before, and I found it to be very reassuring and proactive. Dr. Woodman wasn't spending a lot of time making David feel bad about his diagnosis; instead, he was speaking about it in clinical terms that helped both David and myself understand that we were dealing with a brain chemical imbalance—no more and no less. We were introduced to the concept of having a "team approach" to this disease, which immediately gave us a sense of togetherness as we navigated this uncharted territory.

As I reflected on this new information about bipolar disorder that had always been a part of my life, I found myself seeing my mother through a different lens. During my childhood, I often related to her inconsistencies in behavior to the Crazy, which always supported the suggestion that it was something that was beyond anyone's control. She had been put on lithium at the time she was diagnosed, but in those early days of this disorder there were very few courses of treatment to choose from.

Many years had passed, and the choices of medications had expanded to attend to the fact that different physical systems needed support in different areas. It felt like a diagnosis of this kind now had choices in the courses of treatment that could be tailored to the particular brain and how it responded to treatment. This gave me a sense of power and strength in the path we were now on to find the perfect cocktail for David's brain to find the balance he and I were so desperately seeking.

David was not responding with the same optimism as I was. He didn't like the idea that he would need to take medication for the rest of his life for this issue. He expressed that it made him feel weak and somehow broken. He didn't like the process of me calling the doctor with my own story of how things were going because it took control of the narrative out of his hands. He didn't appreciate the fact that finding the right cocktail of meds was an imperfect science and was largely trial and error, with more error than success. He wanted the doctor to look at his blood work and know exactly what he needed to take and in what dosages, and he wanted to be able to stay on that prescription forever. It wasn't that simple, and it gave him the perfect scapegoat for frustration that led to his often refusal to take his meds without reminder from me.

David had been using drugs since he was seven years old. He had done so much damage to his already imbalanced regulatory system that even when we found the right dosages and the right medications, his system could become imbalanced without any warning. The doctor was very clear from the start that keeping his system balanced was going to be part of David's daily routine for the rest of his life. If he started to feel a little "off" on any given day, he was to call the doctor's office immediately and schedule blood work to examine his levels. If dosage changes were indicated, that would be the next step.

In order for any of this to work, David would have to accept that this was the reality of how his brain worked and then decide to be proactive and self-aware enough to try to nip in the bud any spiral he might be heading into before he bottomed out. It took commitment on his part, and he did not have the stamina to see this through.

Enter my codependency. It was now my job to assess his daily mood and start encouraging him to call the doctor if I started to see him slide either into depression or mania, and I accepted this position with enthusiasm. I had now been a member of Alanon for a couple of years, but I was not "working my program" with enough consistency to avoid such a classic trap. I told myself I was working to help him stay balanced which, in turn, was going to help the balance of our marriage, but I did not have the natural boundaries in place to ensure my "helping" didn't become enabling very quickly. I didn't have a sponsor whom I could call to discuss deeper issues, and I would find any reason not to go to a meeting, even though I had found good meetings in Boulder. The methods to live a healthier life were there for the taking, but David's resistance to Alanon was all the push I needed to relinquish this lifeline for myself. I was living my life trying to hold everything together with my butt cheeks tightly clenched. What I didn't realize was that only served to give me a very toned butt. It did nothing to move me through space with a sense of my own agency and purpose. I was still living through his lens—all interactions with the world had to go through him before they got to me.

I had gotten a job at a local preschool as the two-year-old teacher, which was working well for me, but David was not happy at his job at the halfway house. The overnight schedule was wearing on him, and having opposite sleep patterns was becoming problematic with his new medication regime. His doctor advised him to find a job that didn't require him to be up all night, as he was already struggling with his new diagnosis, and having reversed sleep patterns was making it tougher to adjust. Now that he had more time in recovery under his belt, and had done well at the halfway house, he interviewed at the Boulder Detox Center as a case manager.

His charming ways always worked for him in these situations, coupled with recommendations from the new circle of friends in recovery, and he was hired fairly easily. He was still complaining about recovery and those who worked the program as being weak and a replacement for addiction, but he continued to surround himself with meetings—conducting them multiple times each day and having to speak about the benefits of program to his clients as he processed their intake. I took comfort that this was his higher power's way of immersing him in this new way of life and giggled to myself; he could complain all he wanted, but he was still working the program—or it was working him.

I had settled into a routine at the preschool and had moved up from the two-year-old teacher to the Assistant Director. It was the first time since graduating college that I had a career, and that felt really good. I had avoided being around children for so long after graduation while I worked on myself around the abuse, and now I was working with children just as I had always wanted to in an environment where I was excelling. I had a sixth sense with children that I really couldn't explain. I understood what they were thinking and deeply respected them, which they sensed and responded well to. My training was in special education, but I was able to use that training with this age group because it was all about behavior at this age. I felt fulfilled and understood my purpose for the first time in my adult life. My sense of accomplishment began to follow me home which brought new challenges. David had mostly relied on me not having a "life" outside of managing all things him. He had often chided me for not having a purpose or a life outside of our marriage, but when I got one, he felt threatened by it. It is the paradox of a codependent and emotionally abusive relationship; they want nothing more than for you to get a life. Then when you do, they want nothing more than to destroy your confidence in it.

One day I was sitting at the dining room table eating breakfast, and it occurred to me. I don't remember the last time I got my period. We had discussed having a child and had made the joint decision to stop using birth control to see what happened, but since we didn't have sex very often, we weren't sure how long it would take to get pregnant. David had never had a strong sex drive, probably due to his drug use in the early days. Of late, it was all about the medications he was on for bipolar and the disruption to his schedule when he was working nights. There always seemed to be a reason to not have sex, and I was not going to push the issue. Sex had never been fun or enjoyable to me, so it wasn't anything I searched out. Of course, if you are trying to get pregnant, you kind of have to touch each other, but we figured if it was supposed to happen it would.

I got the calendar out and counted the weeks. I was two weeks late. I sat staring at the calendar and worked to remember when was the last time we had sex. Since we didn't do it very often, it was usually easy to remember the instances. Sure enough, the timeline lined up. Oh my god, this might be happening! I went to work in a bit of a daze that day and then went to the drugstore to buy a home pregnancy test at lunch. When the plus sign appeared, I was over the *moon*! I fantasized all day about how I was going to tell David that night. What would his reaction be? What words would I use? Would I string him along, or just come out and say it?

That night, I got home before he did and started cooking dinner. When he got home, it was the usual routine—obligatory questions about each other's day while he went upstairs to change and get comfortable before dinner. As we sat at the table, eating in relative quiet, I was having a hard time focusing. I had so much expectation wrapped up in what his reaction was going to be that when the time came to deliver the news, I almost couldn't do it. It was like when you receive a letter from a university or program that you know is either an acceptance or denial and you can't bring yourself to open it, because once you do, you can't unsee the answer.

Since words were failing me, I got up from the table and went to retrieve the pregnancy test. If I couldn't find the words to tell him, I would show him. He was so busy eating he didn't even notice me leave the table; and when I returned and placed the test next to his plate he dropped his fork.

"What...what... WHAT?"

"Yes" was all I could say.

"Oh *my god!*" He leapt from his chair and scooped me up in an embrace so quickly it caught my breath.

I had to see his face before my heart could process what he was feeling. He was happy! He asked me a million questions which included asking how I was feeling. I don't think I ever remember him asking me this simple question before, and that meant *everything* to me in that moment. It was like he was seeing me for the first time through his narcissistic haze. Maybe I had found the magic ingredient to our marriage? Only time would tell for sure.

We told everyone in our family immediately. I knew about the wisdom of keeping news like this to ourselves until the second trimester, but our giddiness was so overwhelming we didn't care. The dynamic in our household changed immediately. David talked nonstop about how much he wanted it to be a girl so he could name her after his mom and how he was going to dress her up in beautiful dresses and she would be his princess. Even though he wasn't gushing about me, I got to enjoy this enthusiasm as the vessel that was carrying and creating his princess. He asked about my eating, worried about my sleeping, and spent more time in any day thinking about me than he had during our entire time together.

It was intoxicating to be on the pedestal where he had placed me, and I was enjoying every minute of this newly found attention. I had a purpose that lifted me to a higher level in the eyes of those around me than I had ever experienced before with my family of origin or within our marriage.

My first "pregnancy appointment" was approaching quickly, so I went to the book store and got *What to Expect When You're Expecting* to learn about where our baby was in their development and to create a list of questions to ask the doctor when I saw him on Monday. My boss at the time had become a dear friend, and we were so excited about the baby that we made a date to go "baby shopping" on Saturday to start dreaming about cribs and rockers and all the new things I would need to get before the baby arrived. I was six and a half weeks along, and I was walking on air.

When I got up that Saturday morning to get showered and dressed for my outing with Christine, I noticed I wasn't dragging as much as I had been in the couple of weeks I had known about the pregnancy. Just the day before, one of the parents at the preschool asked me how I was feeling, and I had exclaimed to her that I didn't feel sick or tired at all. This was going to be a breeze for me, and I was going to have the easiest and most worry-free pregnancy in history! I got into the shower, and as I was washing my hair, I started to feel slight cramping in my abdomen. It wasn't intense at first, and I figured it was just part of the process of my body acclimating to this new state.

After finishing my routine, I went to the bathroom and noticed a hint of red blood in my urine. My mind started swirling about what could be happening, and I went downstairs to call the doctor's office. The cramping had increased by this time, and I was getting really scared! David was at work that morning, so I was alone and had to go through a couple of steps to get ahold of the doctor since it was a weekend and the office wasn't open. I hadn't even met him yet; that was supposed to happen on Monday.

When I finally got a call back from him, I was in tears. The cramping had increased, and I'd had to place a pad in my underwear because I was spotting. I had just gotten on the phone with him when Christine arrived at the house to pick me up. I opened the garage door for her to come in, and all she saw were my tear-streaked cheeks as I tried to relay to the doctor what was happening to me.

"Hello, Mrs. Boudreaux, what is the issue you are having?" His voice was flat and completely detached from the fact that he was talking to a woman who was afraid she was losing her baby.

"Hi, Doctor, I have my first pregnancy appointment with you on Monday, and this morning, I started cramping and spotting. I'm scared!" I felt like I was babbling, and Christine, hearing this for the first time, was standing in the kitchen with a horrified look on her face.

"So you have cramping and bleeding," he asked. "How would you describe the cramping? Is it sharp pain or dull and aching?" He hadn't offered any words of comfort yet; he was all about diagnosis. I described my symptoms to him as best I could between the sobs as my diaphragm spasmed over and over from crying. I wanted to know if I could come into his office right now and get examined. I wanted to know what we were going to do as a team to fix this.

"Well, if you're bleeding and cramping, you are probably losing the baby, and there is nothing I can do about it. You already had an appointment with me on Monday, did you say? Then you can just come in on Monday, and we'll decide if you need to have a D&C[3] or if your body has taken care of it for you. If you are soaking more than three pads in an hour, I want you to go to the emergency room because you might be hemorrhaging. Otherwise, I'll just see you on Monday."

I was dumbstruck! He acted like I was interrupting his golf game and couldn't be bothered to spend any more time with me than it took for him to say "See ya Monday!" I stammered and sputtered trying to ask more questions, but he was not interested in answering any of my concerns.

---

[3] D&C, dilation and curettage, a surgical procedure involving dilatation of the cervix and curettage of the uterus, performed after a miscarriage or for the removal of cysts or tumors.

"I'll see you Monday," I said in almost a whisper and hung up the phone. I took one look into Christine's eyes and fell into a puddle; she caught me in her arms and held me tight. Our worst nightmare was coming true. So many feelings and thoughts were running through my mind that I couldn't even finish one before another would begin. I had to tell David his princess was gone. Would he blame me? Did I blame me? We had to tell the family and friends, coworkers, and neighbors. Now I know why they tell you to wait; it is excruciating to go through a miscarriage *and* have to tell the story over and over again.

When he got home from work that day, he knew something was wrong as soon as he looked into my eyes. I fell into sobs again as the words escaped from my lips, partly from heartache and partly from trepidation of how he would react.

"I lost the baby," I said in a whisper between the tears.

"What do you mean?" he responded. His eyes were wide and disbelieving of what he was hearing me say.

"I started bleeding and cramping this morning, and the doctor said there was nothing we could do. She's gone!" The words were tumbling out now, almost like ripping a Band-Aid off. It hurts less if you do it quickly, right?

He was quiet for a minute then, to his credit, he wrapped his arms around me and held me as I wept. We sat together and rocked for a long while, processing the feeling of immense loss of this little miracle we had gotten so excited about joining our family. My tears were about the loss, but I had been crying all day and had exhausted much of that well. These tears were more about his tenderness and the sense of connection we felt as we mourned the loss of our future with this blessing. I was completely vulnerable at that moment, and I did not allow myself that luxury often, as it was not a safe place to be. I was grateful that at that moment he thought it more important to be with me in this grief rather than blame me for it. The anger may yet come, but for now, he was as close to nurturing me as he had ever been before.

We took on the daunting task of calling everyone together. He called his relatives, and I called mine. It was a harsh lesson in why couples wait to tell, but you never think the worst will happen to you. I still had my first pregnancy appointment on Monday that I had to get through. I was dreading the fact that this appointment had changed from excitement to sadness, and I didn't want to have to tell my story over and over. I called the office first thing in the morning to inform them that I had miscarried over the weekend and to please let everyone know so I didn't have to say it multiple times. The receptionist was very caring and assured me I wouldn't have to say it anymore.

When I arrived at the office, I knew immediately that my preparation had not worked. I went up to the receptionist's window to check in, greeted by a woman with a big smile on her face.

"Good morning," she said with glee in her voice. "Welcome to your first pregnancy appointment!"

I looked at her with a mixture of disbelief and anger. *Really, people? You have got to be kidding me!*

"I am not pregnant anymore," I said in almost a whisper. "I called this morning to tell you all that so I didn't have to go through this!"

"Oh, I'm so sorry. Please forgive me. I will put a note on your chart so you won't have to say it again." She put a yellow sticky note on the front of the folder and wrote in big letters: "Miscarried over weekend."

I stood there for a minute, looking at the words. It feels different to see them in print. She told me to have a seat and that they would be with me in a moment. I sat down and closed my eyes, praying that this would be the end of that story. I just wanted to see the doctor, find out if I had to have a D&C or not, and go home to curl up in my bed.

When they finally called my name, I took a deep breath and followed the nurse back to the station to have my blood pressure checked before going into a room. She held the folder in her hand with the sticky note on the front, and she showed me to a seat for some questions before we go into the room.

"How old will you be when the baby is born?" She rattled off the question with such routine that I knew she hadn't seen the note. She was on automatic pilot, and this plane was going down.

"I'M NOT PREGNANT ANYMORE!" I screamed at her as I slammed my finger into the sticky note on the folder. "I called this morning so that I would specifically not have to go through this. WHAT IS WRONG WITH YOU PEOPLE!"

The color drained out of her face as she read the note I was pointing to as I screamed at her at the top of my lungs. I didn't care who heard me anymore. I was about to lose it right in the middle of the office.

"I'm so sorry. I see that now. Please come with me, and the doctor will be in to see you very soon." She shuffled me into a nearby room and quickly told me that the doctor would be in to see me as soon as possible.

This was my first time meeting this doctor. I had been referred to him from a friend when I found out we were pregnant, and this was to be our "get to know you" visit. I had already had a shitty exchange with him over the phone when he acted as if he couldn't care less about my situation, so I was curious to see if he would now be more empathetic now that I was sitting right in front of him. I had wished that David was with me for the support, but I was now glad he wasn't. As much as I had lost it on the nurses, his reaction would likely have gotten someone arrested. He made me wait for what seemed like forever, but finally, he appeared. This was the moment of truth.

"Good morning," he said as he swept in and took a seat, barely stopping to shake my hand. The sticky note still prominently on the front of the folder he had in his hand. "Tell me about your bleeding. Do you think the miscarriage has run its course?"

Wow! Nope, you're a dick… There is no other way to judge you. He proceeded to tell me that most women miscarry at least once and that it was probably just due to my body not knowing what to do with the pregnancy. He asked me about morning sickness and whatnot, and I told him that I had experienced a little, but that last day it had lifted. He told me that was the moment when my body decided to expel the pregnancy. He talked about it like I had gotten a cold, and now it was clearing up. We talked about how heavy my bleeding was, and he determined that my body had "taken care of it" for me and that a D&C would not be necessary.

"Go home, rest for a couple of days, and you'll be back to yourself soon."

I didn't tell him how horrible my experience had been with him and his staff. I didn't give him feedback about his fucked up bedside manner and how inconsequential I felt in his presence. I simply took myself home and cried for the rest of the day. I didn't know how to stand up to people, especially men, when I felt like I was being violated. I had immense anger about the experience, but I swallowed it and internalized it because I didn't think I was worth the effort to express it. There was a part of me who believed he wouldn't listen or care; partly because he was a man (and I didn't give them much credit for caring) and partly because I was not a person worth listening to. It was a double-edged sword that cut me coming and going.

Presence

In the stillness,
presence is.

In the quiet,
I am source.

I am the space
around the matter.
I am the whispers
between the molecules.

Breathe and know
that being still
is moving at the speed of light.

In the heart space,
where time isn't counted
and love surrounds your cells,
softening the walls
to allow the healing to penetrate.

I will presence you
with my eyes
as I stare deep into your soul,
as I hear your stories,
and feel your sorrow and joy.

You cannot become
what you already are.
You can only remember
and welcome that long lost friend
over your threshold
to your warm embrace.

Mend the wounds of this earth,
not by drugs and time,
but by love and forgiveness.

Know you are not of this body.
Know you are of the greater energy
that is connected to all others.

I am you.
You are me.
We are one
in the continuous presence
of the divine.

Chapter 13

It was my routine to put my purse and papers down on my desk and move through the school to check in with the teachers before I started any work. I found if I sat down at my desk and started the work of my day, it would be lunch time before I laid eyes on the teachers or their kids. As I ambled down the hallway with my belly fully obscuring the view of my feet, I had to chuckle to myself. I had always been a thin person, so this experience of being 33 weeks pregnant, with all the challenges that come with it, was comical at times. Sneakers were no longer an option, because I couldn't reach down far enough to tie them. I no longer helped the teachers pick up their rooms, since getting down on the floor often meant not getting back up. Still, I was thrilled to be pregnant. The pregnancy had been textbook all throughout, which I felt blessed to have experienced after miscarrying a year and a half ago. Lately, I had noticed my ankles and hands were swelling, and I got incredibly tired doing daily routine activities that had not bothered me to this point. Just one lap around the school left me tapped out, and I was grateful for the excuse to sit down to recover.

After the miscarriage, I wanted to get pregnant again immediately! I wanted to recapture the bliss I had felt within my soul and within my marriage as soon as possible—but life had other plans. David tended to a homeless man who had fallen in the parking lot of the Boulder Detox Center and had gotten a head wound, without wearing gloves. His hands had small cuts and scrapes on them from doing yard work the weekend before, and with the amount of bleeding you get with a head wound, his hands were covered in the man's blood. When they transported the gentleman to the hospital, they advised David that he had been exposed to possible Hepatitis C and/or HIV and would be informed once testing was done on the man he helped from the hospital. Unfortunately, the gentleman left the hospital AMA (against medical advice) without getting the blood work done, which left us guessing about David's status. The hospital advised him, per protocol: no sexual contact until he tested negative. Getting pregnant again was not going to happen, at least not for six months.

When he was finally cleared, we were ready to start trying again. We got pregnant pretty quickly, and the pregnancy so far had been really easy. I had some morning sickness in the beginning, and I actually welcomed it, remembering what that horrible doctor said to me on the phone that day. I knew the more pregnant I felt, the better chance of it staying viable. I hated feeling nauseous, but for this I was willing to deal with it. I decided I was *not* going back to the same ob-gyn after my last experience. I didn't have the courage to tell him how horrible he was to his face, but I wrote a very strongly worded letter to him expressing all my feelings when I requested my records to be transferred to my new doctor. I never got the closure I wanted, but it felt good to write down how he made me feel and to implore him to treat his patients better. I have no idea if it made any impact on him, but I felt like I had done my part. For obvious reasons, I chose a woman doctor next and had a much better experience with her. She was caring and compassionate from our first meeting, and I knew I was in good hands for this pregnancy.

I had enjoyed shopping for baby stuff, eating anything I wanted and basking in the glow of impending motherhood. David had been so excited when we first found out, as he was the first time, and even after our horrible experience he *still* wanted to tell everyone instead of waiting. I told him he could tell people if he absolutely had to, but *he* would be on the hook to call them if something went wrong. I wasn't going to go through that again. In the beginning, I enjoyed him doting on me and taking care of some of the chores around the house that I normally handled. Over time, his enthusiasm waned, and we settled back into our old routine, but now he added his little comments about what I couldn't do (now that I was fat) or made fun of the changes that were happening to my body as my belly grew.

On this day as I moved through the school routine, I couldn't shake the fatigue. I sat down more than I stood up, and nothing I did helped me feel more energetic. I figured it was just what happens at this stage in pregnancy and really didn't give it any more thought. We had an infant room in our school and were blessed to have an RN working in the baby room named Melissa who was always open to answering any medical questions we had throughout the day. Every day I couldn't believe my luck that I was the director of a preschool with a baby room and a full-time RN, where I could bring my baby when I decided to go back to work.

Toward the end of the day, when Melissa was cleaning up the baby room to close for the day, I wandered in to ask her a question. I told her about the fatigue I was feeling, and she looked at my hands and ankles. She kept her voice very calm and asked me to do a simple thing.

"When you are on your way home, I want you to stop by the drugstore near your house and take your blood pressure with that machine that is over by the pharmacy. Then I want you to call me and tell me what the numbers are, okay?"

That sounded like an easy thing to do, so I did. When I called her and reported my numbers, she responded in the same calm voice, "I want you to hang up with me and call your doctor immediately. Don't get flustered. Just do it now, okay?"

I moved so quickly I didn't give myself a lot of time to worry. I was in the parking lot of the drug store and called the doctor right away. They got me on the phone with my doctor, and as soon as I told her my numbers, she echoed Melissa's concerns.

"Okay, Dee, I need you to meet me at the hospital. Your blood pressure is high, and I need to monitor you and the baby for a couple of hours to see if it goes down while you rest. Can you meet me?"

"Can I go home and get my husband?" My heart rate was starting to climb, and I was just a few minutes from the house.

"Sure, but come straight in after you get him. I'll see you soon."

I pulled into the driveway and moved as quickly as I could into the house. His car was parked outside, and I was relieved that he was home. As I came into the house, I found him on the couch, watching TV.

"I don't want you to freak out, but my blood pressure is too high, and the doctor wants me to come into the hospital to be monitored." I didn't even say hi before I started relating the situation to him.

"How long are you gonna have to be there?" he asked, barely looking up from the TV.

"I don't know, maybe a few hours."

He didn't respond right away, and I knew what was happening. He didn't want to go. I was scared, and I wanted him to go with me. But more importantly, I wanted him to *want* to go with me. I felt myself start to crumble.

"You know, it's fine. I'll just go, and I'll either let you know what they find out, or I'll call you if I have to stay. You've had a long day, and there is no sense in both of us being stuck at the hospital for God knows how long."

I was talking really fast now. It was like his excuses were being fed to my brain and coming out of my mouth like a ventriloquist manipulates their puppet. When I finished, he looked up at me and said, "If that's what you want. Sounds good to me. Drive safe."

I turned slowly and headed back to the car. I don't remember driving to the hospital. The next thing I knew, I was in a hospital room with a heart monitor strapped to my belly. The nurse instructed me to lie as quietly as I could to see if my blood pressure responded to rest and left me alone with the TV remote in my hand. I lay there for quite some time, staring out the window as the sun began to set.

Why didn't he want to come with me? Why didn't I insist he come? The committee was getting louder and louder with each passing minute, waiting for someone to come back and check on me. I wanted someone to comfort me so much, but I didn't know who I could call. I began to think about calling Mom, but I didn't want to lead the conversation with "I am at the hospital alone because David couldn't get off the couch to take me in." I devised a reason to call, telling her the doctor needed to know if there was any family history of high blood pressure during pregnancy. When I dialed the phone number of my childhood, I was saying my opening line over and over in my head. Mom was two hours ahead of me, and I expected she would still be awake.

When she answered the phone with her signature greeting "Nyell-ow," I tried desperately not to burst into tears. Just hearing her voice brought the enormity of this moment crashing down on me and the depth of my solitude was palpable. She asked me where David was but didn't linger on that point. She seemed to intuit my sadness and didn't want to contribute to the situation. We stayed on the phone until the doctor came in to tell me I could go home. I was so relieved to have someone with me during such a scary experience.

It turned out that my blood pressure was high, but responded to rest. There was talk of bed rest, but I didn't want to start using my vacation and sick pay this early because that had to get us through after the baby was born. I pleaded with the doctor to let me keep working and she agreed, but only if I sat with my feet up as much as possible and took my blood pressure every couple of hours. Having an RN in the school was a benefit, as I knew Melissa would be there to help if I needed it. I tried to settle into a new normal at work of resting as much as possible and taking better care of myself. The teachers were super helpful, but at home, it was business as usual.

David didn't appreciate the doctor's concerns and pushed back every time I suggested I needed to rest and put my feet up. He needled me every day about how "I didn't look sick" and even suggested I was milking it for attention. I got tired of saying the same explanation over and over and stopped telling him when I needed to rest. On Sunday, August 31, 1997, I got tired of staring at the box that contained the baby's crib and decided if I paced myself, I could put it together. I had asked David to do it over and over, but he was full of excuses. I felt like time was running out, now that I had a condition that could mean the baby could come earlier than expected if it moved into pre-eclampsia. As I worked up in the nursery to put the crib together, slowly to avoid overexerting myself, a breaking news report came over the television: *Princess Diana has been in a fatal car crash.* I remember screwing the crib together, trying to read the instructions through my tears.

When I think back to situations like these, I feel a sense of embarrassment. The imbalance of power is so clear in hindsight, and I would hope I would not put up with the behavior and choices he made during that time if it were happening today. This particular story is a culmination of years of destruction of my sense of self-esteem and my understanding of where I stopped and he started. I did not have a clear sense of how I should have been treated, and ultimately, I did not think I deserved any better. He had convinced me that I was not worthy of care and concern and that asking him to rise to any occasion was selfish and heartless of me. If he tried to tell me when he met me that I was unworthy of love and care, I would have sent him packing. Being with a person who destroys your sense of self is a slow grooming process. It happens bit by little bit, and before you know it, you have such little understanding of your worth that you accept every guilt trip, every insult, and every abusive act while making more excuses for his behavior than he ever has to offer.

All throughout the pregnancy, David reminded me that he was not going to be present for the birth. He went to Lamaze classes with me, but he wasn't going to be there. He toured the birthing center with me, but he wasn't going to be there. Every step of the way, I was reminded that I was on my own and that his discomfort with seeing "all the gross stuff" was more important than me having support as I brought his baby into the world. His disconnection to the event was a foreshadowing of his role as father. I think a lot of his push-back was linked to his opinion about his abilities as a father. It was clear he didn't think he would be good at it. We talked about his role in parenting, and he was vocal about being unavailable for getting up in the middle of the night for feedings, that discipline would be all my doing, and I could forget about him changing any shitty diapers. As a preschool teacher, I was skilled at doing any and all these things, so I didn't get upset about his lack of participation, but it did bother me that he wasn't willing to be a part of the raising of his child. He wanted the bragging rights without any of the work.

We both wanted to know the gender of the baby as early as possible. After growing up in a house full of girls with a family that was largely made up of estrogen, I wanted a girl because I had no idea of how to raise a boy. I felt comfortable with the developmental stages of a girl and thought that would be the best fit if I was going to be shouldering the bulk of the responsibility. David wanted a girl from the start because he wanted to name her after his beloved (yet abusive) mother and have his little princess to spoil. We both went to the twenty-week appointment (it was one of the few he attended) to learn the gender of the baby. When she gave us a clear "butt view" where it was obvious no penis was present, we danced in the room together because we both got our wish! We had been calling her Peanut up to this point, but now she was Mimi.

*****

I had been following the doctor's rules while still being at work. I put my feet up anytime I was sitting down (which needed to be most of the time) and I bought a blood pressure cuff so I could monitor my numbers regularly throughout the day. It became very difficult to keep myself sitting down and not being able to get involved directly with the kids was hard. I was a hands-on preschool director who had now been sidelined. But this was the only way I could continue to work, and I didn't want to take any time off before the baby so I could have all my leave time for after she was born. Plus, I had Melissa in the baby room to help monitor me and keep me in balance.

Ironically, work was the place I got the most rest. When I came home, I was expected to still manage the housework, and we were still getting the nursery ready for Mimi's arrival. David was not open to hearing my explanation, yet again, about why I couldn't do this or that around the house. Even the words "doctor's orders" had no impact on him. He was convinced it was all in my head and that I was just making excuses to get out of doing my "chores." I had been managing my high blood pressure for about four weeks so far and was just trying to get as close to forty weeks as I could before Mimi made her appearance.

Mom wanted to be present for the birth of her first grandchild, which touched my heart. She was excited to be there and witness this experience, especially since she had been anesthetized for two out of three of her own childbirth experiences. I came into the world in a drugged stupor and had to be woken up for the first few days of feeding due to the amount of anesthesia that was in my system. They have perfected the system with epidurals so that the baby doesn't experience the anesthesia unless absolutely necessary, but that was not the case back then. As a result, Mom had no real recollection of the births of her children, and really wanted to be in the room for the birth of her first grandchild. We had been back-and-forth about when she would come out to Colorado, trying our best to guess when the best time would be so that she wouldn't miss anything. When the doctor put me on bed rest at 36 ½ weeks, I told her to get on a plane. I was going to need the extra support. David was not going to handle me not being able to do anything. Plus, my blood pressure issues were worsening, so the baby could come at any time. She was with me for the week of my trying to maintain the "bed rest" requirements, playing a lot of card games and watching a lot of TV. I had gotten the nursery ready before this directive, which gave me such a sense of relief. Now all I had to do was wait, but even that was anxiety producing. My use of my leave time had started as soon as the doctor said the words "bed rest" and now all I could think about was the fact that I was using my paid time to sit on the couch. That meant I would have to go back to work after she was born that much sooner. I knew she needed to cook as long as possible, but I really wished she would just get the show on the road so I wouldn't use too much of my paid time waiting.

One day, I had gotten up and showered (thank goodness) and spent most of the day lying on the couch in the only position I could find that was comfortable, but I didn't feel well. I'd been checking my BP all day, and it had steadily gone up all throughout the afternoon. It finally got to a level that concerned me, so around 4:00 p.m. I called my doctor's office to check in and see if they would have the same concern I did. As soon as I told them my numbers, they said, "We'll see you soon." I took my bag that I had packed for the hospital with me, since we didn't know if we would be coming home pregnant or with a baby in tow. Mom drove me to the hospital, and David told us to call him when we knew what was happening. He was not going to be bothered until he knew it wasn't a false alarm.

When we got to the hospital they took me back to an exam room and hooked me up to an automatic blood pressure cuff and a baby heart rate monitor. I had strict instructions to lay still and quiet for an hour to see if complete rest caused the numbers to change at all. The room was cold, and I had a million thoughts running through my mind.

I might meet my little one soon.

I might have complications that might cause me to have an emergency C-section.

I might be sent home to sit on the couch for another week.

Mom tried to make small talk, but we both knew we might be getting close, and the anticipation was palpable. It was important for me to stay calm, but inside I was anything but calm. On the outside I was joking, sounding more like a stand-up comedian than a pregnant woman about to become a mom for the first time. I made some of my best jokes when I was sick, hurt, or nervous. I always had.

After an hour of waiting, the nurse came into the room and said, "I'm glad it looks like you've showered today, because it's time to have a *baby!*" It was 5:00 p.m., and I had not slept since the night before. I was wishing I had taken that nap Mom and I had talked about earlier that day. They unhooked all my monitors and sent us to the birthing wing of the hospital. After getting settled into the sexy hospital gown and all the monitors they wanted for me and the baby, I called David to let him know we were on the launch pad.

"Hey, just wanted you to know they've decided she needs to come today. So I am admitted, and they are going to start labor soon."

"Oh my god!" he said, screaming into the phone. "I'll be right there!"

I heard screeching then the phone disconnected. I learned later that when he came bursting into the room, he had done a U-turn where one wasn't allowed and had broken all kinds of laws to get to the hospital. I was touched by his enthusiasm. For a guy who *swore* he wouldn't be in the room for the birth, he was so excited he almost crashed several times getting there.

Once I got in the room and hooked up to all the monitors, things happened pretty fast. They applied Prostaglandin on my cervix, a medication to induce contractions. The plan was to start an intravenous drip of Pitocin to complete the medication needed, but my body seemed to be ready to go! The Prostaglandin was all that was needed. My contractions got intense very quickly, and I was making good use of all the breathing techniques I learned in our Lamaze classes. Mom was engaged in helping me focus on my breathing and giving me encouraging words. David was stationed in the corner of the room. I actually don't really remember talking to him at all. I had never felt that kind of pain before, and I knew this was just the beginning.

About a month before this exciting day, I had begun to have pain in my sciatic nerve that ran down my right leg. The doctor determined that Mimi had moved down enough and had put the piriformis muscle (which encases the sciatic nerve) into spasm, essentially squeezing the nerve causing enough pain that I couldn't sleep more than 4 or 5 hours at a time without it waking me up. It was one of the conditions I was looking forward to being over after her birth, but now it was in full force. Not only did I have the contraction pain, which was so fast and furious that I thought I was being turned inside out, but my right hip felt like someone was stabbing it with a hot ice pick.

I hadn't been feeling the contractions for more than an hour or so when I began begging for an epidural. I had no intentions of doing this the natural way and was ready for the relief I had been promised by an epidural as soon as I could get it. I remember in the classes when they explained what the process was for receiving an epidural, that I would have to bend myself into a fetal position (easier said than done with a basketball in your abdomen) and lay perfectly still as the anesthesiologist put a needle into my spine to administer the nerve block. I was laughing, thinking there was no way I was going to be able to do that. But now, as the pain of these contractions were coming so quickly, sometimes with two peaks before I got a break, I was asking everyone with scrubs on that came into the room when I was going to get the epidural. The nurses were concerned at one point that I might have placenta previa, a separation of the placenta from the uterine wall, which could explain why I was having such intense contractions so early on with very little break. Everyone agreed getting the epidural on board as fast as possible would be the right course for me and for those around me who were concerned about my situation. I could have kissed that anesthesiologist when he came into the room, and I had no trouble lying as still as possible even knowing he was inserting a needle into my spine. It is amazing how your focus changes when you have bigger fish to fry.

The epidural did give some relief to the contractions, which was welcome by me and all those in the room, but it never covered the sciatic nerve in my right hip. As a result, I felt every contraction in my hip and got no sleep that night. I could hear David snoring in the chair over by the window, but I had to breathe through every spike on the monitor, and all I could think about was how I was going to be so tired by the time I was ready to push that I wouldn't be able to get her out. What would happen if I couldn't push? It was decided a second epidural would be given to try to give some relief to the hip, but relief was nowhere to be found. I would just have to tough it out and try my best to rest when I could.

I lay in the dark room, with David and Mom snoring in their respective chairs, and I felt so alone. I was scared to know what the morning would bring, and I was weary of being in such pain. I was swirling in a world of unknowns, and even those who were there to help me through it didn't offer the comfort of knowledge and wisdom to ease my fears. Childbirth is such an enigma of an experience. I read all the books and watched the movies and made a birth plan, and *still* all that went out the window when the ride began. I had the framework of what the experience would be like, but no one could tell me about how it was all going to go down. I was on a roller coaster with a blindfold on, and I had no idea what the next hill and drop would look like until I felt it in the core of my being. I held such resentment toward David for sleeping, and tried to wake him up a couple of times by moaning so loud I was sure he would stir. His deep restful slumber only served to infuriate me. He was in the room, but I was still going through this alone. Somehow feeling like I was doing something by myself when there was a "partner" near me who was supposed to also be involved, but wasn't, just served to increase the loneliness. I found myself wondering if I would be less resentful if he wasn't there like he had always promised. This was a pattern that I was no aware of yet, but would factor in when the real parenting began.

The next morning, when David and Mom woke up to the bustle of the morning shift nurses taking vitals and helping me find a comfortable position, they learned we were no closer to meeting our little one and that I had not slept. As the morning went on, the doctor decided to break my water since that had not happened yet. She was hoping that in doing so, my body would progress naturally and we could encourage this process along to a conclusion. About 11:00 a.m., I started to get the urge to push, and we were off to the races! The problem was the normal position for a woman's knees during the pushing phase were up by her ears, but I couldn't bear the pain of that on my right side. All the nurses knew to leave my right leg alone as we tried to make this part of the process as productive as possible. It seemed every time I went into a push, the blood pressure cuff on my arm inflated rendering my arm useless; it was going to be a long day!

At some point, when we were well into hour two of pushing, we had a shift change with the nurses. I had just sat up in the bed to push when a young new nurse walked in the room. She assessed the situation and ran to my bedside grabbing my right leg and jacking it up to my ear as you do to help a mother push. No one had given her the memo. As she grabbed my right foot and pulled it back to my ear, I let out a scream loud enough for them to hear on the sidewalk outside!

I reached over to her perfect blond ponytail and grabbed it, pulling her head backward to my face and screamed, "DON'T DO THAT!"

She looked up at me in horror and began apologizing profusely, "I'm sorry, I'm sorry, I'm sorry. Please let go, let go, *let go*!" I released my death grip on her hair, and she ran out of the room in tears. I never saw her again.

At the end of three hours of pushing, I had alienated about everyone in the room. In between pushes, Mom was at my bedside, offering what she thought was encouraging words, "You're doing great! Keep it up!"

I finally said in my best Linda Blair impression, "You can *count*! That is all you can do! I don't want to hear your voice unless there are *numbers* coming out!" I wasn't doing great, and I knew it. Pushing should last just a short time, not three hours. There are many theories about why it took so long, but I couldn't hear her say I was doing well anymore because I knew it wasn't true.

In the end, it took the use of a "baby vacuum" to get her out, but she arrived! She had one hell of a cone-shaped head from the vacuum, but she was here! Ten fingers, ten toes, and a great set of lungs on her! They say you forget the pain of childbirth as soon as you lay eyes on your miracle—well, I exclaimed pretty early on that I was never going through that again, and I meant it!

She was born at 2:06 p.m., 21 ½ hours after admission to the hospital, at 6 lbs., 8 oz., and 19 ½ in. long with a 13 ¼ cm head. No wonder I couldn't get this child out! When they laid her on my chest and I got to look at her the first time, I looked up to realize that David had stayed in the room the whole time.

Mothers and Daughters

The universe
gave me a soul
to nourish and house,
sharing blood and energy
through the cord of life
for 388,800 minutes.

When did our breath
become plural?
Was it when you
inflated your lungs
for the first time?

Or has it ever become
a divided enterprise?
Have we ever inhaled
to the beat of our own hearts?

I felt disconnected early,
not knowing how
to surrender
to the grip
your love
had on my soul.

We can't recognize
the imprint
when remembering
the love of our mother
doesn't manifest in
hugs and
comfort and
peace.

I judge myself
for not believing
that I deserved you,
repeating the pattern
handed down from all the mothers
that came before me.

A lineage of estrogen
wrapped in pain and abuse
that hindered the connections
we each felt
to the previous,
degrading the possibilities
of breaking the cycle
for one more generation.

When my mirror became
the eyes of my daughter
and all I could see
were the incomplete visions
of a life not well lived,

every day became a chance
to let go of the shadows
of the past,
to allow for sunshine
to disinfect the soul.

I do the work now
so my second heart
can beat with her second heart,
blending the rhythms
in love.

Life continues to give
new chances for wisdom
to infuse and heal.

I hope you try, my love,
and I hope I have done enough
to strengthen your journey
and teach you that

you are love,
you are worthy,
you are complete.

Because when you meet
your second heart
and she stares into your eyes,
looking for recognition,

I hope you will be able
to see and feel
the threads of time
and say to her
with love

"Thanks for coming.
I got you."

Chapter 14

Taking care of a child was something I knew how to do. Many new mothers struggle with how to change a diaper, *when* to change a diaper, how to hold the baby, and how to dress the baby without breaking them; but I had been doing all these things for years. I was an "expert" on caring for other people's children. I even knew how to take notes about the various caregiving activities throughout the day to keep track of feedings and changings. My instinct and training kicked in immediately, and I was even cocky enough to blow off the nurse who wanted to give me the 411 on how to change my first diaper. I laughed and told her to give Dad a step-by-step lesson, but I had this. I wasn't sure about the breastfeeding part, but I got lucky with a child who latched on well right away, so even that went smoothly, even though it was new to me. The outfit we had brought for her to wear on the journey home was huge on her, and David made jokes about how I couldn't choose her size right. I was confident in my abilities, but I was not confident *he* believed I could handle it. We said goodbye and thank you to all the nurses on the hall and headed for the car—with a family of three instead of two. As David drove us home, I remember looking out the window and realizing that this was different than caring for other people's children. I didn't have to ask anyone's advice before I decided about her care, and I didn't get to send her home with someone else. They let me take her home. What were they thinking?

One of the exciting things I had learned after finding Mimi's pediatrician was that there was a renowned author in the practice. His name was Dr. Ronald Bucknam, and he had co-written a book with Gary Ezzo called *On Becoming Babywise*. It was a best-selling book on how to establish schedules for your infant to allow for a more regulated and predictable flow for the household. I had seen the benefits of babies who were on a schedule for feeding and sleeping versus those who weren't, so I determined early on that I was a schedule-type of Mom. It made sense to me to help the baby establish a rhythm of eating and sleeping that would not only help her adjust to life outside the womb, but would allow Mom to get some much-needed sleep in the early weeks and months. In the first couple of weeks, Mimi's sleep schedule was flipped. She wanted to sleep all day and be up a good bit at night. This book, and the suggestions inside, were helpful in getting that schedule reversed quickly, allowing for a better flow for her and for us as we settled into our new normal.

We had a bassinet at the foot of our bed that we intended her to sleep in for as long as she was willing, and it worked for us all. I did not believe in cosleeping, and David was afraid he would roll over on her and kill her by accident, so that was never under consideration. The first week, I would put her down in her bassinet swaddled in an expert burrito (if I do say so myself), but we saw early we were going to have some issues. Every time I rolled over in our bed, she woke up. If I started snoring, she woke up. If I got up to go to the bathroom during the night, she woke up. With each peep that came out of her, I was up immediately to scoop her up and get her out of the room before she woke David up. He had told me numerous times he had to be at work in the morning, unlike me, and needed his sleep. I knew the dangers of establishing patterns of picking up a baby every time they whimpered, but I didn't see an alternative. In less than a week, I decided she needed to sleep in her room to allow her the chance to get consistent sleep and for me to get some relief from trying so desperately to keep him from getting woken up. If she cried in her room, I could turn the monitor down as low as possible and sleep with it next to my ear so that I could hear her and he couldn't. She wasn't waking up in response to my movements anymore, but she still wasn't sleeping well. I knew babies were intermittent sleepers, especially early on when feeding was every three hours, but there seemed to be something else going on. She slept so beautifully in the swing or in her car seat all squished up like she was in utero, but she did not like to lay flat in her crib. About week three, I had the idea to try something. When it was time to put her down to sleep for the night, I put her in her car seat, and put the car seat in her crib. She was in what I called the "rutabaga stage" where all she did was eat, sleep, and poop, and movement was very limited. If she liked being all squished in her car seat, why not for the night? She was in her crib, safe and secure. It was worth a try.

It worked beautifully and from that moment on, she only ever woke me up once a night to feed. I thought I was *brilliant*, and everyone was getting better sleep. I still learned early on that I could not go into her room to check on her without waking her up. She would be in a dead sleep, and if I walked in, no matter how stealthy I was (and I could be super stealthy), she would pop her eyes open as soon as my energy entered the room. This would not change until she became a teenager and slept like the dead. I even went to check on her at preschool during naptime, and as I was standing outside the classroom watching her sleep from the window, she popped her eyes open and sat up on her cot to stare right at me! We had a connection that was obvious very early on, and I had to trust the monitor to know how she was doing because I could not go into her room for even the quickest peek.

The "unknown" for me when it came to being a new parent was how I would feel as a mom. I had heard women say throughout all my years as a preschool director "I can't imagine my life before I had my little Susie" or "I would jump in front of a bus for my child!" These platitudes seemed logical when I heard them in passing, and I eagerly awaited those feelings in me as I watched her sleep in her bouncy seat, but they didn't seem to arrive. I knew how to go through the movements of the day, making sure she was fed and clothed with a clean diaper, but I didn't feel *connected* to her like I heard the other moms relay. I didn't feel this overwhelming sense of "Oh my god! I didn't start *breathing* until she came into the world!" And I judged myself harshly for it.

What was wrong with me? Was I some monster Mom that would never feel a deep connection to my child? I knew how to *do* parenting—but I didn't know how to *feel* parenting. She was this beautiful little human who looked exactly like her father with big beautiful blue eyes and a smile that lit up the room, so why didn't I feel the way these other mothers described?

I went through the motions of caregiving with little fuss from myself, but David had a lot to learn. He was thankful for my knowledge because that meant we weren't both struggling to learn the basics at the same time, but I also felt a level of resentment from him. I wasn't sure if it was because I knew more than he did about something or if the *not knowing* made him feel more inadequate. I remember feeling a level of confidence that I rarely felt in our relationship. I knew how to change diapers, feed a baby, recognize developmental milestones, identify her cries, and move fairly quickly to address them, and I could do all this with seemingly little effort. There wasn't any other avenue in my life through which I could move with such confidence, and he bristled at the "new me" he was experiencing. Out loud he gave me props for knowing what I knew, even exclaiming more than once, "I'm happy you know how to do this shit, 'cause otherwise she'd be dead by now if it were left up to me!" He, of course, was not suggesting he would harm her intentionally. It was a backhanded compliment that I took to mean that he would be lost without me, which I ate up like a starving person standing at the edge of a buffet with an empty plate in my hand. It was an ego stroke that I rarely got from him but felt *so good* when it came. The mechanics of caregiving for an infant were easy, but there were patterns percolating in me that motherhood had unleashed that I was unprepared for.

I had never liked horror movies. I watched *Poltergeist* when I was a kid, and I think I tried to get through *Nightmare on Elm Street* at one point because Mary liked to watch horror movies, and I wanted her to think I was cool, but I just couldn't handle the gore. I had never shared with anyone that I had my own horror film going on in my head on a regular basis. Not only were my dreams vivid and often full of horror, but I had what I thought of as a horror film going on in the background even during my waking hours. In today's language, it was like an app that never closed out, and every once in a while, it would notify me that it was still running. It did this by showing me snapshot images of horrific scenes at completely random times. Many of them were recurring, and I don't remember them having anything directly to do with the people or circumstances that were around me at the time.

One of the most prevalent was the image of a disconnected hand holding up and stretching the eyelid of someone else to reveal as much of the eyeball as possible, and then branding that eyeball with a branding iron. I don't recall ever knowing the identity of the brander or the brandee, but it was an image that would show up in my head causing me to catch my breath and pull back as if the branding iron was coming for me. These flashes had been happening for as long as I could remember; they were as much a part of me as a memory might be of a childhood experience that pops into your head because you smelled a familiar smell or someone said a name or a word that sparked the memory. I don't recall being aware of the person receiving the pain being me, but the flashes seemed to be in the "first person," which would suggest I was the recipient. I didn't need to see movies that offered more horrific images to put into my memory bank, so I steered clear of them—I had enough of that going on all by myself.

When Mimi came into the world, the flashes shifted. I was no longer imagining someone (possibly me) being hurt. Now the flashes were more along the lines of "I wonder what would happen if…" and they usually concluded with something being done to Mimi.

What would happen if I dropped her while walking down the stairs?

What would happen if I let go while she was getting a bath?

I've never talked to a professional about this phenomenon, but I am pretty sure it came from the anxiety I felt as a new mother. Even with all the confidence I felt with my ability to care for her basic needs, I was now in charge of raising a human, and deep down, I wasn't sure if I was qualified for the task.

One of the first flashes came when I was walking down the stairs in our home. Mimi was in her "bouncy seat" taking a nap, and I was moving about the house doing chores, taking advantage of the quiet. Halfway down the stairs, it entered my brain. I wondered what would happen if I was walking down the stairs with her in my arms, and I dropped her. I could see her swaddled body leave my arms and fall to the stairs, bounding all the way down to the floor below. I don't recall whether that drop would be intentional or accidental, but it scared me just as much either way.

I froze immediately, in midstep, and was overcome with a feeling of nausea and terror. I hadn't had one of these horror flashes in quite a while, and this was the first that included my new human. When it had passed, I went to the couch and sat staring at the backyard for the longest time. The fact that they now included Mimi heightened my sense of repulsion and fear. What if I was even more of a monster than I thought? Not only was I having trouble connecting with this little person, but I was now having flashes of hurting her.

After a time, I realized that all the years I had been having the flashes about branding someone's eyeball, I had never done it. Having these visual experiences didn't mean I would act on them. I slowly felt my heart rate return to normal, and I decided that this was going to be my new normal; as long as I didn't act on it, everything would be okay.

I suppose this might be considered a "normal" state for those of us who have lived through, or grew up in, trauma—this idea that I would be continually processing something and trying not to act on it. When I was drinking, I was less aware of what was going on, to the point of not really knowing there were any "apps" running in the background. This is likely what drew me to "checking out" at the level that I did. The level of disconnect from the discomfort was easier to attain through alcohol. Now that I was sober, my "checking out" behavior was codependency. If I was focused on someone else, I didn't have to concentrate on what was going on behind the scenes in my own psyche. Having a child filled this compulsion beautifully. Now it was my *job* to focus on someone else's needs 24/7. I was responsible for her care every moment of the day, which allowed me to get swallowed by that compulsion without feeling guilty about it.

When Mimi was eleven weeks old, we decided to go back to my hometown in North Carolina, to introduce her to more of the family. I was still on maternity leave, and the doctor said she could fly on an airplane as long as she was old enough to get her first shots, which were at ten weeks. Flying was easy as she was not a fussy child and making sure she had a passy in her mouth during takeoff and landing was enough to keep her ears comfortable. David was going to come for a short time but had to work, so we flew out by ourselves and he would come later.

It was an interesting time being back in that town, as I had only been there a time or two since confronting Dad about the abuse and it held many demons for me. I didn't leave the house that often because I was worried about running into him and I certainly didn't want him to meet Mimi. Dad was remarried and was still working at the private school we all attended, which meant I couldn't go there to visit and reminisce, but that was a small price to pay for the comfort of knowing I wouldn't see him. I had decided early on that he was not going to be in Mimi's life, and I didn't even want him to lay eyes on her. He had chosen to walk out of my life that day sitting in Susan's living room, which meant he was not going to have the pleasure of knowing his first grandchild. Anytime I thought of him, my "mama bear" would surface, and I knew I would do serious harm to him if I ever thought he had access to her.

There was another new phenomenon that manifested being in Mom's house with her first grandchild. We now had two mothers in the same space. This was not completely foreign territory, as I had watched Mom encroach on other mother's space all my years growing up. In any public space, she had never hesitated to express her opinion about the behavior of other people's children, and we were always horrified at how she took it upon herself to parent children who did not belong to her. I don't know why it didn't occur to me that this might be an issue for us, but it still blindsided me when her lack of parenting boundaries reared its ugly head. She had opinions about how I dressed her, fed her, and how I put her down to sleep.

Our first big showdown was in the kitchen one day after I had put Mimi down for her nap.

"I noticed you are putting her to sleep in her car seat," she said in that tone that lets you know she has already formed a judgment about the very behavior she is questioning. It's not so much a question as it is an accusation.

"Yes, I realized she sleeps better being all squished up, and since she isn't moving around yet, she's perfectly safe," I said, realizing the trap I was walking into as the explanation began to spill out of my mouth.

"You know she's going to have a flat head in the back, and when she grows up, she won't have any friends. You need to get one of those straps from the doctor to reform her head. Otherwise, she will be permanently deformed."

I stopped spreading the peanut butter on the sandwich I was making and felt the fire erupt in my belly like a volcano.

"Do you realize what you just said!" I asked in a louder tone than expected. "What the *hell* do you think you are talking about? Who do you think you *are*?"

And the showdown began. Insults were flying, and before we knew it, we were arguing about all the judgments she had about my parenting style that she had been storing up since we arrived.

After some back and forth, she finally looked at me and said, "Well, I guess you could grow her hair long to cover up her mis-shapen head," and she walked out of the room.

This was going to be one of the toughest periods in our history as mother and daughter. As a person, Mom had no natural boundaries. They were never taught to her when she was growing up, and she never taught them to us. She did not know how to be in this kind of relationship with me where she was not the primary parent. She did not know how to watch from the sidelines and not offer suggestions, either directly or indirectly, as she watched me navigate these waters.

In the early days when Mimi was an infant, she would spend most of her time criticizing and judging my parenting choices. When Mimi became a toddler, she would jump in and call Mimi down for behaviors with me sitting right there. At the time, I would get so aggravated by *her* behavior that I could only be around her in small doses. In hindsight, I think she was reacting to an enormous level of anxiety that came from the lack of control she felt she had over the situation.

When Mom was growing up, children were to be seen and not heard. When I was growing up, she tried to change this assumption in her parenting, but when push came to shove, it was her default position. Now that she was watching one of her children parent their own child, she had even less if not *zero* control over what was happening in front of her, and it left her in a place that she did not like to be.

David was dealing with his own shadows when it came to parenting. I realized early on that on many levels I was grateful I did not have to navigate a relationship with his mother. She had passed in 1983, and I had always had a feeling that she and I would have struggled to have a meaningful relationship, given how much she worshipped her baby boy! I could only imagine how parenting her grandchild might have been, but I think she and I would have clashed on technique and philosophy.

David's stories about her parenting style left no question in my mind that she was an abusive parent whose undiagnosed and untreated mood swings manifested in very unpredictable boundaries. My concrete awareness of this history was solidified when we attended the funeral of David's father's third wife. It was the first time I had met all the siblings (after I learned the truth about David's family life), and we gathered in the kitchen of their dad's house after the service. While we had just buried their stepmother, the conversation quickly turned to Mimi (their mom's nickname), and the stories came tumbling out.

"Do you remember that time," David started to say, "when I had just gotten my report card and I was afraid to show Mom because I knew she was gonna be pissed about the one C I had in history? We were driving home after school, and she asked me to see the report card because she knew we were getting them that day. I showed her the card, and she started yelling at me so loudly she ran the car off the road and into a ditch! I didn't have my seat belt on, so I hit my head on the dashboard. After the car stopped, she realized she had gotten a run in her stockings when she wrecked the car, and she hauled off and smacked me with her right hand! Then she started yelling about how I had made her wreck the car and get a run in her stockings! Remember that?"

He was smiling and standing up acting out the wreck and the smack like it had just happened yesterday. When he finished, all the kids started laughing and looking at one another with a sense of knowing, like soldiers in a platoon who were reliving a battle they had fought next to one another in the foxholes.

I must have been sitting at the table with my mouth hanging open. I had my suspicions about "Big" Mimi's abusive behavior as the kids were growing up, but this conversation solidified my worries. These grown adults were reliving stories that many would deem horrific as a loving memorial of the woman they all idolized. Even David's dad walked into the kitchen and joined the conversation, and we had just buried his most current wife! The legacy of "Big" Mimi's behavior was palpable in this family, and they all seemed oblivious to its significance on their lives as adults.

A major legacy piece that David brought into fatherhood was his refusal to discipline Mimi. He was able to give voice to the *why*—when asked in exasperation by me why he wouldn't help me with the discipline—that he was afraid he would go too far and hurt her, so he wasn't going to even go down that road. I got it, but it didn't help me at all with my propensity to go too far down my own legacy road. He was proud of himself for making a conscious decision to not abuse his child, but all I could focus on was that I was on my own for this part of parenting. This not only always made me the "bad guy" within the family dynamic, but it opened me up for the inevitable rage that surfaced in me when my strong-willed child pushed back against what I felt were very reasonable boundaries I had set for her.

The rage was so scary to me. It came on so fast some days that I felt like the main character in a Dr. Jekyll / Mr. Hyde movie. It was a switch that got flipped, and I would just go off on her. I felt like I was on a runaway train, and once it began steaming down the track at full speed I had no control of when it would stop. These episodes were my adult version of dissociation, most often happening when I was alone with Mimi, and they really didn't escalate until she became a toddler with the ability to express herself and resist what I wanted her to do. Before this, she was the perfect child for me. She had a sense of autonomy that I was so proud of, often being the child sitting in the middle of the floor of the baby room at the preschool, quietly playing with a toy while all the other children were screaming at the top of their lungs. She didn't seem to get ruffled about many things, and she had a smile on her face more often than anything else. I couldn't believe how lucky I had gotten to have such an agreeable child, and I decided early on that I would likely not get this lucky again, so I was "one and done."

I think the early days of our lives together were God's way of helping me connect with this beautiful soul who had chosen me to be her mom. I am not sure I could have handled a baby who cried all the time (having colic or some other issue) and I have a deep respect for those parents who go through that type of experience. I mentioned that I didn't feel an overwhelming love for her in the "heart bursting" sense in the early days. I loved her as I did the kids at the preschool who I was charged with caring for, but there was a deeper love I expected to feel that just hadn't seemed to manifest yet. I remember the moment that shifted that for me. Mimi took her naps during the day in her bouncy seat in the living room. One day I had wrapped her up in her Winnie the Pooh blanket and had put her down for her nap while I sat on the couch and watched some TV. She was such a good baby that most days when I put her in this position she would drift off to sleep, enjoying the gentle vibration that the bouncy seat provided when I remembered to turn it on.

This day, I was watching a show, and I got the sense she was looking at me. When I turned my eyes to her she had a look in her eye that caught my breath. If you've ever watched the movie *Terms of Endearment* (spoiler alert), the moment when Emma (Debra Winger) looks at her mom (Shirley MacLaine) and you know she is about to die, then you know the look Mimi gave me. I locked eyes with her and felt my heart open in a way I had never felt before.

I identified the look immediately and thought to myself, "If she is about to take her last breath, what am I gonna do?"

I felt such a deep sense of peace and love that there was no time for panicking. She had made a contract with the universe to be in my hands for whatever time we had together, and she was okay with that choice, knowing something I didn't yet know about who I was going to be as a mom. That was the day my heart began to burst for this beautiful soul who had come into my world at just the right time. I will be forever grateful for her faith in me.

*****

When I returned to work at the preschool, I was grateful every day for my situation. Suddenly I had a deeper understanding of the trust parents were putting in me when they dropped their child off in the care of my teachers. I also couldn't believe how blessed I was to have my baby just down the hall from my office. I could visit her any time I wanted, and I could easily peer through the window to see her at each milestone she achieved. She settled into group care well, and her teachers adored her from the moment they met her. It was fascinating for me to see Mimi side-by-side with babies who were just days different in age, yet their maturity level and ability to manage their environment was clearly different than Mimi's. When other babies were crying over the smallest change in their environment, Mimi would just be looking around the room and smiling. She didn't get ruffled by outside noise, and when she was upset, she was easily calmed.

The job of preschool director had always been more than a forty-hour work week. I rarely had consistent time in my office to do my job because of the constant interruptions by children, teachers, and parents throughout the day. I was good at multitasking, and this job was that on steroids, but I often didn't get significant parts of my responsibilities done until after everyone had gone home and I could lock the door. I could get so much done if I stayed an extra hour or two after closing; it was amazing! When the phone stopped ringing and no one was demanding my attention, I could get shit done.

David was the cook in the family so he didn't have an expectation of me coming home at a certain time each day to prepare his dinner. It was always my responsibility to clean the dishes, which could get done any time (as long as it was before bedtime). Hell hath no fury like a husband with bipolar and OCD who wakes up to dirty dishes in the sink, so I could roll in after putting in a couple of extra hours at the school and sit right down to eat. This got complicated when I added motherhood into the equation, as I now had this new human who wanted a little piece of that pie too. Each day brought new challenges at work, and it seemed harder and harder to get home within a reasonable time, spend time with Mimi before she needed to go to bed, and give any attention to David who seemed to need something from me all the time. He had been asking since even before Mimi was born to move back east, and I had resisted at each request. For him, it was largely about a geographical fix. We had been in Boulder for a few years now, and he was getting bored. I finally had a career that I was excited about and proud of, and so I said no every time it came up. But I was starting to think more about Mimi's relationship with her extended family. Mom and her new husband Bob had come to visit once, as had Mary and Chris, but I was worried we wouldn't see them enough for Mimi to truly know them. Living that far away from everyone meant they either had to incur the cost of a plane ticket or drive two days to get to us by car, which seemed more and more implausible as time went on.

One day, at the end of a very long and hard day at school, I came to clarity about this situation. Our cook had quit, and I had not hired another after many interviews with unqualified candidates. I found myself in the kitchen after everyone had gone home, cleaning the dried spaghetti dishes from lunch several hours before. The place looked like a bomb had gone off, and I had to move about the room in a methodical fashion until I started to see my way clear of the mess that cooking spaghetti for eighty students creates. To keep Mimi occupied, I dragged one of the baby swings from the nursery and put it in the doorway to the kitchen so she could see me while I scrubbed the caked-on pasta from the plates and pans. She was not as taken with the swing this night as she usually is, and within minutes, the screaming began. I talked to her, cooed to her, and sang nursery rhymes to try to soothe her, all the while up to my elbows in dishwater and muck. It was not long before my tears began to join the bubbles in the sink below. How could I have let it get this far? What kind of a mom was I that I treated my child like this? It became clear to me that I was not doing the best I could for her with the demands that this job placed on my time and attention. It was that night, with

258

the tears streaming down my face and hers, that I decided we needed to make a change. I went home that night and told David to get out the map so we could decide where on the East Coast we would find our new home.

11/11

Today is the day
of manifestation.

Lift your eyes
to the heavens,
allow your breath
to fill every cell
in your human universe.

Open your palms
to receive
the energetic bounty
that is yours
for the claiming.
Silence the chatter.
Allow the true wisdom
to be heard.

You are a never-ending particle
in the fabric
of source.

Take each step
with intention,
each breath
with openness
each whisper
with love.

Manifest today
the love that you are
to each soul
you see with your eye,
hear with your ear,
and feel with your touch.

Raise up the vibration
of your inner self!

Manifest!

Chapter 15

After living close to the Rockies with such wide-open spaces, I couldn't do the dark and dingy Smoky Mountains. I didn't want anywhere inland where there wasn't a mountain range or coastline, so somewhere on the water was the focus. Much like we did when we decided to move to Boulder, we got out the map and looked at what the options were. Charleston, South Carolina, was an early favorite because of its coastline placement and because it was centrally located to everyone we loved but far enough away from all of them to be somewhere new. As much as we loved our friends in Florida, we knew moving back would not be good for our recovery. My hometown in North Carolina was never an option for me. That town had way too many demons for me to move back. Charleston was about a three and a half to four hours away from all family and friends in the south, which seemed like a good distance. Looking it up on the internet told us about the culture and more about what the area had to offer, and all of it looked really promising!

We decided to go back to North Carolina for Christmas that year, which would give me a chance to travel to Charleston with Mimi and Mom and look for a house for us. David came for the holidays, but he returned to Boulder to go back to work and get the Boulder house ready for a move and to put it on the market. David and I didn't mind being apart from each other for long stretches, as our marriage had settled into a roommate vibe. Parenting was also easier when I could make the calls without unending discussion or his judging eye overseeing what I did as a mom.

It's curious to me how when we were in proximity to each other, I resented his disconnection, essentially making me a single mother with a partner. But when we were apart, I welcomed the break from trying to coparent with a partner who only saw the benefit of his control when he decided to engage and otherwise lay all the responsibility at my feet.

After our rocky time together during my maternity leave, Mom and I had made a little progress in how to share space as two mothers without getting on each other's nerves too much. I welcomed the help she gave me when she was willing, so after Christmas we packed up Mimi into the van and headed down to Charleston for a long weekend of house hunting. We were lucky to find something in Mt. Pleasant that suited us, and the ball was rolling on financing and logistics.

David had secured a realtor in Boulder who took care of getting the house ready to sell there, and it wasn't long before we had a viable offer to sell. I am a firm believer in the affirmation from the universe when things fall into place. It was confirming in my heart that this move to Charleston was in alignment, and all was going along without a hitch. Famous last words...

After the first of the year, David had told me that his stomach had been bothering him. He was a typical man who never went to the doctor until he was on death's door, and this experience was no exception. After a disturbingly incoherent conversation with him on the phone one day where he would not follow my direction to go to the doctor, I hung up the phone and called our neighbor, asking her to go next door and check on him. What she found alarmed her so much that she called the ambulance immediately and let me know he was on the way to the emergency room at Boulder Hospital.

I was beside myself, being so far away, and it felt like an eternity to hear from the doctors about his condition. David had Diverticulitis[4] that was so bad his bowel had perforated, and he was

---

[4]   Diverticulitis causes pea-sized, bulging pouches—diverticula—to form in the inner lining of the colon or large intestine and become infected and inflamed. Diverticulitis is distinct from diverticulosis, a condition where bulging pouches form in the colon but are not inflamed. In some cases of diverticulitis, the diverticula grow and place pressure on the internal walls of the colon. This can lead to serious digestive complications, such as rectal bleeding and blockages (https://

heading into emergency surgery. They would try not to end up with a colostomy bag,[5] but they couldn't promise me until they got in there and assessed the damage. David was very sick, and all I could do was wait.

He made it through the surgery avoiding the colostomy bag, but it was touch and go. His intestine had perforated, and he was dangerously close to sepsis when he came in. If I hadn't called our neighbor who got him to the hospital immediately, he would have died during the night. I was so grateful they had caught it in time, but I was also so mad at him for letting it get to this point! I spoke to him when he was able to talk, and we discussed what our options were. After much deliberation, we decided Mimi would stay in North Carolina with Mom and Bob, and I would fly back to Boulder to help David when he got out of the hospital. There was much to be done and flying Mimi back and forth was too expensive and difficult. He wasn't going to be able to do any lifting or packing, and the house had to be prepared for the movers.

He asked his buddies from Florida, Ronald and Bryan, to come out to Colorado and help him manage the movers packing up and loading all our furniture. Then they rented a U-Haul truck to transport all our plants, the dog, and various small items across country. David was healing, but he wasn't allowed to drive, so Ronald and Bryan would do the driving and make sure he didn't overexert himself while he was healing.

When Mimi and I had flown to North Carolina for the holidays, we already had a plan in place to get the car and cats across the country. Mary was going to fly out to Boulder and drive cross

---

facty.com/conditions/diverticulitis/10-diverticulitis-signs/?style=quick&utm_source=adwords&utm_medium=c-search&utm_term=diverticulitis&utm_campaign=**FH-Search-Diverticulitis-Signs&gclid=Cj0KCQjwwODlBRDu-ARIsAMy_28X4pxMm53sM-G8D_0TDZV70e9-8LkxoSyiYnNLjr2RFo_nyvUfpCjAaAg1YEALw_wcB)

[5] A colostomy bag, also called a stoma bag or ostomy bag, is a small, waterproof pouch used to collect waste from the body. During a surgical procedure known as a colostomy, an opening, called a stoma or ostomy, is formed between the large intestine (colon) and the abdominal wall (https://ada.com/colostomy-bag/).

country with me and the cats to get our car to Charleston. The first night we spent in the house in Charleston, there was no furniture, but our new washer and dryer had been delivered. As Mary and I lay on the floor in the master bedroom, trying to go to sleep, we began to giggle as the washer started the spin cycle for the load of clothes I had put in earlier. Because the house was empty, every sound was amplified as if it was being shot through a megaphone. When the washer started to spin, it sounded like a 747 jet airliner was taking off in the living room!

As we lay on the floor in the dark, I had a realization.

"David is going to shoot me if that thing makes that kind of noise after the furniture is here!"

We burst into uncontrollable laughter at the absurdity of the noise coming from this machine and didn't realize how messed up it was that I was worried about his explosion at me when he would inevitably blame me for the loudness of the washer that I had picked out. When you are in a volatile relationship, the simplest things can spark anxiety about reactions to otherwise innocuous experiences.

David's doctors had warned him that he would have issues with Diverticula chronically for the rest of his life, and it was possible the next attack would be just as bad, if not worse, than what he had already endured. Of course, he paid little attention to these warnings, and by October of that same year, he was in trouble again. In one year, we had moved to Charleston, evacuated for our first major hurricane (which went up the coast and didn't hit us), and now he was back in the hospital, facing a bowel resection due to acute diverticulitis.

As the Boulder doctors had predicted, he was facing a larger surgery this time where they would have to cut out a large section of his bowel which had become too infected to save, and join the two fresh ends together. Of course, a healthy adult man has about 25 feet of intestine, so cutting out a foot or two is not a big deal in the grand scheme of things. David was phobic of hospitals, partially stemming from his mom going into a coma and dying of unknown causes back in 1983. David's father did not demand an autopsy at the time, so the true cause of death is unknown. It was long said in family lore, however, that she had been given an incorrect dose of a medication that led to her coma and untimely death.

After this experience, David literally began to hyperventilate when the idea of a hospital visit was upon him. This was further complicated by the fact that he had to go off his bipolar meds while healing because he could not ingest anything after the surgery and they did not have an intravenous option for his meds. It was going to be a roller coaster time immediately following surgery, and I was trying to brace for impact while juggling a toddler on my own.

He checked into a local hospital for his surgery, and we both heard the *tic, tic, tic* you hear as you climb the first hill on the ride. The surgery was uneventful, and I was able to see him as soon as they moved him to his room. As expected, he was super grumpy any time I came in to see him, and there was no answer that satisfied him about anything.

"Why does everyone keep asking me how I am? THIS SUCKS!"

"What do they think my pain level is? I need more pain meds, and they won't give me any!"

Every time I walked in, there was a new barrage of complaints. The nurses were getting weary, I could see it in their eyes. One day, he was in a particularly irritated mood telling me about the respiratory therapist who doesn't like him (that was always his take on things) and who came into the room and yelled at him for not doing his breathing exercises with the plastic breathing machine that he called the sucker. He went on and on about her, telling me what a bitch she was and that everyone in this hospital had shitty bedside manners. After letting him rant for about five minutes, I asked him what I could do.

"I want you to find some paper and write on it 'Where is Dr. Kevorkian when you need him?' and put it on the wall above my bed so when they come in and ask me what I need, I can just point to the paper and not have to *tell them again!*"

So I did what he asked. I got a yellow legal pad from the nurses' station and wrote the following signs for his wall:

I FEEL LIKE SHIT!

WHERE IS DR. KEVORKIAN WHEN YOU NEED HIM?

No, I won't fucking shut up!

I taped them to the wall behind his bed, and he calmed down. It was a balancing act to find the right combination to make him feel heard, seen, and understood, while also supporting the folks who were caring for him. I knew he wasn't an easy patient, and I was embarrassed by how stressed out and verbally abusive he could be to those who were assigned to him. I imagined they drew straws, and the loser got assigned to his room on any given shift.

The first time his "favorite" respiratory therapist came in to check on him after we did the sign exercise, she stopped dead in her tracks, reading the words on the wall. She was visibly angry and marched over to the signs and tore them all off the wall! As she did so, she was saying that that kind of language was unacceptable and inappropriate and she would not tolerate it in this hospital! I expected there to be some push back, but I didn't think any of the staff would get that angry. He was in pain and off his meds. What did they think he was gonna do?

When I couldn't be at the hospital, he was calling me multiple times an hour begging me to get him out of there and exclaiming they were trying to kill him. Because of his phobia of hospitals and how I knew he could be, I didn't believe his cries. He was "the boy who cried wolf" to me, and I did everything I could to calm him down and assure him that he would be home soon. When they finally told me he was going to be released, I was so relieved! I envisioned we were on the back side of this process, and I was hoping he would calm down when recuperating at home. I wouldn't have to go back and forth to the hospital several times a day while trying to parent a toddler. Life was going to get back to some semblance of normal.

Once David came home, I became his nurse and medication police. He was given Oxycontin for pain, and I was doing everything I could to keep him from taking more than he should. This was in 1999, so there was very little understanding of oxycontin's potential for addiction compared to today. All I knew was that I had to keep hiding the pills in different places because he was so good at figuring out where I was hiding them. Within three days, we had an idea that something was wrong. His pain was not lessening In fact, it was growing, and I didn't like the drainage and smell that was coming from his incision. Day five had me taking him back to the hospital, where it was determined he had contracted MRSA[6] (methicillin-resistant *Staphylococcus aureus*) in his wound. They rushed him off to surgery to clean out the incision, and all I could do was wait.

After being in recovery for a couple of hours, they moved him to a room on the same hall he had been on for his previous surgery—7 South. He was across the hall from his last room, and you could tell this new room was special. It had dark wood furniture and curtains on the windows. When I asked the nurse about the room, and she said this was the VIP room for surgical patients.

At the time, I thought it was special they were treating him with such care. Over time, I realized why he was getting such "special" treatment. He had contracted MRSA on their hall, probably because someone didn't wash their hands properly. He was a lawsuit waiting to happen, and they knew it. The trouble was, I didn't.

Because he had MRSA, he now had to be quarantined in his room. There were signs on the door with infectious protocols, and everyone had to put a gown and gloves on before entering the room. As a result, the nurses would only come in the room if they absolutely had to, and his meals didn't get brought in when delivered to the floor. They would often be left outside the door for hours and would always be cold when they finally got delivered.

Each time I came to see him, he was more and more irritated. His anxiety was through the roof, because his worst fears were being realized. He had always said they were going to kill him, and now he had contracted a dangerous infection because of their negligence. They thought he was difficult before; they were really in for it now.

---

[6] Methicillin-resistant *Staphylococcus aureus* (MRSA) is a bacterium that causes infections in different parts of the body. It's tougher to treat than most strains of staphylococcus aureus—or staph—because it's resistant to some commonly used antibiotics. The symptoms of MRSA depend on where you're infected (https://www.google.com/search?ei=uDC_XIbKF-K-ggeF87v4CQ&q=MRSA&oq=MRSA&gs_l=psy-ab.3..0i67j0i131i67l2j0j0i13 1i10j0i67l2j0j0i67l2.285578.286532..287191...0.0..0.139.402.2j2......0....1.. gws-wiz.......35i39j0i131j0i10i67.aY0xUIyGYfA).

I would always check in with the nurses at the station when I arrived to get their take on things before going in to hear his version. One day they informed me that the doctor had prescribed Ativan[7] to combat his anxiety, which I thought was a good idea at the time. They had cleaned out the wound in the operating room, removing all the infected tissue until they found healthy tissue underneath. The tricky part about this was that they couldn't just close the wound like they did before.

I was told that because of the nature of MRSA, they would have to allow the wound to regranulate naturally, meaning the new healthy tissue would have to develop over time and the wound would become closed as the new tissue filled in the space. It was going to be a long process, and they would try to get him home as soon as they could, but they had to make sure not to send him home too soon.

I was fine with a bit of a wait. I knew I was going to have to step up my game and do dressing changes several times a day for months. I was not looking forward to this new level of nursing I was headed for, so I was okay with him staying until some of the more immediate challenges had passed.

Each day I arrived at the hospital, I wasn't sure what I was going to find. Would I arrive to find his food sitting outside his room getting cold, or would he be in a rage because he was cooped up and no one would speak to him? All the nurses remembered him from when he was on this hall before, and they did not show empathy to his plight, even though they might have had some responsibility for the MRSA he contracted when he was in their care. I took a few deep breaths as I put on the paper gown and gloves that were on a table outside his room, placing a smile on my face as I walked into the lion's den.

When I came in and said hello, he didn't answer. I walked around the bed to see if he was asleep, which would have been a rar-

---

[7] This medication is used to treat anxiety. Lorazepam belongs to a class of drugs known as benzodiazepines which act on the brain and nerves (central nervous system) to produce a calming effect. This drug works by enhancing the effects of a certain natural chemical in the body (GABA) (https://www.webmd.com/drugs/2/drug-6685/ativan-oral/details).

ity, as he didn't sleep well when he was in the hospital. His eyes were barely open, and he was very loopy. I tried to ask him the standard questions to determine how he was this day, but he couldn't really answer any of them. I was so concerned that I went out to the nurse's station to ask if any of them had noticed how out of it he was.

"Excuse me," I asked with the growing tone of irritation I had for all these nurses on this floor. They had shown me over and over that their concern for him as a person was almost nil. "Have you seen him today? Do you know why he can barely speak to me?"

The nurse looked up from her paperwork with an irritated look on her face aimed at me for interrupting her work and said, "He's probably just had his Ativan recently. At least he's not yelling at anyone." She dropped her head back to her work, and our conversation was over.

Over the next couple of weeks he was in the hospital, there were days when I arrived to find him almost climbing the walls and others when he was basically incoherent. I understood the relief she expressed at him not yelling at anyone, as I felt a similar relief when I could sit in his room and have it been filled with a stillness that one rarely felt when in David's presence. I had registered many complaints about his food not getting to him in a timely manner, but they all seemed to fall on deaf ears. He was calling me several times a day and night when I wasn't with him to tell me they were killing him and I had to get him out of there.

I kept telling him I didn't know what to do because he wasn't ready to be released yet, so where was I going to take him? I thought all his anxiety was due to his hospital phobia, and I knew that no nurses would be able to give him the type of care that he wouldn't complain about since he just seemed to hate everyone on the floor. I would find out weeks later that he was stashing the Ativan they were giving him and taking multiple pills at once to increase the high. He was behaving exactly like an addict, and the nurses were too much in their own feelings to notice. We were lucky he didn't overdose in their care. All this was made worse by the fact that he contracted the MRSA on this very floor. You would never be able to convince him that these nurses were anything other than evil.

After another blank conversation with one of the nurses about his food not being brought into him, I had reached my limit of patience. I sought out the patient advocate at the hospital and filed a formal complaint. I didn't know if it would get him any different care, but I had to do something. I was angry about how they were treating him, but I was also fully aware of how hard he was to care for and how much he was abusing them every chance he could.

But I told the advocate that I couldn't understand why they didn't have any compassion for him. He was a person with bipolar disorder, was phobic of hospitals, and was in for a second time in so many weeks because he had contracted a very bad infection due to inadequate care. I didn't feel like they had the right to treat him the way they were, and I had him calling me (when he was lucid) over and over again, exclaiming that they were killing him. My mind was in a swirl of feelings. I wanted to be his savior, but my subconscious was also considering how quiet it would be if they were to succeed.

They finally got him well enough to send him home. He still had a huge wound on his abdomen that would have to be cleaned and rebandaged three times a day. The first week, we had a home nurse come to the house to change the dressing and give me instructions on how to do it, but it was up to me to manage the rest of the time. I packed and changed the dressing on that wound for two months. We had a table set up in the bedroom with all the fixings for his dressings, and I became quite good at the whole process by the time it was done.

We were convinced Mimi would be a doctor when she grew up because she was not bothered at all by the wound. She used to call it his "pizza boo boo" because it was shaped like a slice of pizza. I was also in charge of his pain medication, which I managed with the same protocol I did when he came home the last time. I would give it to him only as directed, no matter how much he begged, and I hid the bottle each time somewhere different. I had two toddlers in the house. Thank God I was good at multitasking.

David had gotten a job at the local detox center that he had started just days before his latest diverticulitis attack. They were so understanding, especially when I had to call after the second admission to the hospital for MRSA to let them know that I had no idea when he would return to work. Since he hadn't been there long enough to be off "probation" and qualify for medical coverage, we were paying for COBRA from his job in Boulder, which was super expensive.

I had decided it was time for Mimi to start going to preschool for some socialization and to get her out of this heavy house. David had been house-bound for over a month, and we were all going stir-crazy. We had settled into a routine of me being in charge of his medications for pain and his bipolar disorder, which fed my need for codependent caretaking, but I was ready for whatever break I could get.

I didn't have control over when David would be ready to go back to work, but I could get Mimi into preschool. I knew she needed it when we went next door to play with the neighbor kids, and within five minutes, she was in the kitchen hanging out with the mothers. She was more comfortable with adults than she was with kids; I knew then it was time.

Getting Mimi into a preschool gave me some breathing room. When she was gone, I could focus on David without feeling like I was neglecting her and I knew she was having fun and learning things that I couldn't teach her in an "only child" setting. It was a win-win for all of us. David finally was ready to go back to work, but it had been so long he took several weeks to settle in. He didn't have the same excitement about the work as he had shown before getting sick. He would come home most days, complaining about the patients and his coworkers in a never-ending cycle.

He had been done with the pain meds for a while, but I noticed something different about him. Being on the pain meds for such a long time had left a residual imprint on his personality, and he didn't return to the same "recovery" David he was before his illness. He was never into recovery as fully as others might go in, but he now seemed to have nothing but irritation about it all. Every day seemed like the same story over and over about how fucked up everyone was at his work and how stupid they all were. All his stories were cyclical, and they never seemed to end.

I learned pretty quickly when I was researching and touring preschools for Mimi that I was not going to like the system in South Carolina. Colorado was very progressive in the early childhood arena. For a teacher to be a lead in a preschool classroom there, they had to have a four-year degree. For a teacher to be a lead in South Carolina, they only needed a high school diploma. Early childhood is an area of education that many don't take seriously, but the difference between the two states was glaring, and I knew it wouldn't be a good fit for me. I wasn't sure what my next steps would be in terms of a career, but it was getting to be time for me to figure it out.

I joined a "mother's morning out" group that I found online. They would meet once a week at different locations, usually places like Panera Bread, and the moms would sit and talk while the kids played. I enjoyed meeting other moms from the area, and it was good socialization for Mimi outside of her time at the preschool. The organization had a program once a month that met in the evening, and they would put together speakers and topics that mothers of young children could benefit from.

One month, the topic was volunteering. The organization had asked representatives from different volunteer opportunities in the Charleston area to come speak about their programs and inform us of their volunteering choices. I was finding it interesting but was kind of checked out until one very tall white woman stood up. She said she was on the board of directors of a therapeutic horseback riding center in the area that provided services for children and adults with disabilities. My breath caught in my throat, and I was riveted as she talked about the program. My undergraduate degree was in special education, and I had owned and ridden horses as a child, so this was the combination of two of my deepest loves. I don't know how long she spoke, but probably within two minutes of her talk, I was hooked. I decided then and there I would get involved and planned to talk with her after the event concluded.

When we were done, I looked everywhere for her, but she was nowhere to be found. I was so upset I had missed her, and I couldn't remember what her name was to find out how to contact her. I asked the people who planned the evening, and they were able to tell me her name and give her phone number. I was so excited! The next day, I called her, and we talked for over an hour! I asked all kinds of questions and found out the program was on Johns Island, which is one of the barrier islands off the coast of Charleston. She told me about a volunteer training they were having in a week or two and how to sign up.

The training was wonderful, and I got involved right away. I signed up to help with school groups and individual riders and even came out on Saturdays. It was such a beautiful farm, and I felt so completely happy when I was out with the horses and the kids. One day, when we were at the cross-tie area, tacking up the horses on a Saturday, the volunteer coordinator started talking about how she was getting certified to be an instructor.

I poked my head around the back of the horse and said, "You mean you can get certified to do this?"

"Yes," she said. "I am doing my student teaching hours now, and soon I'll be a certified instructor. If you want to talk to the director about signing up, I'm sure she'd talk to you about it."

I couldn't believe it! My head was spinning with all the possibilities. I knew I didn't want to go into preschools in South Carolina and wasn't sure what I was going to do with myself, especially now that Mimi was in school five days a week. I walked into the office after my volunteering time was finished and asked the director if I could talk to her for a minute. We talked about the process and how it worked to get certified to be a registered instructor. She wasn't ready to commit to me yet, but she could sense my excitement.

We were at the end of the summer session at that time, and everything would be taking a break since it was too hot for the horses and riders in South Carolina. She told me to get in touch with her at the end of the summer, and we could talk about the possibilities. I drove down the long driveway away from the barn with the *biggest smile* on my face! I knew what I wanted to be when I grew up! I wish I didn't have to wait a whole summer to find out if I could do the internship with Charleston Area Therapeutic Riding Inc., but I was not going to let up until they said yes!

Chapter 16

When David's abdomen finally healed, his stomach was a hot mess! His belly button had died during the MRSA situation and he had a thirteen-centimeter divot from his sternum to his pubic bone that he called his "bicycle parking rack" because it looked like you could park a bicycle tire in it. It was very ugly, and he was extremely self-conscious about it. Not only was it unsightly, but it was dangerous. It was a huge hernia, which meant if he got hit in the stomach with a ball or even in a small accident, it could do serious damage to his internal organs. The muscles we rely on to protect our midsection had been so weakened after the MRSA infection and the process of regranulation that he was at great risk of serious injury. As much as he didn't want to agree, he needed another surgery. This time, they needed to repair the hernia and make his stomach look somewhat normal again. He consulted with his gastrointestinal surgeon, who had done the previous surgeries, as well as a plastic surgeon to work on the aesthetics of his midsection.

We had a tentative date for the surgery in mid-December, and I was doing a lot of cajoling to convince him that he would be okay. Then we got a phone call from his brother James's wife, Bee. She told us James had a heart event during an ice storm in Atlanta and that the ambulance had taken a very long time to get to him due to their steep driveway turning into a sheet of ice during the storm. James had suffered a stroke once he got to the hospital, and David was to get to Atlanta right away.

I was so worried about him going back to our old city. He hadn't been back to Atlanta since we had left, and I didn't know if his old drug boss would be waiting for him. It had been eight

275

years since we left, but there is something about going back to a place that holds that much history; you often find yourself right back where you left if you aren't careful. He convinced me I didn't need to go with him. He would be at the hospital all the time, and I wouldn't have anywhere to be with Mimi if I went. My gut was telling me it wasn't a good idea. But he was right about having a toddler in a hospital setting, and I agreed it was for the best. He packed a bag and left that day, and I tried not to obsess about what could go wrong.

I did the codependent wife thing of calling way too often to check on him. He always had excuses why he wasn't available to answer his phone. The hospital had bad service, or they told him to turn his phone off. He told me he was sleeping at the hospital and James was unresponsive. I could hear how freaked out he was in his voice, and I pulled out all the skills my PhD of "talking off the ledge" afforded me. I felt like I was his lifeline, but I didn't know what cliff he was dangling from. When he would talk to me, we would talk for hours, and I would truly feel like I was helping him process his fear. I would get off the phone and feel drained but satisfied. Another crisis averted. And I had saved the day again.

In the meantime, I rather enjoyed the fact of being a true single mother while he was gone. As worried as I was about him while he was in Atlanta, I breathed more than one sigh of relief at being able to parent by myself. I didn't have to run things by him, secretly holding my breath, waiting for the push-back, or trying to undo the bad habits he instilled in her every time I turned my back. Being a single mother is exhausting and draining and sometimes soul crushing, but being a single mother with a partner there to criticize your every move is way worse. Not only did I have the struggle of doing it all by myself, but I resented the *hell* out of him for being right there and not helping.

While he was in Atlanta, he didn't care what time I fed her or what I dressed her in or why I insisted on her having a schedule, because children do better when they have a predictable schedule they can rely on. He was in his own bubble, and he allowed us to be in ours. I was so conflicted the whole time he was gone. I wanted him home to know he was safe, but I was reveling in the bliss of normalcy that existed in his absence.

James was holding his own but was still critical. David's job was telling him he needed to come back to work, and his surgery date for the hernia repair was looming. He finally came home, and I could tell something had shifted in him while he was gone. I tried to get him to tell me more about his time away, to determine if he got into any drug activity, but he was very good at being elusive if he didn't want me to know something. He was jumpy and quick to anger, and I couldn't tell if it was because he had "gone back out" (which is the way we say people are drinking or using again in recovery) or if he was just worried about his brother and his upcoming surgery, which was definitely possible.

Every day became a balancing act as; moment by moment, I tried to hold it all together. Was he taking his meds? Was he going to meetings? Was he going to work? Would he be ready for his surgery? All those thoughts and more filled my days, along with Mimi's care and my own life at the barn. As the surgery date approached, he got more and more anxious. He tried to cancel the surgery many times, but each time I was able to talk him off that ledge and get him to agree to go through with it. By the time we got to the big day, he was beside himself, popping Xanax like it was candy to keep his nerves calm.

The surgery went as expected, and they let me know I could see him once they moved him to a room from recovery. He was on the same floor he had been the other two times, and the nurses were all *so* happy to see us both. He was still on MRSA protocol because he had been previously infected, so everyone who came into his room had to put on a gown and gloves. I was worried we would have the same issues we had before, and I was hopeful that he wouldn't be in the hospital long enough to cause anxiety in anyone. This was a regular surgery. He should be in for just a couple of days, and then we could get him home.

When I got my gown and gloves on and came into the room, he was sitting up and cracking jokes. He immediately began telling me how hungry he was and begging me to go get him fried chicken.

I asked the nurses if that was okay, and they said they checked with the doctor. If David insisted on eating something that heavy, who were they to stop him? I didn't think it was a good idea, but I was tired of listening to him beg, so I left and went to get him some fried chicken. He ate about half of what I brought him and started feeling nauseous, so he stopped.

I chastised him, saying, "I told you it was too soon to eat all that," and he let me harp on him feeling pretty shitty.

He kept hitting the nurses' call button until they finally came to check on him, which took longer than it should because they didn't want to gown and glove up before coming in. When they finally did, he told them he felt really nauseous, and they said they would contact his doctor to ask if he could get prescribed something for the nausea. I waited with him as long as I could, but it was getting to be time to go get Mimi, and they charged a fee for every minute I went past the pick-up time. As much as I wanted to stay until he got some relief, I finally had to go pick up our daughter. He was complaining a fair amount about his stomach now, but the nurses assured me he would get the meds he needed as soon as the doctor called them back.

He called me a few times that night to tell me how horrible he felt and that they were trying to kill him, but there was little I could do. I hung up with him once and called the nurses' station right away, only for them to tell me that he had been given the antinausea medication as prescribed and that he just needed to go to sleep. They told me they would call if anything happened, and my phone blissfully stopped ringing because they turned the phones off in the hospital rooms at 10:00 p.m.

I had to trust that the nurses would do their jobs and call if anything happened, no matter how much they hated him as a patient. I was caught between knowing how hard of a patient he could be and knowing how much the nurses disliked him from all of our stays on this particular hall. I had to turn it over to God and hope David was exaggerating his situation, as he had done time and time again.

The next morning, I dropped Mimi off at preschool and went straight to the hospital. I had called the nurses that morning, and they said he had an uneventful night, but I had not heard from him, so I was ready to see for myself that he was alright. When I walked onto the seventh floor, I saw a lot of activity down by his room. As I got closer, I realized that all that bustling about was coming from his door, and I wiggled my way past all the medical staff to get inside to see what was happening. His doctor was leaning over him in the bed, examining his abdomen and hollering out orders to the nurses and staff in the room as they transferred him from the bed he was in to a gurney for transport.

"What's happening! Where are you taking him?" I called out as he was being rushed out of the room. His doctor finally held my arm and told me the words no one ever wants to hear.

"He ruptured something overnight and needs emergency surgery. I don't know what we are going to find when we get in there, but I need to get in right away. You can wait in the ICU waiting room, as that is where he will go when I'm done. I'll come find you there." And he was gone.

The surgery took three hours. I waited in the ICU waiting room by myself as I paced and watched TV without really focusing on anything. He told me they were trying to kill him. He told me I needed to come get him, and I didn't. This was my fault. I didn't believe him, and now he might die. I had called everyone to let them know what his status was, but I didn't know anything definitive yet. Finally, his doctor appeared from the ICU door and came to sit next to me, taking his surgical cap off as he sat. He was a man with a huge God complex, and he always approached everything with the attitude that it was all going to be fine because he was on the case. This was not what I saw when I looked into his eyes this time.

"It's bad," he said. I had never heard anything that negative come out of him in all this time.

David had ruptured his wound from the abdominoplasty, and his bowel had escaped into his abdominal cavity. The doctor was able to tuck it all back in, and none of it had died in the process, which was good. He would not need another bowel resection as a result of this incident, and the doctor had closed up his wound with a different apparatus that would give it more stability in the initial days of healing. He would stay in ICU for a few days so that he could get the best supervision, and I could go visit him in a little while.

I breathed a sigh of relief as I made all the phone calls to let everyone know his status. They let me go in to see him after about an hour, and he was sleeping in a glass cubicle. He was under quarantine because of the MRSA, so he was in isolation even in ICU. There were big signs on the glass door that said as much, and I remember thinking he was going to hate looking like a diseased animal on display when he woke up and saw those signs in front of his face. I sat with him for a few hours until I had to go pick up Mimi.

He woke a few times, telling me how shitty he felt and asking why I didn't believe him when he told me they were trying to kill him. I didn't know what to say and just sat there holding his hand, apologizing for being a bad wife. When I left that afternoon to go get Mimi before the preschool closed, he was groggy and in and out of consciousness. The nurses in the ICU seemed really nice, and I made sure I had the phone number to call the nurses' station to check on him. I was relieved that he was no longer on that same floor and that even though he was in ICU, I was grateful it seemed he was with folks who would actually take care of him.

The next morning, I came in to the ICU waiting area and picked up the phone to call the station to let them know I was there. Instead of them calling back to let me know it was okay to come back, his doctor appeared in the waiting room.

"David took a turn last night," he said, his face very grim. "He has developed staphylococcus pneumonia. Apparently, he aspirated some of his vomit from the night he ruptured his abdominal wound, and we had to put him on a ventilator to help him breathe. We have put him in a drug-induced coma so that he will relax and not fight the tube down his throat. I'm sorry to have to tell you this, but he is very sick."

I don't know how long I sat there, staring at him. I heard what he said, but it wasn't resonating in my brain. Why didn't anyone call me? What time did all this happen? My head was swirling, and I finally got out of my mouth, "I want to see him."

They took me back to his cubicle, and I got my gown and gloves on and slowly slide the glass door open. There he was, with a tube coming out of his mouth and his eyes taped shut. The cubicle was full of beeping machines that weren't there the last time I was here, and it all seemed so scary. How in the world did we get here? This was supposed to be a simple surgery, but nothing was ever simple with this man.

They didn't know how many days we would be in this state of suspended animation. They were encouraged by the fact that he was so young. As one nurse told me, "If he was in his sixties or seventies, we'd be more worried," but they couldn't tell me when he would be able to come off the vent. It was December, Christmas was right around the corner, and I had a toddler at home who was excited about Santa and was wondering when Daddy was coming home.

I called my mom and asked her to come. I just couldn't handle all the details of life by myself. That was the year I bought a fake Christmas tree because I couldn't do the real one by myself, and I wasn't sure how long it was going to need to stay up so that he could see it when he came home. Every day was spent at the hospital, looking at the numbers on the machines and asking questions. A visiting specialist asked me if I was a nurse because I knew all the lingo and could answer her questions with confidence.

I said, "No, but I will deserve a nursing certificate when this is over!" She laughed.

Every time I came into his room on a new day, the radio was tuned to the local public broadcasting station, and there was classical music playing. David *hated* classical music, so I would change it to the classic rock station, which he would have preferred. The nurses would change it every time, and every time, I would change it back. On day two, one of his regular nurses came into the cubicle and promptly walked to the back to change the station.

"What are you doing?" I asked with more of a raised voice than I intended.

"Well, we prefer soothing music to be playing so the patient stays quiet and relaxed. Rock and roll is not soothing music. We want him to stay under sedation, not get excited and start to wake up."

"Believe me, if he can hear this shit you have on, he's in there *begging* to wake up and wring your neck! He hates classical music. If you want him to stay asleep, you need to play the music he actually would want to hear."

She looked rattled that I had spoken to her in that tone, but she left the station alone, and I never had to change it again.

On the third day, I walked in to find the ventilator, not behaving the way it needed to. The nurses were shuffling around, trying to find the solution. When the doctor showed up for rounds, it was found that the ventilator had been unplugged for a time. I was beside myself. These were supposed to be the *good nurses*, the ones I didn't have to worry about?

On day eight, while I stood at the bedside and was holding his hand, I swear I felt him move. I had been talking to him every day about Mimi and what was going on in her life, and all that time, he was so deeply asleep that I never felt one bit of energy coming back to me. This day, his hand moved, but it was so slight I had to convince myself I wasn't imagining it. I was living my own version of *Groundhog Day*, and I was questioning everything I thought I knew.

After the twitch in his hand, I thought I saw his eyebrow move. I told the nurses, and they said they had been concerned that he was building up a tolerance to the sedation they had him on. They had increased the doses already and were almost to the cap of what they could give him. True to drug addict form, he was gonna make it hard for them to keep him under.

They told me not to talk to him anymore when I was in his cubicle. They said my voice might encourage him to fight the sedation, and they were not ready for him to wake up yet. They told me that he had extubated himself three times before they put him under and didn't want to go through that again while he was healing. It was so hard not to talk to him anymore while I sat at his bedside, as I had grown accustomed to telling him Mimi's events of the day to keep him updated. We had a new nurse, who tried the radio thing again, and I let her know that if they didn't want him to wake up, they better not play classical or new age because he *would* work hard to come out of his stupor to turn that shit off!

We were now racing the clock for his antibiotics to work and heal his infection before his tolerance brought him out of the drug-induced coma needed for his healing. Meanwhile, the world was bracing for Y2K on December 31, 1999. He was going to miss the turn of the century.

On January 2, 2000, the doctors determined they couldn't keep him under anymore. He had been on the ventilator for eleven days, and he was becoming more and more awake every day. It was time to extubate and wake him up and see whether or not he had spent enough time healing. When I came into the cubicle after they extubated him, he was disoriented, and his voice didn't want to work. I had a wallet-sized picture of Mimi in my hand, and as soon as he saw it, he began to cry. It was one of the more touching moments of our time together. I could tell he was afraid he was never going to see her again. He was insistent to communicate, so I asked the nurse for a pad of paper and a pen so he could write his questions. He let me know that he had been aware for days, and he thought he had suffered a stroke like James had, which scared him to death. I hadn't been able to tell him that he was paralyzed because of the medication they were giving him. All he knew was that he couldn't move or wake up.

He asked me why someone had been electrocuting his eyes. I had no idea what he was talking about, so when I asked the nurse, she looked at me wide-eyed. There was a machine they used to test the patient's level of sedation, and it sent electrical currents into the temple. The depth of the sedation was determined by how much the eyebrow reacted to the jolt. They were doing this several times a day in the past few days because he was trying to wake up and they needed to know his status.

They were amazed to know he knew what they were doing and could express it so clearly. Later that afternoon, one of the younger nurses was in his cubicle, making some IV changes and tidying up his space. When she walked out, he scribbled something on his pad and insistently motioned to me to pay attention.

On the pad, he had written: BJ $?

He pointed at the pad, then pointed at the nurse. When I didn't understand, he pointed again to the pad, then emphatically at the nurse. I finally figured out what he was asking. He thought he owed the nurse money for giving him a blow job! It turned out she had given him a sponge bath, and in his drugged stupor, he had remembered a more intimate exchange. I laughed so hard when I realized what he was saying and assured him he didn't owe her any money. He always had a hell of a sense of humor, and this was a particularly funny version of his twisted mind.

In the coming week, something called ICU psychosis set in, where he was even more "imbalanced" than normal because his circadian rhythms had gotten all upside down from not seeing daylight for an extended period of time (the windows to the outside world were behind his bed) and always having the lights on on the floor. He told stories of hay people with red eyes who were smoking, and he was worried about them catching themselves on fire (we figured out this was inspired by the nurses call button on the bed that was a profile of a person with a red light as the eye). He also rambled about how the nurses were making Russian pastries behind the nurse's station and there was flour all over the floor as proof (he had a line of sight to the microwave they used to heat up saline bags and made his own determinations about its use). Every time I arrived to the hospital, there was a new story that was grander than the last. It kept us all laughing, which was good medicine at the time, but I was ready for him to get to a regular floor, where he could get his regulatory system back on a normal rhythm.

I had a long talk with his doctor one day in a "family quiet room" before he was to be moved from ICU. I told him all about the incidents of the vent not being plugged in to the respiratory therapist whom I kicked off his case when she came in, recognized him from his first surgery, and pointed out the "Dr. Kevorkian comment" and said, "Oh, he's the difficult patient." I told him he was *not* going back to the seventh floor with those horrible nurses whose negligence landed him here in the first place, and he wholeheartedly agreed.

It was decided he would go to the cardiac floor for his stepdown care, and the nurses on that floor were wonderful! They treated him with dignity and compassion, and it was the most relaxed I had ever seen him in a hospital.

This whole situation ended up with a lawsuit against the hospital.

David's doctor agreed to testify for us regarding the hospital's negligence, and the hospital retaliated by revoking his privileges. The hospital settled with us in the end, and we learned a lot about how messed up South Carolina's laws were for the protection of patients and just how strong the "wall of silence" was to protect the managed care companies that owned the hospitals. That process would take another couple of years after he was released, and it didn't do a lot to help him put the situation behind him, as he hung on to the anger and resentment while we slogged through the depositions and legal proceedings.

The events of the past couple of years had taken a toll on his already fragile sobriety. The multiple surgeries, prolonged pain medications, and ongoing anxiety had ripped apart any hold he had on living a life of recovery. Not long after his near-death experience, he decided he didn't want to work at the recovery center anymore, not because he would admit he couldn't handle it, but because everyone there was "too fucked up to be helped." The time spent in caretaker mode had also laid waste to my recovery and had kicked me into a familiar place of monitoring his every move, including whether or not he was taking his bipolar medication.

Since diagnosis, he had cycled through the familiar territory of getting balanced and regulated, deciding he didn't need the meds anymore because he was fine, bottoming out after a couple of weeks of being unmedicated, going back on the meds until he felt better again, and then starting the whole cycle over. This had become so routine to me by this time that I was watching and counting his meds every chance I got so I could confront him when I knew he wasn't taking them. What little healthy boundaries we had established were eroding fast, and the Crazy began to be a regular visitor in our household again.

David's obsessive-compulsive disorder had never really left him, but he had learned how to manage it better and not let it take over our lives or be the cause of fights for quite some time. With the slip of everything else, this also returned, and I found myself trying to second guess what he would obsess over next to stay one step ahead of him, which never really worked.

One fight that stayed with Mimi for a long time was over the cat box. We had a laundry room at the end of the hall that lead to the garage. The washer and dryer lived in there, as well as a utility sink, and it was a great out of the way place to keep the cat box. We had a chain lock on the door so the dog and child couldn't get in, but the cats could, and it worked for everyone.

When David was feeling especially antsy, he loved to do laundry, which I was not going to argue about! As a result, he spent most of the time going in and out of the laundry room and was particular about cleaning out the cat box. He would almost go in right behind the cats to clean up the box, which was excessive, but if it made him happy to do it, I wasn't going to worry about it. On this day, it was the battleground to which he was determined not to relinquish his stand.

"Why the *fuck* am I always the one who cleans out this god-damn cat box?" he bellowed down the hall, causing my heart to stop in its tracks. I knew that tone and wondered how thick the tornado would be today around his head. When he stormed down the hall to the kitchen, because no one answered his seemingly rhetorical question, I knew it was going to be a big one.

"What do you mean?" I said with as calm a tone as I could muster.

"You have to clean it *every day*! I am *always* the one who cleans it out. You haven't touched that shit in *weeks*! Do you want these cats to be here, because if you do, you have to clean up after them! Do you think we live in a shit hole?"

"David, I often don't get a chance to do it before you get in there, because you spend more time in the laundry room than I do. If you always get there first, then I can't clean what isn't there."

The bipolar tornado around his head was pretty thick, and I couldn't see much of him through the spin. Mimi had stopped watching her show and was listening intently from the sunroom to see where this was going to go next. She was five years old.

"You don't give a *shit* about the cleanliness of this house! If it were up to you, we would live in a fucking *pigsty*!"

286

I stood quietly looking at him because I knew anything I said would fall on deaf ears at this point. I wasn't sure how to diffuse this situation, but I felt my anger rising up to meet his, which was never a good sign.

"I *try* to keep this house clean, but you are *impossible* to please, and I can't keep up with your OCD! If you're so worried about the fucking cat box, then by all means, *clean the damn thing every day!*"

He could see I was getting mad, but I wasn't getting to the level of mad his Crazy needed to feel satisfied. He had to up the ante.

"I think we should just take both cats and have them *put to sleep* since you don't care about taking care of them! If you can't care for these stupid animals, then they may as well be dead!" As he said this last sentence, he went to pick up Louie, who was sleeping on the back of the couch, oblivious to how his life was hanging in the balance at that moment.

That was it. He had me. He also had Mimi. She started screaming, "Nooooooooo!" from the sun room and came running in to try to wrestle Louis from his grasp.

I jumped into action when I saw her near him, as I never knew what he was capable of doing when he was in this state, and I wanted to make sure she was safe. He had found the button that brought both of us into his tornado to share the spin with him, and with that knowing, it began the release of pressure.

Mimi was crying and pleading with him not to kill Louie, and I was trying to pick her up and console her while yelling at him for being a monster. I don't know how long this particular screaming match lasted, but he eventually stormed off to the garage to mess with his motorcycle, and Mimi and I were left to recover from the storm. Thankfully, he loved those cats as much as we did and never brought it up again, but Mimi talked about that episode for years after it happened. It deeply impacted her sense of safety to hear her father talk so flippantly about putting her cats to death.

The Crazy of my thirties looked different than its other iterations. I now had a child, who was the light of my life, and the Crazy became a combination of an outer being I needed to protect her from, and an inner being I needed to protect her from. The Crazy would flip-flop from the bipolar husband raging for hours (sometimes days at a time, as I would stand between Mimi and the storm to shield her from harm) to the rage coming out of *my* mouth as I yelled at her for being a child who had tested my patience to its brink.

Some days, this shift would be many times an hour. Some days, the Crazy would stay entrenched in one host, spinning into a tornado so thick you couldn't see the human inside its funnel. This Crazy looked like "Come see Daddy's motorcycle… I promise I won't turn it on," "If you don't go to sleep, I'm going to *fucking lose it*!" or "I'm just going to kill myself and get it over with."

I had my suspicions that David had begun drinking again. I often thought I smelled beer on him when he returned home from being out on the motorcycle with his friends, but he was always able to convince me that he had been drinking nonalcoholic beer, which smelled exactly like the real thing. I always thought it was a convenient explanation, but it was one I couldn't argue with. I was trying so hard to keep the boundaries I had worked to establish by going to Alanon meetings as often as I could and talking to my sponsor. Between the erratic behavior and the fights that seemed to be escalating, we were in a troubling spiral that only seemed to have one conclusion.

The evening he came home after a long day on the bike with his buddies, I knew it immediately. His face was red from the cold, but his slurred speech was not because his lips were cold from the ride. As he took off his leather gloves and began his rambling about the day's events, I was listening to the details intently so I could question him and catch him in inconsistencies to prove I was right, and he was wrong.

I took a deep breath during the "Alanon kiss" and smelled it right away. I had been smelling the nonalcoholic beers for quite some time and this smell had a sweeter tinge to it. This smell included hard liquor. He was getting bolder in his choices. He was anxious and talking a mile a minute about the day's events, rarely taking a long enough breath to allow me to get a word in edgewise.

Mimi ran up to him with her arms stretched up to the sky, saying, "Dadddddddyyyyy!" I must have looked at him with a look of knowing, and I saw his eyes change. The Crazy had entered, and I knew what was coming next. He started peppering questions at me like "Why don't you believe me?" and "How the fuck do you know anything, you haven't seen me all day!" I didn't even have to say a thing, we both knew exactly where we were going next. My body kicked into the familiar position of defender and stealth interrogator.

I had more on the line than just myself. Mimi was in his arms and listening to everything we were saying. A big part of me wanted to avoid the conflict altogether to keep the peace and save Mimi from what promised to be an ugly showdown, but I had just been talking to my sponsor about this the week before after our Alanon meeting. I had said to her then, "If he 'goes back out' [starts drinking again], I will have the courage to leave him this time for sure." With all the Crazy we had been sliding back into these past few years, the one saving grace I held on to was that he wasn't drinking—that I knew of and could prove. I had drawn the imaginary line in the sand just a few days before, and now that line had manifested in my kitchen as bright red as if drawn in blood.

After a ten-minute barrage of how fucked up I was for questioning his time out with his friends, he concluded he would change and go back out in his car because he wasn't gonna stick around "for this bullshit." He put Mimi down at some point, which allowed me to breathe a little, but he did it because she began to cry, which could trigger further anger directed at her for being too loud and having nothing real to cry about. He'd give her something to cry about, if we weren't careful.

He changed clothes and left with a last-ditch verbal attack as he headed out the door. I don't remember what he said because I was holding my breath until I heard the garage door close behind him. We were safe for the night.

Later that night, Mimi spiked a fever which had her awake and crying most of the night. She rarely got sick, so I was quite worried and began calling him to tell him she was sick and ask him to come home. He wasn't answering his phone. I sat on the floor of the doorway of her room listening to her whimpering as we waited for the pain reliever to kick in. Meanwhile, my "committee" was having a knock-down, drag-out argument in my head.

"When he comes home, I am going to tell him to pack his bag and *leave*!" said one member.

"But I can't be the one to break up her family! What kind of mother would I be to do that?" said another.

"He's a *dick* and will never change! I have to do this for *her*!" said yet another member.

These conversations went on and on and on inside my head. When the sun finally rose the next morning, I waited until it was a reasonable time to call my sponsor. I gave voice to all the arguments my committee had been making inside my head all night, along with the awareness that I knew what it was like to be without a father, and I didn't want to do that to my little girl. The resonance with that level of abandonment was so real, and every cell in my body was screaming at me not to do that to her.

After listening intently to me, she offered one sentence that has stuck with me the rest of my days: "If you leave him, you will be teaching her not to accept unacceptable behavior. She may not understand now, but she will someday and that is one of the greatest gifts you can give her as her mother."

When he finally came striding in at noon, I was ready for him. He had been out all night and was hungover, so I felt like I had a slight advantage going in. In the hours since I had spoken to him to tell him about Mimi's fever, I had gathered a level of courage and strength I didn't know I had. In the years we had been together, he had always reminded me that he would make my life a living hell if I ever tried to leave him. Meanwhile, he had held me emotionally hostage by threatening to kill himself so many times I had lost count. The juxtaposition of living under threat if I ever left, while simultaneously being responsible for begging him to stay, had me so twisted up inside I rarely understood the ground that was immediately under my feet. But on this day, I had a clarity that I don't think I had ever experienced, and I knew I needed to take advantage of that moment and speak my truth as I had rarely spoken it in my lifetime.

We began with small talk. He asked how Mimi was feeling, and I let him know that her fever had finally broken and she was sleeping since we had both been up most of the night. I was grateful that she was asleep for this difficult conversation, but I knew on some level that her psyche was listening to every word.

"We need to make some decisions," I said to him to indicate I was done with small talk. "I cannot do what we are doing anymore."

"I know," he said, standing in the kitchen with his head down in a position of defeat. "I've been drinking again for a while."

"I've known for a while."

We were off to a good start, but I knew this was not going to be that easy. Over the course of the day, we had moments of tenderness and anger, tears and laughter, moving from room to room as we seemingly dissected every ghostly, diseased molecule of this relationship. It was Super Bowl Sunday, and we spent the entire day talking through the inevitable conclusion of separation.

He wasn't hearing me, or I wasn't being clear enough to understand that I was at the end of my very long rope and I could not hold on anymore. At one particular moment, as the sun was setting on the day, I was standing in the living room, and he was in the kitchen, which is actually where the conversation had begun.

I uttered the words that seemed to break through his impenetrable shell, "I'M DYING! Can you not see that I am standing here, *dying* in front of your eyes!" The tears were falling, and I had bared absolutely everything I had in my being at his feet. I had claimed the depth of my pain and had shouted it from the rooftops so that all could hear... "YOU HAVE TO GO!."

The Birth of a New Heart

Eggshells crack
from the tapping of new life,
longing to thrive.

Light cannot penetrate
until openings allow
for rays to enter
the depths
and shine its radiance
where darkness reigns.

My pleading for
a new heart
always fell on
deaf ears,
first and foremost,
my own.

I must create the cracks
within my own shell.
I must find the courage
to speak
my new heart
into existence.

My light does not come
from outside my shell.
The light of my God
flows from within.

Allowing the knowing
of my connection to spirit
reflects my light back
to my soul,
illuminating my new heart
right where it's always been,

here, in the center of life,
in the heart of my being.

Chapter 17

When I hear people who have not lived in toxic relationships say things like "Why doesn't she just leave?" or "You can't tell me she didn't see this coming!" I get immediately angry. As a person who has lived through this process, I understand the complexities of these relationships and want to jump to the defense of any woman or man who is being accused of not doing enough to protect themselves.

The bottom line, which I have come to understand through my own experiences, is that it *always* looks different from the outside, looking in. There is a clarity and a reasoning that lives in the brain of the person who has not been taken apart bit by little bit over a span of time that is not always available to those of us who find ourselves energetically buried by another's narcissism, ego, and anger.

I look back on my separation with David, and I see more clearly now that when I asked him to go, I was not asking him for a divorce. In fact, if you asked me that evening after he left if I thought this would end in divorce, I might have given you some blustery answer that made me look big and bad, but the true ultimatum was not "You better get out of my life or else." It was more like "Please, dear God, just leave for a little while so I can catch my breath."

In retrospect, I do not think I truly believed our relationship would end up in divorce at that moment. I was still too committed to keeping our family together, to making sure Mimi had her father, and to not do anything that would anger the bear too much that I couldn't retract if it became necessary. For many women and men trying to get out of toxic relationships, it looks more like two steps forward and ten steps back, as we slowly regain our sense of self and connection to the ground beneath our feet in order to stand tall when the winds begin to blow.

Just as the "grooming" process is slow and methodical as they tear us down, the process of building ourselves back up takes time and happens in small increments. If you find yourself loving someone who is walking this path, know that they are doing the best they can with what they've been left with in the wake of this slow moving tidal wave, and your judgment of the speed in which they are moving will not ever help them find their acceleration; often it will do the exact opposite.

David got a furnished apartment about twenty minutes away, taking only his clothes and personal items when he left. It seemed like the best thing to do, and it didn't involve splitting up furniture, which would be more obvious to Mimi, possibly causing more trauma. I was ready for him to go. The moment when he left the house with a car full of personal items, I realized I had never heard that level of silence in our house before. It was an energetic silence, not just auditory, and the calm felt in my heart was tangible. I was actually surprised the act of him leaving had even happened since I never thought he would allow us to get to this point. He had always warned me of how hard he would make it if I asked him to leave, so it baffled me that he had complied at all to my requests.

We began the task of figuring out our "new normal" when it came to communication and co-parenting. In the early days of the separation, he was calling me several times a day to see how Mimi was doing and wanted to know every detail about her day. I found myself excited by his enthusiasm and started to feel the familiar pull on my heart that maybe I had made a mistake in asking him to leave.

But it wasn't long before he began picking fights with me during each phone call. The most common complaints were:

"Why are you doing this to me?"

"You get some sick pleasure out of making me miserable, don't you?"

"You fucking anyone yet? I know you are…and I'll find out who it is."

These accusations started happening during every phone call. Sometimes the calls would begin in a nice tone and devolve to the abuse, and others would be abusive right out of the gate. Sometimes I would have the patience to try to talk him off the ledge, and other times I would hang up and not answer again. Since David did most things in circles, the cyclical pattern of these phone calls was not a surprise, but he became just as successful in draining me through the phone as he had been in person.

When I had found the courage to ask him to leave, I made a commitment to myself to be more consistent about attending Alanon meetings. I had been "sober" for nine years, but I was still challenged to put meetings first in my life to practice working a better program. My home group at the time was on Tuesday nights, and a group of folks who went to the meeting had been going to dinner before to deepen their connections with one another.

My sponsor had often asked me to join them, but I had always refused. When David was still in the house, I was lucky to get out for the meeting itself, so dinner was too much to expect. But with my newly found freedom, I decided that dinner with "Alapals" and then a meeting would be a great way to spend an evening, so I arranged for a babysitter and met them at the restaurant.

Spending time with these folks outside of meetings really helped me deepen my understanding of the principles of the program I had been learning for nine years but was still struggling to make a part of my everyday life. We tried to follow the guidelines of meetings, incorporating anonymity and trust with what was shared during dinner. I began laughing again, which fed my soul.

Not long after I began my new Tuesday night routine, David began calling on that night to discuss our relationship. I agreed because I was out of the house and could speak freely about things without little ears hearing, but it wasn't long before I noticed the destructive part of this new schedule. Tuesday night had become my "therapy" night. Dinner with Alapals, followed by a meeting, helped me keep my head screwed on straight and keep the focus on me while I figured out who I was and what I wanted. I had difficulty knowing where I stopped and he started, and Tuesday nights were a clear step toward delineating that boundary.

After a few weeks, I realized that we were getting into *huge* fights on Tuesday nights, either on the way to the restaurant or to the meeting or both. I would sometimes find myself sitting in the parking lot of the restaurant, screaming at him, followed by hanging up on him, followed by him calling me all through dinner. (Phones were different then. Putting them on silent was more difficult). If he didn't call before the restaurant, he called on the way to the meeting. I would often walk into the meeting late and in such a spin that I had a hard time focusing on what the topic was or offering anything other than venting about what a state I was in after speaking with him.

Most of the time, the accusations were directed at me hurting him. I rarely heard him talk about what he was doing to contribute to the chaos or taking responsibility for any of his choices (surprise, surprise). I decided after about a month of this pattern that I would no longer speak with him on Tuesdays. Those nights were for my healing and my progress, and I was not going to let him sabotage them any longer. We both had a lot of growing and work to do on ourselves before we could entertain the idea of reconciling and I had learned two very important lessons:

1) I was worthy of setting the boundary with him and the importance of safeguarding my Tuesday nights.
2) The indicator of David's readiness to come back home would be when he stopped begging me to return.

That indicator would take four months to appear. In that time, we got connected to a great therapist where we finally started to do some real work on our marriage. He got an opportunity to open a bail bonding business in Charleston, and it was exciting to watch him be enthusiastic about a career opportunity. David had always understood how people accused of crimes navigated the world. He would be good at finding them if they skipped, and he had a way of connecting with them and helping them to feel like whole human beings when everyone else had turned their backs on them.

He worked under a bail bondsman from another city as an apprentice, then studied to take the test to get his license. He was gone a fair amount of time working with this new adventure, but when I spoke with him on the phone, he was excited about life and this new journey he was on. He stopped asking me when he could move back in, therapy had begun to take hold, and we were discovering things about ourselves and our patterns that could be a game changer for us both. I had a huge revelation during one of our therapy sessions that has stuck with me all these years.

"I want each of you to tell me four adjectives that describe yourself. David, you go first."

"Smart, clever, handsome, and funny!" He rattled them off so fast it made my head spin.

The therapist turned to me and said, "Your turn."

I sat staring into her eyes and froze. David was waiting with the type of silence that you could feel as he anticipated my answers, which never came.

"Now, tell me four adjectives to describe your spouse. Dee, you go first this time."

I didn't hesitate for a moment. I rattled off about ten adjectives to describe him until she held up her hand to ask me to stop.

"Why do you think you were able to tell me all about David, but you couldn't offer any words about yourself?" She knew the answer, of course, but she wanted to see if *I* knew.

I truly could not think of one adjective to describe me. I could give you a dissertation on him, but my mind went completely blank when asked to describe myself. I walked out of that session with a brightly lit light bulb above my head. I realized in that moment that I had lost track of myself. I had lost connection with who I was and what I wanted. It was the first time I truly internalized my lack of boundaries and personal knowledge of what I wanted in this life.

I was growing and changing a lot with my newfound dedication to working my Alanon program, and David was learning from our therapy sessions, showing personal pride in his new work as a bail bondsman that I had not seen in him before, and for a time, life was good. In the brief moments when I considered asking for a divorce, my own abandonment issues from my father walking out on me came to the surface just enough to convince me that I didn't want to break up Mimi's family. I worked harder than he ever did to have him stay in her life, and I wasn't ready to give up that fight yet. As crazy as it sounds, we began having conversations about what reconciling would look like, and then we planned for him to move back in.

*****

During the four months of separation, I had been on a journey of discovery about myself. The silence I felt in the house, even with a five-year-old, was soul nourishing. I had experienced an awakening to myself during the time in my life when I discovered the memories of my father's sexual abuse and then further when I began walking through my life without the anesthesia that alcohol provided. Both had prepared me for this third moment of rebirth when I could discover what my life could look like through the eyes of faith and hope.

Growing up in the Episcopal Church, where attendance was about punishment, I grappled with the idea that there might be a loving God who could accept me for the child of light others suggested I was. How could a loving God allow the suffering I had endured, unless I was not worthy of their protection? I remember questioning my Sunday School teacher when I was young, daring him to provide evidence that God existed with the stubbornness of a child determined to be proven right. It was easier to accept that God didn't exist than to think they might think me unworthy of love and safety. I believe I was trying to convince myself that I was okay, because God didn't exist and life was happening to me just because I was there.

When I joined Alanon, I was told it was not a religious program. That was good, because I wasn't going to accept religion being pushed down my throat, but I struggled with some of the writings in the daily reader, *One Day at a Time in Alanon*, that quoted scripture from the Bible for us to ponder. Dr. Bob and Bill W. were of the Christian faith when they started Alcoholics Anonymous, and the Bible was their source of comfort as they crawled through the early days of their sobriety and then began to help others. The one saving grace of the program, for me, was the suggestion that my relationship with my higher power (as it was often referred to) was my own to determine. Step three of the twelve steps of Alanon says, "Made a decision to turn our will and our lives over to the care of God as we understand him." That last part was where I took a deep breath: *as I understand him*. It had never been suggested to me that I could formulate an understanding about what God is or was. I didn't know I had that kind of power over this seemingly omnipotent process, and in many ways, learning about that power unlocked a door to *my* power in many parts of my life that I had never considered. I was learning boundaries *and* how to own the power of them. I was learning communication *and* the power of clarity of expression. I was learning to let go of control *and* the power over my peace that release provided.

My sister Mary had been experiencing some amazing results in her own life through energy work. She had been sharing what it was like to go to a Reiki practitioner and move some of her blocked energy out of her body. One day, I woke up and decided I wanted what she was having, so when I went to my chiropractor appointment that day, I asked the receptionist if she knew anyone who did energy work. I had been going to this chiropractor for quite some time because I held all my tension in my shoulders and my hips, so my back was almost always out of alignment. The folks in this office were the most "woo-woo" people I knew at the time (which is how I referred to folks in the new age belief system), so I thought they would be a great place to start.

When I asked her if she had any recommendations, her face lit up like a Christmas tree! She gave me the names of a couple of people she knew who did this work but highly recommended one woman in particular who did craniosacral therapy.[8] She worked in Mt. Pleasant

---

[8] CranioSacral Therapy (CST) is a gentle, hands-on approach that releases tensions deep in the body to relieve pain and dysfunction and improve whole-body health and performance. It was pioneered and developed by Osteopathic Physician John E. Upledger after years of clinical testing and research at Michigan State University where he served as professor of biomechanics. https://www.upledger.com/therapies/faq.php

out of her home, and I called her on the way home to make my first appointment.

The day of my first appointment with Debi, I was nervous. I had talked to Mary about what to expect, but this was so far out of my box that even knowing what Mary had shared did not prepare me enough to quell the jitters. Not only was I unsure about the experience in and of itself, but my "committee" was busy worrying about how I would describe the experience to David, who was as far from understanding anything "woo woo" as one could possibly get. I anticipated judgment and ridicule and spent a bit of time on the drive to Debi's house, exploring the idea of not showing up to avoid the ultimate bashing I would receive from him on my choices.

Even though we had been separated for a couple of months, my brain still continued the negativity that he brought to the relationship in his absence. It was my internalized Crazy that I was as yet unable to turn off. Even with all those distractions, I found myself pulling into her driveway on time.

Her house was blue, with a chain-link fence surrounding the front yard that was covered with all manner of ivy and flowering vines. When I opened the gate to enter the space, I found a garden that immediately caused the word "Eden" to pop into my head. There were wind chimes singing in the wind and a bird bath with ceramic garden creatures at its base. I remember taking a deep breath, inhaling the beautiful breeze that filled my lungs with a deep sense of calm. I rose to the door and knocked, causing small dogs to begin barking inside. A little voice said "Just a minute," and I could hear rustling as she put the dogs away in their space. When the door opened, I locked eyes with a soul whom I felt I had known all my life.

Debi's home was as I would have imagined it to be. Images of spiritual beings lined the walls, crystals were on every surface, and incense was burning, filling the rooms with calming energy. We sat for the obligatory paperwork and a little small talk to put me at ease. Then she asked me to follow her to her "healing room," where we found a massage table draped with sheets and blankets. She instructed me to take my shoes off and lie on the table fully clothed. She would step out as I became comfortable and would be back in just a few moments. She spoke barely above a whisper, and I felt I was hearing her with my heart instead of my ears. I complied with her instructions and was laying on the table when she entered the room.

To describe the experience I had with her on that first day, and for the many years since, remains a challenge for me. She didn't have to say anything, and I trusted her with every fiber of my being. As her hands hovered above my body, or when she was surrounding my energy centers with one hand above and one below, I felt her hands get so hot I thought she would pull back in pain. She would ask about whether or not I had fallen out of a tree and landed hard on my feet (which I had), because she could hear my cries. Or she would twist my head and neck in such contortions, describing what she was experiencing as "taking me through the birth canal."

She was reading the book of my soul experience through her hands, and I could only marvel at the sensations and emotions that were moving in ways that I had rarely, if ever, felt before. Some days I was locked so hard we both felt like we had run a marathon after our sessions. Tears would come during some sessions, and as she lovingly asked me to explain the pain, I felt I was not only expressing the memories verbally but could *feel* them leave my body through my lips. In all the years of traditional talking therapy, I had never felt such a powerful release. She was unlocking the doors to my soul, and I was allowing the pain and trauma to actually leave my body, never to return.

I would get off the table in what I called a Debi trance. She would offer me a glass of water and sit with me as I gathered myself before I needed to get behind the wheel and navigate home. When I was in the bathroom, washing my hands, I would look at myself in the mirror and marvel at my eyes. I had never seen them so clear. It was as if I had undergone cataract surgery and was seeing myself with clear lenses for the first time. One day, at least two years after my first appointment with her, I was leaving and looked up to see a graveyard across the street from her home.

I exclaimed, "Hey! When did that graveyard get there?"

She started laughing in her gentle giggle. Of course, the graveyard had been there all along. I was just finally clear enough to see past the end of my nose and acknowledge it existed. We decided that would be her litmus test for her client's progression—how long it would take for them to notice the graveyard.

Debi helped me understand the nature of holding trauma inside our cells and how that holding causes disease inside the body and the mind that can be with us for our lifetimes if we don't let it go. My body began to heal itself in ways I didn't know were possible. Not only was I letting go of the trauma I had stored up over the years of my journey, but I was making space for other healing energies to come in and nourish me. I had more patience with Mimi on days where I would usually find myself raging at her, and I began to have deeper understandings about concepts like boundaries and personal responsibility that allowed me to begin to incorporate them into my life more regularly than I had ever been able to before.

One of the main principles of Alanon that I have always appreciated is the idea of doing the work on ourselves, not to change the alcoholic in our lives, but to shift our relationships to and with others. Even if David continued to drink, if I was doing *my* work and changing how *I* related to the world, it would shift our relationship in often positive ways. I began to see that dynamic working the longer I continued my sessions with Debi, David's and my relationship was changing because *I* was shifting. As a control freak, who always thought it was my only way of survival to change others, I was surprised and delighted to begin to see that what everyone had been telling me all these years was true. I do not have the ability to change anyone else but *myself*, and if I focus on changing myself, my relationships *will* change.

Between David's excitement about his newfound profession as a bail bondsman and my work with Debi, plus more focused time in Alanon, our marriage began to take a turn toward health. When we decided to get back together, we enjoyed a honeymoon phase of time where he was working and making money to contribute to the family, which he had never done consistently before, and I was flourishing in my work at the barn, taking on more responsibilities in the office besides teaching, which expanded my skills and my investment in that career. Mimi had been attending a local

Montessori school and was surrounded by loving teachers who were allowing her intellect to soar. The three of us seemed unstoppable for a time, but as in all phases of our lives together, this one didn't last for long.

2003 was the year of our tenth wedding anniversary, and we were eager to celebrate. We couldn't believe we had reached this milestone and were grateful for all the folks who had helped us along the way. David had opened a bail bonds business, and it was a quick success. We had taken a loan against my trust for the start-up costs and had crafted a great office just down the street from the local jail, which was always prime real estate. Location, location, location. He had built a reputation of fairness and respect among the community he served and was proud of his accomplishments, as was I.

But there was a downside to his success that was beginning to show itself—he was gone a lot. If he wasn't working late hours at the shop, he was out "chasing a skip," spending many hours sitting in cars on stakeouts to catch the person who had run away from their bail obligations and who represented thousands of dollars to his office if they went uncaught. At first, I was so proud of him using his skills for good instead of evil, as I used to say, that I didn't have a problem with him doing this part of his job, even if it meant I went to bed alone many nights. His time living on the other side of the law was invaluable to this work, and I saw he had a confidence in himself that I had not seen since our first meeting when he was one of the biggest drug dealers in Atlanta.

What I wasn't seeing behind the scenes was the briefcases of cocaine that some of his clients were giving him as payment in lieu of cash. He would tell me about these incidences as if they were super rare, and he always told me that he insisted they take it away immediately and only pay in cash. But once an addict, always an addict. It wasn't long before he began accepting those briefcases, and then it wasn't long before that product was going up his nose. I believe I could correlate his longer absences from our lives with the increase in his drug use. He was still making money and loved throwing cash at me every chance he got, but he was now in the throes of his addiction, and it was quickly spiraling out of control.

Remember when I talked about how people continue behaviors as long as they still get a pay off? Well, I was not immune to contributing to the spiral David was caught in. As much as I might have thought I could complain about him not being around, I have to admit it worked for me for him to be gone. I had the best of both worlds: our marriage was "good" again and I could claim that as a success, *and* he was gone all the time so I could parent the way I wanted to.

He was making money, which made me happy and kept my family off my back for having a "deadbeat" husband, and I could move through space with little push back from him. We settled into a comfortable routine where Mimi and I would see him only if we went to the shop to visit. We might meet for the occasional dinner out, where he would give me a wad of cash and play with Mimi a little as he showed her how much her daddy loved her, then we would go our separate ways. Sometimes it would be three weeks before we would see each other in person, with our only contact to be a phone call every once in a while. I was living as a single mother within a marriage again, and it was working for me—until it wasn't.

I was getting my haircut one day, spilling all the details of how messed up my life was having a marriage to a man who was never around, when I had a revelation. After listening to my long diatribe, my hair stylist said, "You are the most long-suffering woman I know."

In that moment, I looked at myself in the mirror and something shifted. I didn't want to be long-suffering anymore. I didn't want to be the wife everyone felt sorry for, the saint to his forever sinner. These roles had been what I had thrived on for our ten-year marriage, and I realized in that instant that they no longer served me. I was ready for this marriage to shift in the same direction that my sense of self was shifting. I no longer wanted to be fueled by fear and loathing. Instead of waiting for our actual anniversary in October, we had decided to take a trip in July to celebrate. We were originally going to take a cruise, but the very ship we were booked on had a massive fire in the engine room three weeks before our departure and would not be sailing anytime soon. I had to scramble to find an alternative, and we ended up at a beautiful resort on the French side of St. Maarten, which is an island in the Caribbean.

I was determined that this trip would jump start our connection and we would rediscover our union—returning home with a newly found dedication to each other and our relationship. It would be a ten-day journey to paradise.

When we arrived at the resort, it was everything we dreamed. The beaches were quiet with crystal blue water lapping at the shore, the buildings were white stucco, and the rooms had rooftop lounges where you could sunbathe and relax if you didn't want to be at the pool or the beach. The rooms were full of rattan furniture with white linens and Tolle curtains that blew in the breeze. We decided to have dinner in the resort restaurant overlooking the sea, as the sun set seemed to perform just for us, filling the sky with pinks and purples as the sun dipped below the horizon.

Soon after the waiter took our drink and dinner order and left us to enjoy the view, it began. David looked me straight in the eye and said, "So tell me about this woo woo bullshit you've been doing. I gotta tell you, you've become really weird the past few months, and I'm not sure you're right in the head anymore."

It was as if the oxygen had been sucked off the balcony and time was suspended. What was he talking about? Where in the *hell* did this come from? It had been some time since he had launched an attack like this, and my missile launch detector had gotten rusty. I no longer had a well-honed skill set for navigating this territory without blowing myself up, so I blew it up before he had the chance.

"What the fuck does that mean?" I said in a much louder tone than he anticipated.

"You're just doing all this freaky stuff now, and I gotta tell you, I'm worried about whether or not you've lost it. You're doing yoga and listening to creepy new age music and talking about intuition and shit. You'd think you're the Dalai Lama or something! You're not the same woman I married, I gotta tell you."

"Well, of course, I'm not the same woman you married. People change! We've been going to therapy to change and make this marriage better. How the hell else do you think we're gonna keep this together? Where is this coming from?"

"I don't know! I don't know if you are a good mom anymore because you believe in all this goofy shit. I don't know if I want that around my daughter. You just aren't the same woman I married."

"You're right! I'm not the same woman you married, and she ain't coming back. So you either need to get to know *this* woman, or get the hell out of the way! We were in Charleston *five hours ago*, and you waited until *now* to have this conversation? What the fuck, David!"

I was shaking. He had me so mad! He made me come all this way to blow up our trip! It was just like him, but I didn't see it coming because we had both made such progress in our relationships with ourselves and each other. We ate our meal in silence, barely noticing the transition to darkness as the sun went to sleep over the horizon of the beautiful crystal-clear water. We returned to the room and went to sleep facing away from each other in the bed, trying not to notice we had ten days together on this island, and I wasn't sure how we were gonna make it without killing each other!

The next morning, true to form, we rose to greet the day as if nothing had happened. I explained it away in my head that we were both just tired from the travel and that today would be better. We decided after a lovely breakfast in our room that we would go lie by the pool for a little while. After getting settled in on our lounge chairs in the glorious sun, it wasn't long before he got antsy.

He started asking about going into town and bugging me to shift gears to go shopping and see the sights. To do that would have meant showering, which would have taken longer than he wanted. I really didn't want to move. We were supposed to be there to relax!

He began to needle me with comments like "You stupid Americans just want to sit around. I want to go meet the locals and see how they live! You can sit in the sun at home. Why don't we go see the sights!"

After thirty minutes of this, I finally snapped, "Why don't *you* go into town? I am happy here and don't feel like moving. We've got ten days here. We've got plenty of time."

That seemed to be exactly what he wanted. He jumped up to grab his towel, and off he went, saying he would see me later over his shoulder. I was happy for the quiet, but it wasn't long before loneliness set in. We hadn't been here twenty-four hours, and he had already abandoned me. This was feeling familiar, but I resolved myself that we were both doing what made us happy, which was a sign of a healthy marriage. My "committee" was working overtime to keep my heart from knowing the truth about this landmark trip. Even though we were here together, I was alone.

As the days went on, David got more and more agitated. Cell phone service on the island was spotty at best, and he had found only one spot outside in the parking lot where he got the clearest connection. He was calling the office all the time, seemingly solving all the world's problems that cropped up immediately after our airplane left the ground. He befriended a taxi driver that was always the one who picked us up to go anywhere. I always thought his ability to befriend people was one of his greatest skills. What I wasn't in touch with was *why* he befriended these people. He knew if he was going to score drugs; he needed to have local connections. I was oblivious to this behavior and just thought he was friendly and liked by all. My naivete was still so strong about the lengths he would go to have access to drugs even after all these years.

We would go into town in the evenings and visit the local casinos. I didn't want him to gamble, but he begged and begged, so a compromise was met. He could gamble as long as he didn't lose more than a certain amount, and we were both drinking our water and sodas as we strolled through the shops. He was desperate to buy me something expensive, and we could not walk past a jewelry store without him dragging me in to look at all the incredible necklaces and bracelets. I didn't wear flashy jewelry like this, but he was insistent.

There was this cash he had earned burning a hole in his pocket, and I was tempted, only because I liked the idea of him buying something expensive with his money that wouldn't impact my trust for once. Days and days of shopping yielded nothing I could accept, until we found the shop that sold Rolex watches. This seemed to satisfy both of our needs; it was expensive for him and practical for me. After days of negotiations, he finally bought me a woman's Rolex watch for more money than I had *ever* considered paying for myself.

We fought off and on, usually about him calling home too much or going off by himself and seemingly forgetting about me, and we never touched each other intimately even once. There was the obligatory peck on the lips at hellos and goodbyes, but in that beautifully romantic setting, we never made love. There was always one excuse or another. In hindsight, I can honestly say I was relieved to not have to perform. It was an excruciating ten days of exile on this island, and both of us were eager to get home.

The day before we were set to leave, we were gathering our clothes together for packing when there was a knock on the door. A steward of the hotel handed David a sheet of paper with a note on it, and he read it as he slowly closed the door. Then he exploded.

"WHAT THE FUCK IS THIS! WE CAN'T LEAVE?" His eyes were popping out of his head as he shook the paper in the air and threw it at me.

I picked the note up off the floor and read the message. It read:

> Dear La Samanna guest,
>
> Due to the volcano erupting on neighboring Montserrat Island, the government has grounded all flights in the area for at least the next twenty-four to thirty-six hours due to the danger of flying with ash in the air. We know you are due to check out tomorrow to return home and that this will affect your plans. Rest assured La Samanna will allow you to stay in your room for as long as it takes for the airport to clear and you to return home.
>
> Please stay in touch with the airport for updates on flight availability, and if there is anything we can do to make your extended stay more comfortable, please do not hesitate to ask. We are sorry for the inconvenience.

He was beside himself. During the time it took for me to read the note, he had stormed outside and had started making phone calls. He didn't even hear me when I called out to him to discuss what we were going to do, as his tornado had formed in a nanosecond and there was no turning back.

I waited for him to finish his phone call and come back inside to discuss what our next steps were. He was pacing, saying he had court he had to get back for and skips to chase that were costing him money every day we were gone, and that *he couldn't stay here anymore!* My PhD kicked in, and I started trying to talk him of what looked like a very high ledge, suggesting that there was very little we could do about a volcano erupting and that there might be worst places to be stranded. But he wasn't having any of it. He decided we were going to pack as scheduled and that we would take ourselves and our luggage to the airport tomorrow and wait for them to reopen the flights so we would be one of the first to get on.

I didn't think this was the best course, and I didn't look forward to sitting at an airport all day, but he would not be dissuaded. He spent the rest of the night perseverating on how fucked up his life was and that this could only happen to him. I kept waiting for the tornado to subside, but it didn't look like it was going to until someone told him he could get on a plane.

The next morning, we called our friendly taxi driver / drug dealer, and he picked us up with luggage in tow to go to the airport. We told them at the desk what we were doing and made sure our room wouldn't be given away in case it didn't work, and they were kind enough to agree, probably because they thought we were being silly for trying so hard. Why didn't we just go sit on the beach and enjoy our extra days in the sun? We must have looked insane to them.

When we arrived at the airport, it was a madhouse! There were tourists everywhere, wandering around with their luggage, demanding to be put on a plane like irate Americans can do. It was like looking at an entire building full of Davids, which made my head hurt and my stomach do flip-flops. We stood in line for three hours while our taxi driver took care of our luggage at the curb. He wasn't going anywhere because David was paying him to wait, so he was just fine with this arrangement. We thought we saw some folks who had success getting a ticket, and we were hopeful we would have the same luck. They had not made a formal announcement that planes were flying again, but it did seem like there was hope. When we finally got up to the counter and David began his spiel about how he desperately needed to get home (which he had been practicing on me over and over and *over* while we waited), our prayers were semi-answered.

"We have one seat left that you can have today."

"I'll take it!" he yelled at the ticket agent, then spun around to me and said, "Legs, you'll be fine! Our taxi guy will take you back to the hotel. Then I will pay him to pick you up tomorrow and wait with you here while you try to get on a flight. I *have* to get back, legs. I can't stay here. It's costing me too much money! You'll be fine, won't you?"

I stood there with my mouth open as he shook me by the shoulders. He was leaving me here. He was taking the single ticket and going home without me. I flashed back to the young girl standing in the doorway of the bathroom with my wedding trousseau on, being told by my new husband the very same statement: "You'll be okay! I'm just going to go out and party for a bit. I'll be back soon."

Before I could mount any argument, he had paid for the ticket, gotten his bags to be checked, and with a peck on the cheek and a palmed wad of cash to the driver, he was gone. I turned slowly to the driver, climbed back into the van, and went back to the hotel.

The whole way back to the hotel my "committee" was talking me off my own ledge. It would be ok, I could sit by the pool all day without having to listen to him bitch. I would enjoy the peace and quiet, and it was kind of nice that I had the place to myself. None of these arguments filled the hole in my heart, but they were a nice try. The driver brought my bags back up to my room, and I stood there in the center of it not knowing what to do. I put my bathing suit on and went down to the pool, but I was afraid someone was going to ask where my husband was, and I was embarrassed to say the truth and too dumbstruck to come up with a good lie. I lasted about fifteen minutes before I finally realized how exposed I felt and returned to the safety of my room. I had a whole twenty-four hours before my flight would leave, and I was in one of the most beautiful places on the planet. I lay on the couch all day, watching TV, and cried.

*****

    I got home to Charleston on a Monday and couldn't wait for my regular Tuesday night Alanon meeting. I hadn't seen nor spoken to David since he left me that day at the airport. He was back in his chaos element of work, and I was happy to be home in my quiet house. The extra day I had on St. Maarten was filled with sadness and loneliness, but returning home, I began to feel a different sort of way. Something in me had shifted since being abandoned yet again by this man whom I had stood by for years at my own peril. I couldn't wait to get back to my normal routine without him underfoot every day, but I didn't have the deeper revelation until I was sitting in that room at 8:00 p.m. on Tuesday.

    The format of Alanon meetings is the same, no matter where you are in the world. The meetings tend to have different flavors and rhythms depending on who attends, but the opening and closing are always the same, and I take great comfort in that. I know them both by heart, and hearing them again after such a harrowing trip is like hearing a familiar song that my mom used to sing to me for comfort when I was sick or upset. After the topic was introduced and we began to go around the room for each person to share, I found my mind drifting off a bit. I realized that I was among my very favorite people, and I knew that I could say anything out loud in this room without judgment or ridicule. I had a deep understanding of the difference between where I had just come from for ten days and where I sat now, and I felt the tears rise to the top of my throat. These were my people. These were the folks who listened to me and allowed me to cry in the safety of their circle week after week. They weren't waiting for me to change or morph into someone more palatable for them to manage; they accepted me exactly as I was in that moment.

    As I took a deep breath in, I realized my marriage was over. I realized I no longer wanted to be in a relationship that required me to be someone other than who I truly was. I realized I wanted to move forward in my growth and understanding of myself, no matter what might come with that knowledge—and I wasn't afraid. I wasn't afraid of being alone. I wasn't afraid of being a single mother or a divorced woman. The excitement about what my life might become outweighed the fear for the first time in my life.

When it came time for me to share, I felt the love being reflected back to me as I described my internal realizations that had just been made clear to me. I felt a smile begin to emerge on my face, and I knew that whatever might come, I was going to be okay.

Legacy

You define my bones,
every sinewy ligament
tying the chapters
of my skeleton together.

The length of my leg,
the circumference
of my skull
dictated by those
who came before.

What part
of my genetic code
came from your
fist hitting my face or
your hand over my mouth,
muffling my screams
as you penetrated
deep inside?

What part
will I pass on
to my daughter?
How will her DNA
be warped by the ills
that came before?

How can I break
the ties that bind?
How can I set her free
from your despicable touch?

I begin
by speaking
my truth.

Part Four

After Dad walked out of Susan's living room that fateful day in 1993, I got busy creating a life without him. He had clearly indicated that he had no interest in having me in his life anymore, and his blatant rejection of me actually helped me in moving on. Mom leaving him helped as well, as I essentially was able to amputate the gangrenous limb that threatened to make my body go septic and take my life. I hear about and know abuse survivors who have to see their abusers at family gatherings, in their workplace, or places of worship; and my heart breaks for them to have to face their monsters with no end in sight. The day I saw him pack up his legal pad and pen and walk out the door was the last day I saw him for quite a while, and I was blessed to have that level of safety. I rarely went to my hometown in North Carolina, and when I did, I wouldn't leave Mom's house for fear of running into him on the street or in a restaurant. I didn't go see Baboo before she died because I was afraid he would appear in the doorway, and I didn't know what my reaction would be to seeing him nor how I would handle rejecting her son in front of my beloved grandmother. When Baboo died while David and I were on our honeymoon, I was able to use my being out of the country as an excuse not to go sit in the church with him and pretend like nothing was wrong. It was as if he and his entire side of the family were just gone—and that worked for a while.

In 1995, Mary was getting married. She was having a big wedding, and Dad was going to walk her down the aisle. In the two years since I had confronted Dad, Mary and I had been through a tough process of forgiveness and acceptance. While the rest of the family rejected him, she welcomed him back into her world with open arms—and I was angry. We had many conversations that revolved around the "him or me" choice, but resolution was not easily attained. Mary and I had only recently become friends, and she had seen me through some very tough times, like when I was considering suicide or when David and I were having such a rocky start. I didn't want to see it as a betrayal that she still wanted to have a relationship with Dad in light of my truth, and I worked very hard to reconcile in my mind why she couldn't just side with me. I didn't want to lose her again, and there were many conversations where she made it pretty clear that if I pushed her to choose, I wouldn't like the outcome.

My perception of the arc of this story is, she felt she had lost her dad to me when I came into the world and his attention had turned to me—and now she had him back. As sick as that all sounds, when children are living in that kind of twisted situation, they don't understand the depth of the sickness. They only understand that the parent they wish they had was no longer showing them the attention they craved. All these years later, he had returned to her focus, and she was happy. I do not know if her story includes any improper behavior by Dad to her. That is her story and not mine to tell. But at this moment in time, it seemed to me that she felt like he had returned to her and she was not letting him go again.

She asked me to stand with her as one of her attendants at her wedding, and I couldn't say no. I had no idea how I was going to handle seeing him again, not to mention being surrounded by his entire side of the family at the rehearsal dinner and then the ceremony the following day, but I was going to try. David and I had a long conversation about whether or not he was going to go with me, and all he could do was bluster about punching Dad in the face the moment he saw him, so we quickly decided he was not going to go. Looking back at that time, had we had a healthy relationship, David might have been able to put his feelings aside to go in support of me and not do anything that might embarrass me in front of the family. But he decided he couldn't control himself, and so I went alone.

I convinced myself I was happy to be alone because I didn't have to worry about him flying off the handle and doing something I would regret. I was newly sober and freshly married without the solace of drinking to numb the pain and anxiety or a husband to lean on for support. It was going to be like walking into the lion's den without a weapon, and I did not know if I had any allies to lean on while fighting for my life.

I stayed at Mary's house in the area of Atlanta called Little Five Points and was so excited that the day had finally arrived for her. She was marrying a great guy, and they were super cute together, but she was nervous when I arrived. We had a couple of days before the rehearsal dinner, and our younger sister, Christy, was arriving soon. Christy was a natural blonde but had gone through a goth period that began in high school and ever since had been dying her hair black.

When I was asking Mary if there was anything I could do for her, her response was simple.

"Please make sure Christy doesn't have a skunk stripe on her head for the ceremony, and I will be forever grateful!"

We stayed up late into the night, talking about the family and Dad and how I was going to feel seeing him again. Mary and I had come to an understanding about her relationship with Dad, and I didn't hold resentment toward her for including him in her life. I understood why she needed him, and I was able to not equate that need with a rejection of my truth. We hadn't done a whole lot of work on ourselves by this point, but we must have done just enough to figure out how to navigate this impasse. I had gone most of my life without my big sister in my corner, and I wasn't going to let him ruin that for me again. If pushing her to make a choice between Dad and me would push her away, I wasn't going to let the choice leave my lips.

That night, in her kitchen, as we talked about everything under the sun, she offered a level of acceptance of my truth that I had never heard from her before.

"In all this time, you have never wavered in your story," she said. "Your father walked out on you, and you never looked back or considered changing your mind. That commitment to your story is the one thing that gives you credibility to me. I'm not ready to say you are telling the truth, but I will say the honor you show in holding your story makes me believe you."

I cried when I heard those words. She was doing her best to be supportive of me and admit that this weekend was going to be difficult for me and she appreciated me being there. I knew she would be surrounded by people who wanted her attention and that she would not be able to safeguard me from a cousin asking me why I didn't talk to Dad anymore, or an Aunt giving me a judging look because she knew I had rejected him for whatever reason. But I knew she wanted to be that protector, and that was enough for me.

When I opened the front door the next day to greet Christy, she did indeed have a three-inch-wide blond stripe starting at her forehead and going all the way back to the nape of her neck. Her roots had grown out, and she had forgotten that fixing this was the *one thing* Mary had asked her to do before she arrived. I let her put her things down, then said, "We'll be right back!" We left to walk down the street to the drugstore to buy hair dye. Christy was not going to stress Mary out with this important detail if I could help it. By the time she made it to the rehearsal dinner, Christy's hair was all one color—black! It was better than a stripe!

As I walked down the drive to the rehearsal dinner, I was having one of my out-of-body experiences. I could hear the chatter coming from the venue and I knew the hall was filled with at least fifty people whom I had not seen since long before our family blew up. I had no idea what explanations had been offered, or if any of these folks knew that Dad and I were even estranged. If they did know, would they ask me about it? If they didn't know, would they notice he and I were not speaking? I had not laid eyes on Dad since watching him walk out of my life two years earlier and I was working hard to feel my feet on the ground as I walked into the space.

It was a beautiful venue that was largely an outdoor space, like being on someone's open deck. There were round tables and chairs filling the space, with a head table at the front of the room where Mary, Chris, and the respective parents would sit. I found a person or two I could talk to and did my best to hide in places where no one would find me throughout the night.

The first time I saw him, I had a visceral reaction in my gut as if someone had punched me, and I lost my breath for a second. He was moving about the space, greeting people, shaking hands with the men, and giving sloppy kisses on the cheeks of the women. Mary's best friend, Lydia, invited me to sit with her when we finally took our seats for the dinner, and I appreciated the support she offered as a friendly and accepting force. Lydia knew the story, and I took comfort in being with someone who understood my discomfort without me having to explain in detail.

I had decided before I came that I wasn't going to tell anyone my story. I wasn't going to lie, but I wasn't going to spill the beans either. This wasn't the place to do that, and I didn't want to risk ruining Mary's special weekend. When everyone sat down and the speeches began, I was riveted just like the rest of the room to honor the blushing bride and the handsome groom with tales of their love together and wishes for a prosperous and happy life. When Dad stood up for his toast, I didn't know what to expect. He started off with well wishes and platitudes that anyone would expect from the father of the bride, then he stepped in it.

"I want to thank Mary for making me a father-in-law for the first time."

You could have heard a pin drop in that room. Then a small disembodied voice rang out in response, "SECOND TIME!"

He paused, regained his composure, and proceeded with the rest of his toast as if nothing had happened. Lydia reached under the table to find my hand and gave it a squeeze. Of course, David and I had been married two years already, but he had not been a part of any of that, and the whole room knew it. I didn't have to say anything that made him look like an ass. He had done that all by himself.

When I walked down the driveway later that evening to my car, I had a smile on my face. I had walked into the lion's den, and just by virtue of my presence in the room, I had made the lion so uncomfortable that he had stepped in his own shit without any help from me. It was a victory for me that I did not anticipate getting or needing, but it gave me the power to get through the following day with my head held high and my shoulders back.

The wedding was a beautiful event. Mary and Chris enjoyed their day and no one tried to talk to me about Dad. I ignored him, even when we took family photos together. I believe there was an element of dissociation for me during the day, but I stayed present enough to be happy for my sister and her new husband while still protecting myself and staying in my power. I was happy I didn't have to see him for a long while after this day, but I got through the first major encounter after becoming estranged with my dignity intact.

My next encounter with Dad was seven years later at the birth of Mary and Chris's son, Tyler, in 2002. Mary and I had deepened our relationship during her pregnancy since I had been through it with Mimi five years prior, so it was never a question whether or not I would be present at the birth of my nephew. I had crafted a world without my father that allowed me to move through space, knowing he wouldn't be lurking around every corner, but this was different. Mary was the only one of us who still had a relationship with him, and she wanted her father there at the birth of his grandchild. She and I had many talks about what that would look like, and I never considered asking her to not invite him to the blessed event.

The bigger challenge for me was the fact that he would meet and be in close proximity to Mimi for the first time in her life. I had resolved myself that he would never have access to her and had been successful in keeping that distance, but she wanted to be present when her cousin was born, and I wasn't about to say no to those pleading eyes. It turned my stomach to think of him in the same room with her.

It was a victory for me in many ways that I had given him his first grandchild and he had never met her. When he walked out on me in 1993, he walked out on any rights to know her, and I felt power in the ability to keep that promise to myself. This family event was going to bring them together, and there wasn't anything I could do about it. I had to think of how I was going to ensure her emotional safety, especially if I wasn't in the room when they were together.

Mary had decided on hypnobirthing as a birth plan, and she wanted me to be in the room with her for the process. I was honored to be asked, and we put together her bag of candles and CDs for music in the room to ensure the calmest atmosphere for baby Em to come into the world. (They chose to be surprised at the baby's gender, so they called him/her Em, which stood for *embryo* and Emma, which was their girl name for the baby.)

Mimi and I had arrived in Atlanta days before Mary's due date to make sure we were there for the blessed event, and everyone was on baby watch. When her due date came and went with no indication that Em was joining us any time soon, we began to plan each day around activities designed to encourage labor. We took walks, ate specific foods that were supposed to do the trick, and even took Mary on top of Stone Mountain, hoping the energetic vortex it is supposed to house would get things moving—with no luck. As each day came and went with no labor, we knew we might be heading into inducement if she wasn't showing signs by two weeks past her date. As that day approached, we made plans, and family members began to arrive in town.

I had a talk with Mom before the blessed day to ask that she be "on guard" for Mimi. If I was in the labor and delivery room with Mary, Mimi would be in the waiting room with everyone else, including Dad. I needed her to say directly that she would not let Mimi out of her sight and that she would pay attention if he began to talk to her in case Mimi got confused by anything he said. I had talked to Mimi before the day and explained to her that she was going to meet my daddy at the hospital. She didn't ask me why she hadn't met him yet, and I didn't offer why.

Mom had remarried in 1996 to a wonderful man named Bob, and Mimi had always known him as her grandfather. She wasn't missing that element in her life, so she wasn't curious about why she was just meeting my dad now. As I explained this to her, I could feel my gut twisting in fear. I didn't think he would touch her or do anything to overtly hurt her, but just the idea that he got to share the same oxygen with her was more than I had ever thought he would get to experience. If I was going to be there for Mary, I had to trust that Mom had this one and that all would be okay.

After a long labor with little progress, Mary ended up having a caesarean section. Because he was two weeks overdue, Tyler had cooked so long we all joked that Mary had given birth to a toddler. He was 10 pounds, 8.4 ounces! Baby and Mama were doing fine, and it was the first time I had stepped foot in the waiting room, where he and the rest of the family were waiting. I couldn't look at him directly and was grateful for my mommy duties that allowed me to focus all my energy on Mimi. She looked good, was smiling, and didn't seem to have any adverse effects from being in the same room with this monster from my childhood all this time.

When I asked Mom later how the time went between them while in the waiting room, Mom said Mimi kept calling him "Mommy's daddy" as she tried to get him to engage with her with games or books that were in the waiting room. He just sat there and stared at his lap, never responding to her pleas. It was one of the first times I felt sorry for him, as he seemed trapped in a hell of his own making. Whatever his reasoning was for disengaging, I was deeply grateful for that gift.

When Tyler turned four years old, Mary invited me to North Carolina for his birthday party. She and Chris had moved back to our hometown, which astounded me as she would have been the last one of us I could imagine moving back to that small community. Chris had gone into business with Mom's husband, Bob, and they had a nice home among the pine trees of my childhood. Mimi and I traveled to North Carolina for the weekend of the party, and I was looking forward to seeing CC and Skinny (her husband) since they were coming from their home in Boone for the special day.

I loved the fact that we were all close enough to make it a priority to gather to celebrate our kiddos on their birthdays. We had spent many years working on our interpersonal relationships and genuinely liked being with one another. If I spend any time thinking about where we had come from to today's connections, it is truly a miraculous journey filled with lots of tears and lots of forgiveness. Gathering for these milestones further deepened those links, allowing me to be in gratitude for the path walked.

As Tyler's friends began to arrive, we were in the backyard. The kids had swimsuits on to run through the sprinkler and play on the play set. Chris was on grill master duty with hotdogs and hamburgers grilling for the masses, while Mary and I spent the morning putting all the snacks in serving bowls and getting all the coolers ready, filled with Bud Light and Juicy Juice.

Within the first fifteen minutes of guests arriving, he walked down the driveway. I stood staring at him with my breath caught in my throat as his wife and he worked their way in my direction. Mary was usually good about letting me know when he was going to show up, but she had failed to mention his attendance this time. Floods of feelings washed over me—betrayal, fear, sadness and anger toward Mary rose up in my throat as my fight-or-flight instinct kicked in. In past encounters, I had reactions like feeling like I had been punched in the stomach and/or the shutdown response where my eyes would drop to the ground and I would move through the space like he wasn't there. My skill set of self-preservation was not well-developed in past sightings, but this time felt different. Among all the feelings swirling toward Mary, I was feeling something different toward him. I had a sense of strength in my feet as I felt the ground below me, and my instinct was to hold my ground. As he made his rounds, saying hello to everyone, it didn't occur to me to run away. I had every right to be there and was no longer willing to surrender my position to him.

He had also adopted the "ignore her" stance in the past, so when he looked me straight in the eye and headed in my direction, I recognized his choice as new. He had not looked me in the eye since the day he chose to walk out of my life thirteen years before, and for a moment, it was as if everyone else became blurred and we were the only two in focus. He approached with his arms outstretched, as if to ask for a hug, but there was no asking. He went straight into my personal space without recognition of the boundary. Nothing had changed, and yet everything had changed.

I put my hand up to his chest and said, "No!"

Time seemed to suspend. The whole encounter probably lasted less than ten seconds, but in reality, it was thirty-eight years of subjugation falling away, as I expressed my God-given right to a boundary he had never honored. When my fingertips lightly touched his shirt, I realized he was still advancing, having not heard my verbal rejection or, more likely, just not thinking it applied to him. My eyes had to speak to his soul more than my voice to his ears.

I leaned back to avoid his advancement and reiterated my boundary, "No!"

His body began to move backward out of my personal space. The look on his face told me he understood what I was doing, and I felt victory! He had no real ability to harm me in that moment, but I was reclaiming all the times before when my no was lost in ears muffled by power and alcohol. I removed myself to go into the house and catch my breath, and Mary followed me inside. She had watched the whole exchange and wanted to apologize for not giving me warning of his invitation. She also expressed outrage at his audacity to try to take a hug like that and wondered out loud what he thought I was going to do.

He thought I was going to submit to him. He thought I was going to put his needs before my own. He thought I was the same scared girl he had raped at the age of two with his arm across my neck and his demands to be quiet. He thought wrong. I had walked through the process of identifying my boundaries with both David and Dad, and they each continued to give me opportunities to express those boundaries, but I wasn't just trying to convince them. For as many years as I had been violated by both of them, I needed time to rewire my brain and my story to include new reactions of self-protection that I could always rely on and predict. Those boundaries did not start with their respect; they began with me believing I deserved them. I had to know in the depths of my being that I was worthy of protection, safety, and love. Only then would the people in my life understand my value; they would see it reflected in my eyes.

The Victory of a Reluctant Kiss

There are no doors
that lock in my world.
The edges of my curves
give way to your hands
as they always have.

I have been yours
for the taking
since my first breath.

My no falls into the ether,
never being detected
by your ears.

Until one day…

Your kiss goodbye
is rejected
by my childlike resistance,
and I feel the power
of keeping you at bay.

It is my small victory
in this perpetual war,
trying it on for size
to see if you will obey.

Courage grows
in my heart
with each small step
as I strengthen
my arms
to hold you back.

At night, my defenses
are few.
Reluctant kisses
are where I find
the energy to keep going
with the faith to rise
and the knowing that
one day
I will be big enough
to say no to it all!

Epilogue

I started writing my story twenty years ago. It was something I always thought I would do, but I had no idea when I was going to get the courage to do the deep dive. I began by doing what I called a data dump, creating documents on my computer that held random stories from childhood I remembered in sporadic bursts, but I didn't know how to bring them all together or what that might look like.

My goal for this process was to help others, but I realize now that I had not considered how it would help me. When I first sat down with Matthew Foley, my writing coach, he asked me if I wanted to write a chronological story. My answer was I didn't think I could. I had always described my memory as Swiss cheese with big holes in random places. I wasn't sure if I knew how to lay it out in any kind of recognizable fashion that might in any way benefit a reader who dedicated time to read my story. If you have gotten to this page, you are one of those brave souls, and I thank you for spending some of your life with me.

After the first meeting with Matt, when we created an outline for this book, I had tears in my eyes as I walked away. Just sitting down with someone to form a rough timeline of events allowed me to see my life with my inner eye in a way I had never seen it before. Throughout this process, the fog that obscured my memories has been lifted. I feel I have the most complete memory bank I have ever had, available for retrieval at a moment's notice. I did not realize how whole that would make me feel. For those of you who experience similar fog when you reach back into the recesses of your memory, I encourage you to have the courage to write down as much as you can. Even if you never print the words, the process can make you whole.

I have changed some names within the story to protect those who feel it's important to hide their identities and others who might take issue with my perspective. I didn't feel the need to combine experiences and details or to conflate separate situations. It was important to me to speak my truth without trickery or fluff.

As you read this story, you may find yourself having feelings of anger, disgust, and frustration toward some of the characters found within. That is understandable and expected. As you read the words to describe my actions and the actions of my family and loved ones, I have only one request. Please always hold compassion in your heart for our journeys. One of the most important lessons I have learned in life is that *hurt people hurt people.* We are all responsible for our choices and the consequences, intended or unintended, that result. You may find yourself assigning labels to some of these individuals, such as monster or evil, but all these people came into the world with wonder and promise. Some experienced transgressions that forever shifted their course, and I want to honor the reality that they are victims too.

I have had many wise teachers in the half century I have walked this earth, and they have left me with nuggets of wisdom—some I have memorialized in permanent ink on my body and others in sayings I find myself passing on to others to keep the energy flowing. Here are some of these nuggets:

It's just an *is.*
Risk!
Is that in your hula hoop?
Stay in your power.
The difference between God and me is that God's not trying to be me.
They have their own higher power—and I'm not it!
God can dream a bigger dream for me than I can ever dream for myself.

To all who find themselves in patterns that are no longer serving them, you can break away. It's never too late to take a different step, and if it feels uncomfortable, you are likely moving in the right direction! We only stretch and grow in discomfort, so we have to learn to allow that feeling of being cracked open in order for light to get in. If you find yourself struggling with boundaries, not knowing where you stop and someone else starts, buy a hula hoop. Put it on the floor of your living room, and stand inside it. Everything *inside your hoop* is yours to manage, and everything *outside your hoop* is not yours. This applies to children, spouses, parents, siblings—pretty much everyone! Do this physically enough times until you can mentally stand in your hoop anytime you feel those lines getting blurred. It is simple, but it isn't easy. I believe one of the greatest shortcomings of our society is the failure to teach children about personal boundaries.

When I was at the preschool, I used to talk to my teachers anytime I heard them tell a child that they must do as they say because they are the tallest person in the room. We do children a great disservice when we don't teach them how to know and assert their boundaries. We set them up for abuse, manipulation, and life-changing events when we don't teach them how powerful their no is and how and when to use it. The course correction for adults around this takes time, but it is well worth the effort, and it is never too late to learn. This wisdom was passed to me by one of my sponsors, and I graciously hand it to you now, bowing in reverence for the power of the words.

I've spent this time sharing with you my journey toward saying no, so it seems right to also share what I am now saying yes to. I say yes to laughter, adventure, creativity, personal power, authenticity, service to others, rhythm, love, and risk. I say yes to witnessing the pain of others who struggle, holding space for healing and truth-telling in the hopes of shifting the shadow side of our humanity into the light. While I am human—and some days, I fall short of these intentions—I pick myself back up and try again because as long as I am breathing, there is hope.

In the following years after my divorce from David, I would marry again and divorce again. The details of this second marriage might be a sequel to this story, but as what happens often in life, old patterns continue until we release them. I do not believe any time spent with someone is wasted time, and I know that the lessons I needed to learn from my second marriage were gifts to me that I am still unwrapping.

Within the first couple of dates with my second husband, he asked me if I had issues with intimacy. I had been dropping all my "bombs" on him to see if he would run away, and when he asked me that question, I didn't have an answer for him.

I told him, "I had never been in a healthy relationship, and I had done a lot of work on myself. But I believe our old patterns don't surface until we are in a similar situation. I had not been in a relationship since leaving David, so my answer is, I don't know." While that answer may seem unclear, it was actually the most honest response I could give.

After Greg and I got married, David escalated, threatening to kill Mimi and me because he couldn't have access to her the way he wanted, exclaiming, "If I can't have her, then no one will, and I'm taking you down with her!"

After police reports and installing security systems, I chose to terminate his parental rights to protect her from him if anything happened to me. She came with a bank account, and I knew he would do anything he'd have to do to charm the judge into giving her to him. Even with a lifetime restraining order against him, he continues to resurface every once in a while, reminding us that we are still within his reach just in case we get too comfortable.

Nothing breaks a mother's heart more than to hear her child say for the first time at age eleven, "I wish he would just die so I don't have to worry about him anymore."

I understand this sentiment as I have felt it for both my dad and David. In spite of the trauma she experienced during her formative years, which has left her with anxiety and depression, she is thriving in life, and I could not be prouder of the woman she is becoming.

I am in the best place I have ever been with my family and friends. I will always be a work in progress and continue to let go of the perfectionism that lives in my cells so that I can live by "progress, not perfection" as was taught to me in Alanon. In the twenty years since the end of this book, my mom, Mary, CC, and I have continued our journey of self-discovery and acceptance of what we find in ourselves and one another. I understand the deep value of having each of them in my life, and I continue to show up for and with them as we walk this journey together, enjoying the highs and lows that sometimes only family can truly provide.

One of my favorite parts of Al-anon and Alcoholics Anonymous is we don't give advice. One of my longtime Alapals used to say, "There are only two kinds of advice—the kind you shouldn't ever give and the kind no one wants to hear." My goal for this book was to share my experience, strength, and hope on the off chance that you see yourself in my reflection. I believe we are all part of the same energy, and as such, nothing I pass to you is ever lost. Building you up strengthens me in ways I can only imagine. I love you for the extraordinary human you are, and I thank you for taking the time to share space with me.

Acknowledgments

It truly takes a village to give birth to your story, especially when trauma has created smoke-filled spaces that need a light breeze to blow the vision clear. "Thank you" will never encapsulate the truth of my appreciation to all who manifested that breeze, but here I share with you a small portion of that gratitude.

- To Mom, who has stuck by me, doing the hard work of excavation and dialogue, leading to a deep level of healing. Your willingness to allow me to tell part of your story in order to illuminate mine is the greatest gift you have given me. Thank you for sharing bits of you so that my broken pieces can be made whole.

- To my sisters, with whom I have shared every breath, thank you for bringing dimension and edges to my life. You have held my hands through all the anger, joy, laughter, and tears, giving me a safety net that I know will always catch me when I fall. As with Mom, in order to tell my story I had to tell part of yours, and I am truly grateful to you for your openness and participation.

- To my daughter, Mimi, for being the soul I didn't know I needed to love. You have been my teacher, my student, and my reason for making some of the hardest decisions I have ever had to make in my life. When I couldn't find the strength to change for me, I found it to change for you. I have always thanked you for allowing me to be your mom, and that will never change.

- To my writing coach, Matthew Foley, for sitting with me in coffee shops for a year, creating the perfect space for me to spill my guts. You have given me the ability to look into the recesses of my memory and see a life that was obscured by shadows and pain. When I doubted my process, you lifted me up, reminding me that the journey of a lifetime begins with one step.

- To my beta readers, who took the time to read my story and give honest feedback about form, storyline, and what might be missing. Christine Cohen, Charlotte Jerace, and Tanya Sanders, your first-impression reactions gave me life at a time in the process where fear and doubt could have stopped me cold. The experience and love you brought to the dialogue allowed me to dig deeper when I needed to and discover a realistic expectation for what came next.

- To my childhood friends, ex-fiancé, and former therapist, who took the time to walk down memory lane with me in the hopes of filling in the gaps that alcohol and trauma created, thank you. You didn't have to give me your time, and I will be forever grateful to you for your help. I hope our conversations were as healing for you as they were for me.

About the Author

D.T. Shanti is originally from North Carolina and has lived in Charleston, South Carolina, for over twenty years. She has a bachelor's degree in special education from Greensboro College and a master's degree in social science from the Citadel. She has worked in the nonprofit arena her entire career, focusing on organizations that serve children in different ways: as a preschool director, an applied behavioral therapist for kids on the autism spectrum, and a therapeutic horseback-riding instructor for children and adults with disabilities. Along the journey, she has always appreciated the chance to serve, sharing her skills to increase the opportunities for those living on the margins of our society.

Ms. Shanti has unlocked her creative side as an artist, poet, and writer. She is the proud mom to a grown daughter, who reminds her every day of what is important. Her daily focus includes actively unpacking her own internalized racism, in the city where the Civil War began and more than 40 percent of kidnapped Africans were brought to this country to be enslaved, with the intention of practicing anti-racist behaviors to affect lasting change in herself and in the community. She volunteers in her local community wherever she can be of service and recently accepted a new position as Managing Director of The Peace Alliance, a national nonprofit working to cultivate a culture of peacebuilding through community programs and governmental policy. She is a firm believer that you can't change what you don't acknowledge and that acknowledgment begins, for her, with a long look in the mirror.